LET'S BUY A HOUSE
Homeowner's Guidebook for Life

DONALD J. GRIFFIN, MAI, SRA

DEDICATION

For Sarah Griffin, my life partner

ACKNOWLEDGMENTS

This book covers many aspects of real estate and I wish to thank the many professionals with whom I have had the pleasure of working. If the reader finds fault in any section of the book it is mine and mine alone.

Lisa Cremonini, CFP ® a Certified Financial Planner helped to make sure the many calculations were accurate. Dan DeStefano, ASHI, assisted in the role of the home inspector. Rosemary Garcia Frost is a residential bank lender who sharpened my understanding of the APR and other bank lending rules. Matthew Gleason is a Certified General real estate appraiser who reviewed the myriad of financial calculations. Jim Masciarelli is a self-published author and management consultant with tips on structure and making it reader friendly. Julie McQuade Ladimer, Esq. is an elder law attorney, with help in areas of reverse mortgage and options for seniors in their later life. Susan Ledoux is a Para legal who works with the Hud-1 forms on a daily basis. George R. Lonergan is a general contractor who assisted in the construction review. Regina Nieves, CISR is an independent home insurance agent who assisted in the complex area of home insurance. Adam Pachter is an editor who assisted in making the grammatical corrections. Wendy Powell, CPA and her husband reported on a recent upgrade to a larger home and offered several tips as a recent buyer. Bill Ross is an accountant and enrolled agent offering practical tips on making the book user friendly. Frank H. Russow Esq. is a real estate attorney in California and helped educate me about trust deeds. Christopher A. Russow is Vice President of a reverse mortgage company and California real estate broker who helped review the reverse mortgage section. R. Thomas Sanford is a general contractor, who built his own home, and serves on his town's planning and zoning board. Julius Sciarra, CPA offered tips on the tax issues, with second homes, and thresholds on capital gains. Stephanie Watson is a life insurance agent and provided input on the section on life insurance. Sam Webb is a Senior Real Estate Broker with Coldwell Banker, Sudbury, MA with many years of experience. His support and input helped in all aspects of the real estate sections. Lisa Wroble is my editor and writing mentor who completed the final polishing.

PROLOGUE

Owning your own home is fun. It anchors you to the community. There are many tangible benefits in home ownership. Often the intangible benefits are overlooked. You become part of a neighborhood where you make friends. There are events that you take for granted such as the fourth of July picnic and parade.

There are the school sports events and Halloween trick or treating. You have access to your local shopping area with its great restaurants where you relax after a hard week's work. You appreciate the short trip to watch your national sports teams and visit your major cities' arts and cultural centers. Local colleges and universities provide learning opportunities.

So as we proceed through all the hard core technical aspects of real estate that are so important in the front end purchase process, don't lose sight of the main goal of owning a house for the long term.

I am a real estate appraiser and wrote this book to help put you back in the driver's seat. No one is watching out for your best interest in today's real estate market, so you must. I use my twenty years of experience to teach you about values, houses, mortgages, the buying and selling process, contracts, professionals, insurance, credit score, maintenance and lifetime planning.

Knowledge is power, and you will learn real estate details that will help in your purchase. Forces that protected the buyer twenty years ago are no longer in place. The better informed you are the more confident you will be in your purchase.

Many readers may be overwhelmed with portions of this book. Others will find sections simplistic. I have used as my guide William Zinsser's book *On Writing Well* to get the complexity of the subject down to a level of understanding for most readers. As Mr. Zinsser said:

"It's the principle of leading readers who know nothing, step by step, to a grasp of subjects they didn't think they had the aptitude for or were afraid they were too dumb to understand." I do not believe that anyone is too dumb to understand real estate, houses, mortgage, or any topic explained here.

This book is about Life Cycles, the first being your life cycle. Throughout your entire life you need shelter to survive. Shelter costs money. You have to pay for shelter in one form or another.

There will be times when renting is the best thing to do. But, there will be long blocks of time where you will reside in one place. It is during these periods where home ownership makes sense, and it allows you to take the money you are paying for shelter and have it accumulate to a valuable portion of your total investment portfolio.

A home has a life cycle. The home is two major pieces, the land and the house. The house starts out new and wears out over time. The land always increases in value. A piece of land fifty years ago cut out of a farm was very inexpensive. Fifty years later the whole area has built up with highways, employment and shopping centers. That same lot of land is much more valuable. The house value is increased with every update, addition and improvement.

The real estate market has a life cycle. Tied to the overall economy, it fluctuates up and down, but in general the market value increases with time.

Keep the fundamentals in mind as you learn the details that will make you a savvy home owner. I take the guess work out of buying/selling and help you avoid the risks and pitfalls, with the main goal of helping you to maximize your home value.

INTRODUCTION

I bought my first house when I was 25, when I knew nothing about real estate except that we had a second baby on the way and needed more room. I had to borrow the down payment from my uncle, but with much help from friends, family, and professionals, the deal was done.

Since that first transaction, over a lifetime of changes, I have owned and rented a wide variety of homes in several states. As the youngest of six, I have observed my children, nieces and nephews as they followed a similar path of getting married, starting a family, and buying their first, second and sometimes third home.

As a real estate appraiser, I have been the one that documented the values of property as they increased in value at dizzying rates, and documented the declining values that have devastated so many people.

I balance my own experience as a homeowner with the technical skill of valuing real estate to show you how to buy and manage your own home. I provide the supporting education of the underlying forces that create real estate and its value.

In this book, you will learn:
- The buying and selling process
- How to find the house, and inspect it
- How to value the house
- Details on the key contracts you will be using
- Negotiating to a firm contract
- Maximizing your value when you sell a house
- Everything about mortgages, financing, down payments, and credit score
- All about the land, the foundation of value
- Different house styles, construction detail, finishes, quality, and support systems
- Specific discussion on the Condominium form of home ownership
- How to become a critical observer of quality and condition
- How to maintain the house
- Determining when you have sufficient skills to buy a property that needs work
- Lifetime planning, the several paths to reach retirement with no mortgage
- Addendum items on financial calculators, Excel, deeds, budgeting and others

Because laws vary from state to state, readers should check with their local statutes and municipal departments about the rules that are in force in your area. Massachusetts rules and statutes guide most opinions with a note when something applies in another state. For example, some states use a trust deed or deed of trust instead of a deed. I use the term deed throughout the book, but the term includes the similar form of encumbrance found in a trust deed or deed of trust. See the addendum for other conventions used in the book.

CONTENTS

BUYING AND SELLING SECTION

DONALD J. GRIFFIN, MAI, SRA

1 READY TO BUY YOUR FIRST HOUSE

What Can You Afford?

You will probably need to get a mortgage loan when buying your first house. The first step then is to determine how much of a down payment you'll need. If you have saved for a 20% down payment, then the maximum price you can pay is the down payment divided by .20 (20%). For example, a $30,000 down payment should allow you to buy a house for $150,000 ($30,000 ÷ .20).

In addition to the down payment, you will need funds to cover the closing costs and inspections. You must also have the income necessary to make the mortgage payment. Most lenders allow up to 28% of your gross income to be used to cover the principal, interest, taxes, and insurance (PITI) on your mortgage. This 28% is part of the Debt to Income Ratio (DTI) they'll require before approving your mortgage loan.

If you are putting less than 20% down, then the DTI will also have to cover the Private Mortgage Insurance (PMI). The 28% ratio is called the "front-end ratio." The term "back-end ratio" includes any other long term debt payments such as auto loans, school loans, and credit cards. The usual "back-end ratio" is 36%, but can go as high as 45%. The DTI is often stated as 28/36 for conventional mortgage loans. Read this as a front end ratio of 28% and a back end ratio of 36%.

If you are buying a condo, the association dues are included in the PITI total. They are considered a monthly housing payment.

If you are getting a Federal Housing Administration (FHA) loan, the DTI limits are 31/45. If you are getting a Veterans Affairs (VA) loan, they only have a total debt limit of 41%. The VA does not use a debt ratio for just the PITI costs. Most mortgage loan brokers work with many lenders and may be able to offer you a program with a back-end limit of up to 50%. For this analysis I will stick with a traditional conventional loan with DTI of 28/36.

Calculating Your Total Purchasing Power

Author's Note
You may want to brush up on your excel or HP-12c skills found in the addendum before you read this section.

The complexity of calculating your purchasing power is due to variables such as mortgage rates, property taxes, property insurance, down payment percentage, PMI, amount of debt, and the front and back-end ratios. There are formulas that will calculate purchasing power. The easiest way is to look at it from the lender's point of view. The lender needs to make sure that you will be able make your mortgage payment every month. The two ratios measured by most lenders include the 28% front-end ratio and the 36% back-end ratio. Let's walk through a typical loan.

Purchase price		$150,000
Down payment	20%	$30,000
Mortgage		$120,000
Rate	5%	
Term in years	30	
Payment	$644	

Assume you have saved $30,000 for a down payment and have researched mortgage interest rates. You find you can get a 5% rate on a 30-year fixed-rate mortgage and have seen several houses for sale for around $150,000. Using these figures, here is the EXCEL worksheet formula you can use to calculate payment due each month.

[=PMT(.05/12,30*12,120000)]. This is the Principal and Interest expense, or the PI of PITI. The result is a monthly payment of $644.19.

The same information on the HP-12c financial calculator:

	Calculate mortgage payment				
	n	i	PV	PMT	FV
Variables	30 years	5%	$120,000	????	not used
Key	30 [g] [n]	5 [g] [i]	120000	**PMT**	
Answer				-644.19	

4

The next expense is the property tax. You can estimate it by looking at the taxes of similar properties. Tax information is available at the assessor's office and much information is available online or through the MLS sheets available at open houses. Add the estimated tax and insurance to calculate your total payment.

Expense	Monthly	Annual
Mortgage Principle & Interest	$644.19	$7,730
Taxes	$183.81	$2,206
Property Insurance	$50.00	$600
Total PITI	$878.00	$10,536

In the example, for a $120,000 mortgage ($150,000 minus the $30,000 down payment), you will need $10,536 per year to pay the mortgage, property taxes, and homeowners insurance. PMI costs are added if you have less than a 20% down payment.

Using the example, let's say the total annual gross income for your household is $50,000. You may include additional income from sources such as alimony or child support in your gross income figure. You also may be able to count work-related bonuses. If you are self-employed, your mortgage lender will require you to verify your income by providing copies of your federal income tax return for the past two years. Your total income is:

Income	Monthly	Annual
You	$2,083	$25,000
Partner	$2,083	$25,000
Total Income		$50,000

Now list all your other debts. For this example Student Loans are $200, car payment is $225, and credit card bills are $100 (use the minimum payment per month). Do not include expenses for utilities (heat, electric, telephone, cable). Other debt is truly debt and not optional items such as retirement plans, or child care.

Other Debt	Monthly	Annual
Tuition Loan	$200	$2,400
Auto Loan	$225	$2,700
Credit Cards	$100	$1,200
Total Other Debt	$525	$6,300

Your total of other debt is $525 a month:

Expense Summary	Monthly	Annual
Total PITI	$878	$10,536
Total Other Debt	$525	$6,300
Total of PITI & other Debt	$1,403	$16,836

Your total of PITI and other debt is $1,403 a month. The actual ratios are 21/34 and they are less than the loan limit of 28/36, so you qualify:

DTI Analysis	DTI limits	DTI Actual	Debt	Income
Front End - PITI	28%	21%	$10,536	$50,000
Back End - PITI + Debt	36%	34%	$16,836	$50,000

As you can see above the front end ratio of 21% is less than the front end ratio of 28%, and the back end ratio of 34% is less than the 36% back end ratio.

Now, look at the same model with more debt. Your tuition loans have increased to $400, your auto loan is $275, and your credit cards are $200.

Other Debt	Monthly	Annual
Tuition Loan	$400	$4,800
Auto Loan	$275	$3,300
Credit Cards	$200	$2,400
Total Other Debt	$875	$10,500

Total expenses:

Expense Summary - More Debt	Monthly	Annual
Total PITI	$878	$10,536
Total Other Debt	$875	$10,500
Total of PITI & other Debt	$1,753	$21,036

The DTI calculations with more debt are:

DTI Analysis	DTI limits	DTI Actual	Annual Cost	Income
Front End - PITI	28%	21%	$10,536	$50,000
Back End - PITI + Debt	36%	42%	$21,036	$50,000

The back-end ratio of 42% exceeds the 36% limit so you will not be approved for a mortgage loan. Your other debt puts you over the limit.

Points and Closing Costs

You can reduce the interest rate by paying points. Points are prepaid interest. One point is 1% of the mortgage. If the mortgage amount is $200,000, then one point is $2,000. A general rule of thumb is that for each point paid you reduce the mortgage rate by an eighth to a quarter percent. The amount of reduction is dependent on lender and mortgage product. If the current rate is 6% and you pay 2 points, you can get a 5.75% to 5.875% mortgage rate. It takes about five years to break even when paying points. After that the mortgage will cost you less at the 5.75% to 5.875% rate than the 6.0% rate. Points are prepaid interest and are tax deductible.

When buying your primary home, points paid in cash are deductible in the year the loan is closed. If the points are financed, they remain deductible in the first year if the cash contribution by the borrower for the down payment and other costs (total cash) exceeds the amount of the points. Otherwise excess points over your total cash become part of the loan, and are deductible as interest over the life of the loan. If you refinance this loan, you lose the points as a deduction.

When refinancing or purchasing a vacation or rental property, the IRS requires that any prepaid points be deducted over the life of the mortgage. In the first year of a 30-year mortgage, you may deduct one thirtieth (1/30) of the points paid. However, should you sell the house or refinance to a new mortgage loan, the remaining balance of the points is deductible in the year the property was sold or refinanced.

Escrow: Having been approved for the mortgage loan, the lender may require you to include some other expenses at the closing. When borrowing for a mortgage, it is customary to put three months property taxes and insurance into escrow and prepay the first year's home insurance.

Closing costs: Closing costs include the additional fees paid at the time the mortgage loan is granted. Closing costs include the broker's commission, expenses incurred on the borrower's behalf, credits to the seller for items paid in advance, points the borrower pays to reduce the mortgage rate, prepaid amounts for escrow expenses, title charges, recording and transfer charges, and any other settlement charges. All of this is reported on an accounting sheet known as the HUD-1 Settlement Statement. An example is provided in the addendum. HUD is the U.S. Department of Housing and Urban Development.

Calculate Your True Total Housing Costs

Using the example above, I start with the $878 which includes the loan repayment of $644 a month and escrow payments for taxes and property insurance of $234 a month.

Monthly loan expenses	Amount
Total Loan Payment	$644
Total escrow payment	$234
Total Monthly payment	$878

As a borrower, you should have a good understanding of your net housing costs. Federal tax law allows you deductions on the interest expense you pay on your mortgage loan as well as for the amount of your local real estate taxes. *Real estate tax deductions may be reduced by the alternative minimum tax (AMT). This won't affect most people, especially in the first-time buyer category; however, check with your tax advisor if you have questions.*

Tax Deductions: Tax deductions are available on properties with a mortgage up to $1,000,000. In our example, a couple (assume married for tax purposes) with combined income of $50,000 have a federal marginal tax rate of 15%. Assume the couple lives in a state with state income tax of 5%. Also assume that the interest expense on a mortgage is a tax deduction from state income tax. The couple's total marginal tax rate is 20%.

Correct for tax deductions:

Tax Analysis		
Annual Mortgage payments	$7,730	Deductions
Mortgage Interest Portion	95%	$7,344
Property Taxes		$2,206
Deductions		$9,550
Marginal Tax Rate Fed and State		20%
Tax savings	$159	$1,910

In this example, most of the loan payments of $7,730 are interest expense estimated at 95% or $7,344 ($7,730 × .95). The interest expense amount declines over time as more of the payment is paid against the principal and less against interest. In this example, the total deductions are $9,550 consisting of $7,344 in deductible interest and $2,206 in deductible real estate taxes. Annual tax savings are $1,910 ($9,550 × .20). Savings each month are $159 ($1,910 ÷ 12).

Estimate utility bills: Ask the real estate broker or current homeowner for historical costs of the house.

Plus utilities	Monthly
- Water & Sewer	$50
- Electric	$80
- Heating / Cooling cost	$80
Total Utility costs	$210

Estimate Landscaping Expense: For this example I assume the new owners will do their own landscaping. If later you use this model on a larger home, you may choose to budget the expense of additional landscaping services.

Repairs & Maintenance	Monthly
- Supplies	$25
- Labor - self	$0
- Contract	$25
Total Maintenance	$50

Summary	Monthly
Total Monthly Payment	$878
Less Tax Savings	-$159
Plus Utilities	$210
Landscaping - self	$0
Total Maintenance	$50
Net Housing Costs	$979

For this example, a couple buying a home for $150,000 with a 20% down payment with a $50,000 annual income, the total costs for the home should be around $979 monthly.

Ready to Purchase—Setting Up the Transaction

Shop for a lender/mortgage broker: If at all possible, shop for a thirty-year fixed-rate mortgage. Variable rate loans are available, but come with interest rates that increase over time. If you are putting 20% down, a conventional loan is your best option. If you are using a loan program such as an FHA or VA loan, you must qualify to meet their requirements for DTI (debt to income ratios), income threshold, and credit score.

A good place to start looking for a loan is the bank or credit union you use now. Comparing interest rates and closing costs for a number of lenders is always wise. Mortgage brokers have access to a wide range of mortgage products with varying interest rates.

The interest rates a lender charges vary depending on their source of funds. If a lender holds the loan in its portfolio, its interest rate may be different than if the lender planned to sell your loan to Fannie Mae or Freddie Mac. If the loan is sold, it must meet Fannie Mae or Freddie Mac's requirements. If the loan is sold to a third-party investor, it must meet those investment guidelines.

Pre-Qualified vs. Pre-Approval: Being Pre-Qualified means that based on what you have told the lender, you qualify for a certain mortgage level. The Pre-Approval is a more rigorous process and results in a letter that you should get from your lender which will back up your offer on a house. In the Pre-Approval, you submit all of your documentation to support your income, asset and expense data. The lender will run a credit check and get your actual credit score. Your credit score is discussed in detail in Chapter 7. After reviewing your financial situation, the lender will tell you how much they can lend you.

Start the process by getting the lender you have selected to pre-approve you for a loan. A pre-qualification does not carry much weight when negotiating with a seller. The seller's primary concern is that you can get the mortgage.

A pre-approval puts you in a stronger negotiating position. A seller will accept an offer with a pre-approved mortgage.

What Professionals Do You Need?

Professionals supporting you in your purchase include your real estate broker (assuming you are using a buyer's broker), the mortgage broker or lender, your attorney, and your home inspector. Professionals supporting the lender include the real estate appraiser, site plan surveyor, flood plain analyst (if needed), and the lender's attorney who does the title search.

Real Estate Brokers: As you search for a home, you will meet a number of real estate brokers. In most cases the real estate broker works for the seller and has a responsibility to protect the seller's best interest. However, the real estate broker also has a responsibility to the buyer and cannot misrepresent the property.

> **Broker's Nugget**
>
> A buyer's broker is a real estate broker you engage to represent you in your house search. In most cases, listing brokers will share the sales commission with a buyer's broker.

This is not always the case, so be aware of the rules on sales commissions when working with a buyer's broker. A buyer's broker has the same responsibility to you as a buyer as a seller's broker has to the seller.

Buyer and seller brokers work for real estate firms and it is possible that a conflict can arise in an office. Example: If a real estate office has a property listed for sale by John (the seller's broker) and you have engaged Mary from the same office to be your buyer's broker, both John and Mary represent the seller since they both work for the same company. In this instance, Mary also has a responsibility to you as a buyer's broker. This is known as dual agency. It is a tricky situation but it can be handled. In summary, all parties agree in writing to be fair with each other.

Be sure all parties are clear about the role and compensation of any real estate brokers involved. If you are working with a buyer's broker, be sure to notify every other broker you come across in your house search. In most cases the buyer's broker will have you sign an agreement indicating your relationship. This is important since this determines who gets paid a commission.

The following is an excerpt from a Massachusetts Consent to Dual Agency. It will vary from state to state:

Massachusetts Consent to Dual Agency

A real estate broker or salesperson may act as a dual agent who represents both prospective buyer and seller with their informed written consent. A dual agent is authorized to assist the buyer and seller in a transaction, but shall be neutral with regard to any conflicting interest of the buyer and seller. Consequently, a dual agent will not have the ability to satisfy fully the duties of loyalty, full disclosure, reasonable care and obedience to lawful instructions, but shall still owe the duty of confidentiality of material information and the duty to account for funds.

Buyers and sellers should understand that material information received from either client that is confidential may not be disclosed by a dual agent, except: (1) if disclosure is expressly authorized; (2) if such disclosure is required by law; (3) if such disclosure is intended to prevent illegal conduct; or (4) if such disclosure is necessary to prosecute a claim against a person represented or to defend a claim against the broker or salesperson. This duty of confidentiality shall continue after termination of the brokerage relationship.

Broker's Nugget
Key points in the above definition: salesperson may act as a dual agent but shall be neutral shall still owe the duty of confidentiality

Mortgage Loan Brokers: Your mortgage loan broker or lender is the next professional you will need to engage. While you look for a house, you will be talking with various lenders and mortgage brokers, shopping for the best mortgage and rate. The lender or mortgage broker will get you the pre-approval letter to aid in your negotiating with sellers. Once you have selected your financing source and have your pre-approval letter, you are ready to begin negotiating with sellers.

Attorney: You should always have your own attorney to represent you through the Offer, the Purchase and Sales Agreement, and the sale closing.

Your attorney will protect you against a potential disastrous misstep. Don't wait until you have signed an offer to get your attorney. You may be committing yourself in the offer and giving up important rights. Your lender might suggest you use its attorney, but remember the lender's attorney represents the lender. If a sticky situation comes up, you may not get the advice that is optimum for you.

The Home Inspector: This is an important professional supporting you through the process of purchasing a home. These professionals provide a detailed report of everything you need to know about the house. The home inspector should be a member of The American Society of Home Inspectors (ASHI). Most states require home inspectors to be licensed. You can see your state's regulations at the ASHI web site [ASHI.com].

You should plan on going with the home inspector on the inspection. Take a note pad with you, as you will learn a lot about the house from this professional. Be sure to ask questions, there will be no better time to learn about the house. The home inspection report is a standardized document of the home inspector's findings. The inspector can also give you many details on the house that will be helpful to your managing it.

Home inspection reports are limited by what the home inspector can observe. These disclaimers are standard practice. If the inspector cautions you about something beyond his area of expertise, such as a structural issue, he may recommend further evaluation by a specialist.

The fee for the home inspection is paid by you, even if the purchase is not completed. If the home inspection results in you cancelling the purchase, you still pay the inspection fee. It is money well spent, since it protects you from a purchase that might have been problematic.

Real Estate Appraiser: You will not be able to select the real estate appraiser because this professional is engaged by the lender. As the buyer, you can suggest the lender use a professional who holds the SRA designation from the Appraisal Institute. The SRA designation indicates expertise in appraising residential properties. If you need to find a professional real estate appraiser, look to the Appraisal Institute's web site: [appraisalinstitute.org].

Other Professionals: Along with the professionals listed above, the following is a list of professionals you may need when purchasing a home.

Tax Advisor or Certified Public Accountant (CPA): Either can help you with tax deductibility issues of points, interest expense, real estate taxes, capital gains tax, deductibility of PMI, and tax issues on second homes and/or income property.

Insurance Broker: An independent insurance agent can help you purchase the right homeowners insurance policy.

The Certified Financial Planner and/or Life Insurance Agent: These professionals can help you with planning to insure your lifetime financial goals are achieved.

Finding Good Professionals: Most professions associated with real estate transactions must meet state licensing requirements. Also, it's wise to look for designations and memberships in nationally accredited associations such as National Association of Realtors (NAR), Realtor ®, American Society of Home Inspectors, (ASHI), Appraisal Institute (MAI, SRA), and Certified Mortgage Banker designation, (CMB™). These groups provide ongoing education as do state organizations such as the Massachusetts Board of Real Estate Appraisers (MBREA). Attorneys don't have designations but are admitted to the state bar. Look for an attorney who specializes in real estate law. When you are ready to start your search for a house, ask your professionals, friends, and family for referrals to other professionals in real estate, mortgage lending, loan officers at lending institutions, attorneys, and home inspectors.

All the professionals listed have a cost. The real estate broker earns a commission on the sale. The real estate appraiser, home inspector, and your attorney earn a fee for their work. The mortgage broker earns a commission.

Fixer Upper vs. Move-In Perfect

When selecting a house to purchase you will find the best prices are on properties in need of updating. Move-in perfect homes will always command the highest price. Your decision point is what level of work is acceptable to get a discounted price. Some of this will depend on your skills and time available to do the updating work. Another factor is how you feel about managing the sub-contractors required to do the work you don't feel comfortable undertaking.

You as the developer: If the house needs a modest amount of repairs and updates, you may be able to do most of the work yourself. You might retain a few professionals to complete some of the more complex work. If the house needs extensive upgrades but is in a good location, consider acting as the project manager yourself.

HUD-FHA 203K rehab loan program: If you do not have enough cash to handle the down payment and also pay for the repairs, the government has a loan program that may help you. The U.S. Department of Housing and Urban Development and the Federal Housing Administration HUD-FHA 203K rehab loan program targets this exact need. It is a home improvement loan. FHA-approved lenders will have the property appraised in its AS IS and AS COMPLETED condition.

They will make the loan based on the AS COMPLETED value. You purchase the property but the lender holds the rehab funds in escrow. After you take ownership, the lender releases portions of the funds as you start the rehab work.

You need a project plan to qualify for a rehab loan which might look like this:

Task	Contractor	Cost
Permits	Town	$500
Clean out interior / demolition	Self	$1,000
Replace roof	Roofer	$6,000
New windows	Window Company	$4,000
New exterior siding	Siding Company	$8,000
Reframe rooms	Carpenter	$3,000
Upgrade electric & new fixtures	Electrician	$3,500
Upgrade plumbing	Plumber	$4,000
Replace bathroom floor tiles	Flooring Company	$1,500
Bathroom fixtures & vanities	Plumber	$4,000
Replace broken drywall & ceilings	Drywall Company	$8,000
New kitchen cabinets, appliances and flooring	Carpenter	$8,000
Interior painting	Self	$1,500
Refinish hardwood floors	Self	$1,000
New carpeting	Carpet Company	$3,800
New heating system	Plumber	$2,800
New hot water heater	Plumber	$350
Upgrade landscaping	Landscape Company	$3,000
Dumpster	Trash Company	$1,500
Hard estimated costs		$64,950
Contingency costs	10%	$6,495
Total estimated costs		$71,445
Rounded		$71,000

Some people shy away from large rehab projects. However, real estate developers often take on this type of project. To get a developer interested in a property, the seller may discount the price by at least 20%. The government's 203K rehab program described above is only available for owner-occupied properties.

Traditional developers cannot use this program. For some buyers this approach to an upgrade is a great way to increase their equity. Here is an example of the financing on an owner occupied rehab:

Cost	Amount
As-Completed Value	$250,000
Less Repairs	$71,000
Less Developers Profit @ 20%	$50,000
AS IS Value	$129,000

The appraised AS COMPLETED value is $250,000. The AS IS value is $129,000. The AS IS value is the $250,000 less the cost of repairs $71,000, and less developer's profit of $50,000. You buy it for $129,000 with a 203K FHA rehab loan through an approved lender in your area. The loan is based on the AS COMPLETED value up to 96.5% Loan To Value (LTV), or $241,250. You only need $200,000 to make the purchase and complete the actual work:

Mortgage	Amount
Purchase Price	$129,000
Rehab Work	$71,000
Total	$200,000

Rehabbing a property can also provide an opportunity to build "sweat equity" in your home. The more work you supervise yourself, the more equity you build. The 203K program was designed with the concept of a developer handling most of the work. You will add to your equity if you have developed the skills to oversee all or part of the job yourself. There are two loan types.

The Standard 203k is intended for more complicated projects that involve structural changes, such as room additions, exterior grading and landscaping, or renovation that would prohibit you from occupying the residence. A Standard 203k is also used if your project requires engineering or architectural drawings and inspections.

The Streamlined 203K is designed for less extensive improvements and for projects that will not exceed a total of $35,000 in renovation and related expenses. This version does not require the use of a consultant, architect, and engineer or as many inspections as the Standard 203K. As a result, when applicable, the Streamlined 203K generally becomes the simpler, less costly option.

There is no income cap for the program, but you must qualify for the loan. There are limits on the size of the project. Based on the state and county. It is limited to 1-4 living units. Refer to the HUD web site for more information portal.hud.gov. Search for 203K information.

Resources to help you. You will need to hire professionals to do some or all of the electrical, plumbing, carpentry, dry wall installing, flooring, masonry, roofing, and landscaping. You will also need reputable sources for building, plumbing, electrical, and appliance materials and fixtures.

When rehabbing a property, follow these guidelines to ensure you achieve the maximum value for the money you spend.

Don't over improve. Consider the neighborhood before you plan on adding expensive features such as a great room with floor to ceiling stone fireplace, kitchen with cherry cabinets, marble or granite flooring, and counters, or extensive multi-tiered deck. If you over improve the house there is a risk you will be creating something called "super adequacy." Super adequacy includes improvements that cost more than the market will pay when you sell your house later. A property should fit within the range of properties in the neighborhood. If the property is the most expensive in the neighborhood, it may be hard to sell. You may not get your investment back in the sales price if the property is over improved.

Kitchens and Baths. A good plan is to focus much of the cost of updates in the kitchen and baths. A well designed, updated kitchen can add future value. When you are starting with a worn kitchen, think of it as an empty room and envision a correct layout. Consider the work triangle. The work triangle in an efficient kitchen has easy access between the refrigerator, sink, and range. No through traffic flow should have to go through the work triangle.

Take care not to move existing features. The sink is on an outside wall with a window, in most cases. If you move the sink you have to move the plumbing and the window. The range may also be on an outside wall for venting. You may have flexibility in the location of the refrigerator. The dishwasher is next to the sink to access the hot and cold water supply and drain.

Think about lighting. This is a good opportunity to put in recessed ceiling lighting and/or under counter lighting. Depending on the size of the kitchen area, add in the most modern features to make it contemporary for the next 5-10 years. Work with a lumber supply company that sells cabinets. Cabinet sellers may have a design expert with Computer Aided Design (CAD) software that will let you try several layouts to refine it to an optimum solution.

CAD software allows the designer to layout the kitchen with a computer program. It starts with the room dimensions plus window and door locations. The designer will take these measurements so they are exact. You select a line of cabinets you will be using, and the designer places each component on the computer layout. This includes upper and lower cabinets and all appliances. You can then try different component pieces until you get a design you like. If there is a small gap between cabinet units, the program calculates the dimensions of the fill-in piece. The image is a three dimensional view. It allows you to look at the kitchen from all angles and views. . Be sure to check the space between the top of the cabinets and the ceiling, and decide how you will use that space--whether you want cabinets there or will use it for open storage or display. Once you order cabinets, all of the pieces are shipped to your house with everything you need to complete the kitchen.

Baths also present opportunities for improvement. If the fixtures are old and outdated, replace them by adding contemporary flooring and wall finishes. Improve the lighting and venting. Modern bathrooms have a ceiling vent fan that exhausts warm moist air. If the older bath does not have a vent, this is a good time to add one. Depending on the bathroom's size and the overall neighborhood, add a whirlpool tub or steam shower. It will add to your enjoyment of the house and improve resale value.

Depreciation. When looking at houses, look for any potential problems. Functional obsolescence is created when an item no longer meets a market need or when ongoing change renders layouts and features obsolete. The functional issue can be either a deficiency or a super adequacy.

The following descriptions will avoid some of the functional problems found in older homes. People have gotten by with these problems in the past and will in the future. These definitions are designed to help you know when you have an issue. The house may still suit your needs.

Be sure there is a bath on each floor which has bedrooms. All bedrooms must access a common hallway to the bathroom without crossing a living or work area. A bedroom cannot cross another bedroom to access the common hallway (Boxcars). A bedroom must conform to your municipality or state definition of a bedroom. The bedroom must be large enough for a single bed and a chest of drawers as well as a closet and a window. The minimum size might be 70 square feet. Additionally, it is not a kitchen, bath, living, dining, family, den or other defined room type.

The number of bedrooms can become a zoning question. Problems occur when the zoning code requires a certain number of parking spaces per bedroom. Problems can also occur when the size of the private septic system is based on the number of bedrooms. Look at any additions to the house carefully. Does it make the house stand out in the neighborhood as less or more appealing than other homes?

Quality of Materials: You will find a wide range of quality for each component of the project. This will include the very expensive parts such as kitchen cabinets and appliances as well as less expensive items like paint and hinges. Keep in mind the overall neighborhood and try not to exceed the standard too much. It is difficult to get the market to pay for improvements above the average for the area.

Subcontractors: As with all of your professionals, start finding the companies and laborers from referrals from friends, family, and other professionals you know and trust.

18

Containing Renovations. It is easy to get into difficulty when starting a renovation project. For example, your renovation begins with a plan to update the kitchen. Soon you realize the kitchen is small, so you think about making it larger. You then decide to add a family room. Then your contractor tells you that you could add a second story over the family room to enlarge the upstairs master bedroom. With the increase in project scope you now need to update the heating and electric systems. You can see how a simple idea can grow into a large project. Try to make improvements to the existing design plan. It takes a real expert to design and build a major addition, and they seldom pay for themselves.

Remodeling Magazine publishes the annual Cost vs. Value report ©, in conjunction with the National Association of Realtors ® (NAR). This report is an analysis of the cost to construct typical home improvements and compares them with the amount of value expected in a sale. On their web site [remodeling.hw.net], you can see the local cost and value compared to the national. On the next page is a sample from the 2011-2012 report:

2011-2012 National Averages			
Project	Job Cost	Resale value	Cost Recouped
Attic Bedroom	$50,148	$36,346	72.5%
Backup Power Generator	$14,760	$7,009	47.5%
Basement Remodel	$63,378	$42,338	66.8%
Bathroom Addition	$40,096	$20,455	51.0%
Bathroom Remodel	$16,552	$10,293	62.2%
Deck Addition (Composite)	$15,579	$9,780	62.8%
Deck Addition (Wood)	$10,350	$7,259	70.1%
Entry Door Replacement (Fiberglass)	$3,536	$1,990	56.3%
Entry Door Replacement (Steel)	$1,238	$903	72.9%
Family Room Addition	$83,118	$50,004	60.2%
Garage Addition	$57,824	$33,089	57.2%
Garage Door Replacement	$1,512	$1,087	71.9%
Home Office Remodel	$27,963	$11,983	42.9%
Major Kitchen Remodel	$57,494	$37,785	65.7%
Master Suite Addition	$106,196	$62,874	59.2%
Minor Kitchen Remodel	$19,588	$14,120	72.1%
Roofing Replacement	$21,204	$12,257	57.8%
Siding Replacement (Vinyl)	$11,729	$8,155	69.5%
Sunroom Addition	$74,310	$34,133	45.9%
Two Story Addition	$165,796	$103,391	62.4%
Window Replacement (Vinyl)	$11,319	$7,692	68.0%
Window Replacement (Wood)	$12,229	$8,258	67.5%
Total	$865,919	$521,201	60.2%

© 2011 Hanley Wood, LLC

As you can see, most projects do not cover the cost in the value. Overall, only 60.2% of the cost would be recouped in a subsequent sale.

One factor not considered in the above report is the concept of curing functional problems. There are instances when a purchased property is upgraded and then sold for a profit. The market discounts the value of properties with functional problems. When you cure a functional problem with a renovation you recoup the loss. If your project will cure a functional problem, it may add more value than implied in the survey.

Budget. Here is another way to contain a renovation project. Establish a budget for the planned work and stick to it. Create a contingency budget of 10-20% over what you think the project will cost. If you have no experience with the planned project, then make your best estimate and double it.

Now you have a good understanding of the type of property you want and can begin your search. Looking for a house is the fun part of buying a house. The anticipation of owning your own home can be overwhelming and you may want to jump right in and start looking. However, you should also want to look back on buying your home and be able to say you got good value for your money. A good friend in the real estate brokerage business once told me that searching for a house is all analytical up to the end when it then becomes all emotional. At some point in the process, emotions take over and you make the deal. So the better prepared you are for the process of finding and buying a home the more confident you will be in your decisions.

2 START LOOKING AT PROPERTY

Location, Location, Location

Most people have heard this old adage about buying a house. To a real estate appraiser, location means the community, neighborhood, and the home's location within the neighborhood. The community is the city or town where the property is located. One way to rank communities is by average household income. Household income is a main driver for home values in the community. Higher income equals higher home values. If you look at a county in any state there will be a bell curve on the distribution of home values within its cities and towns. Access to employment centers, proximity to highway, commuter train, and public transportation are all factors in a buyer's decision making. Commute time is important. So your first choice in location is the city or town in which you want or can afford to live.

The second location choice is the neighborhood within the community. In a similar fashion neighborhoods are delineated by wealth factors. In most cities and towns there will be an entry level neighborhood and a high end neighborhood. Again there will be a bell curve of home values. Neighborhoods tend to center around schools. The reputation of a neighborhood school is an important factor to buyers with children.

The third location choice within the neighborhood is the particular street and the location of the house on that street. Neighborhoods are bounded by access roads which allow residents to get to employment, shopping, and entertainment. Access roads carry more traffic than inside local roads.

Local commuter roads may have some commercial uses on them. Most buyers would prefer not to live next door to a convenience store, gas station, or restaurant. Some homeowners with children would prefer to be on an inside quiet street. An ideal location would be on a dead end cul-de-sac road with little traffic. Other buyers might prefer to be on the commuter road with access to bus stops or public transportation.

Finally, within a neighborhood there will be schools which may be attractive to families with children. There are a multitude of reasons why a particular location is ideal for a particular buyer.

In the end, all houses sell. The value driver is the demand for housing. The more people who want to buy a particular house, the higher the price for which it will sell. Conversely, the fewer people who are interested in a particular house, the lower the final selling price. What this all translates into is "market segmentation." Market segmentation is the process by which submarkets within a larger market are identified and analyzed. Houses are segmented by style, size, number of bedrooms, age, quality, condition, neighborhood, and school district to name a few. A young well-maintained four bedroom colonial in the best school district will have a large demand, compared to an older run-down two bedroom cottage in a lesser neighborhood which will have less demand.

Look For Nuisance Factors. When driving around the neighborhood it is important to look for nuisance factors such as noise, smell, heavy traffic, or commercial uses. Also observe the appeal of the neighborhood. Are the streets clean? Are lawns well maintained? Is it tree lined and are there sidewalks?

Visit the neighborhood at different times during the day.
Is there a noisy highway or rail line?
Is there airplane or airport noise?
Visit on the weekend day and evening, as well as during the commuter hour.
Do you feel comfortable in the neighborhood?
Can you envision living in this neighborhood?
What would it be like to sell your house in this neighborhood?

Another consideration is how well the house fits into the neighborhood. The neighborhood will have a range of property values and property types including size, quality, and condition. The lowest value house will be the smallest, oldest ranch in the worst condition and in the worst neighborhood location. The highest value will be the largest, newest colonial in the best condition in the best neighborhood location. Place the property you're considering at the bottom, middle, or top of the market.

Ask everyone you come in contact with such as brokers and owners about upcoming changes that might be planned. A planned new park would be positive. A widening of a nearby road may be negative. If you don't ask you won't know.

Things to Know About New Construction

The reputation of the builder is the most important factor in buying a house to be constructed. As with selecting all professionals, seek referrals for a builder from friends and family.

There are two ways to buy a home to be constructed. The first is to buy the lot and then select a builder. The second is to find a desirable subdivision and then buy the lot and the builder as a package. It is unusual for a developer of a subdivision to sell you a lot and let you select your own builder. Builders have money invested in the infrastructure of the subdivision and want to maintain control of the properties built.

Neighborhood Association: In good developments, the developer will create restrictions that buyers must agree to and which become part of the recorded deed. See the section on deed restrictions in the Anatomy of a Lot of Land (Chapter 10). They apply here as well.

In summary, neighborhood association restrictions may include limits on the exterior look and maintenance. They may restrict parking of commercial vehicles, boats, and unregistered vehicles. They may exclude clothes lines and toys or bicycles left unattended on lawns and driveways. Some associations have rules concerning the length of the grass, the need for pooper scoopers, acceptable house colors, as well as prohibitions of fences or satellite reception dishes. You may welcome these restrictions since they create homogeneity in the neighborhood and increase property values. However, they may restrict you from something you thought you could do, so it is wise to read and understand all of the deed restrictions before purchasing.

The developer may have final say on the type of house you may build as well as its size. The developer's objective is to maintain homogeneity which means houses that are similar in size, construction quality and appeal. You may want a simple ranch house in this neighborhood of 3,000 square foot colonials, but the developer won't approve it.

Be sure to understand the developer's contract. The developer is in business to make a profit, so there will be no additions to the contract without additional cost. The contract will spell out what you are getting. This comes in two documents. The first document is the set of plans that defines the size of the house and the room layouts. The second document is the specification sheet (spec sheet) that details what the base price of the house includes. The spec sheet will define the basic construction materials such as a foundation to be 6" or 8" poured concrete walls, poured basement floor, or slab if no basement, 2 x 4 or 2 x 6 framing members constructed 16" on center, exterior sheathing material, roof and insulation.

There will be a budget allowance for some items. Budget allowances are made for appliances, lighting fixtures, and flooring finishes. This means that the builder has included an amount of say $1,500 for all of the appliances. If you choose to select more expensive model appliances, or appliances other than those included in the contract, there will be an additional cost. Using our example, the contract allows $1,500 for appliances and you select $3,000 in appliances. This adds an additional $1,500 to the price of the house.

Another way to experience a price increase is to make changes to the original plans. If you change anything that takes time and/or additional material from the original plan, there will be an additional cost. Sitting down with the design architect to add some bay windows, to move the living room wall slightly, or to reposition the staircase will increase your cost. It will be even more expensive to change something that has already been built. For example, you take a walk through the house after it has been framed and you realize that to see the sunset, the rear facing window should be about 4 feet to the left. You have already paid to have the window built as it is. It will cost more to move the window location at this point in the building process.

When having a home built, keep the big picture in mind. Before the foundation is poured, take a careful walk through the plans and envision each room and how you will use it. Walk the land morning and night to be sure the house is well positioned on the property. Take advantage of southern exposures and natural lighting. Look at the trees that are marked for removal. Are there any nice ones that could be saved? Once you are happy with your decisions, try not to visit the site again until the house is finished.

Broker's Nugget
The builders would love to have you take this advice, but we recognize human nature. You will not be able to stay away. Try to minimize changes for the sake of the budget.

Example: A good friend was having a house built. He wanted to change the size of the garage by 4 feet. This allowed other changes to be made with staircases and interior room sizes. Everything was fine and all the plans were changed. Then one small error caused a big problem. The builder had set the main foundation wall to be set back from the front boundary line based on the depth of the garage at 20'. When it was changed to 24' the garage was now 4' closer to the property line and violated the town set back rules. The town made him cut 4' off the garage, and with all of the other changes it created an expensive repair. Since it was the developer's error, he had to absorb the bulk of the costs, but neither party came away satisfied. Prior to taking ownership of the property, have it inspected. There may be issues that can be pointed out by a professional home inspector.

3 HOW TO INSPECT A PROPERTY FOR SALE

Knowledge Is Power

The more you know about a property, the better armed you will be to negotiate price. So we will learn about data sources to help you understand the market in your area.

Do your homework before you visit a home in which you're interested. The town's assessor's office has a wealth of information on all properties located in the town. A lot of the assessor's material may be available online. (In the addendum of this book, you will learn how to find assessor material online.)

Get the Property Field Card. The field card or property record card includes all the information the assessor has on the property. You can get a copy of the property field card from the assessor's office. Many municipalities have them available online. The field card shows the property location by Map, Block and Lot.

Now find the property on the assessor's maps. Select the map as shown on the field card. On the assessor's map, look for the block number and lot number. Often it is easier to find the street and then locate the house by its address. Ask the staff in the assessor's office for help, if needed. Take a digital picture of the assessor's map showing the site. In its simplest form, the site on the map will show the metes and bounds, the length of each boundary. The map may show some additional dotted lines crossing through the property. Dotted lines indicate a known easement on the land such as a gas line. The site map may also show any wetlands in the area with a symbol resembling grass.

In some municipalities there may be a Sales Book on a counter in the assessor's office. The Sales Book will contain information on sales, which are organized by year. Feel free to ask the assessor how to find recent sales in the neighborhood of interest. Ask when the properties were last revalued and if the assessed value is based on 100% of the market value. This will help in understanding the relationship between the assessed value and the current market value. If the last revaluation was ten years ago and the assessed values are 50% of market value, then the assessed value will not be close to market value. On the other hand, if the revaluation was done two years ago, they used a computerized statistical update each year since, and the assessed value is based on 100% of market value, then the assessed value should be close to market value. If a question on zoning arises, visit the zoning or planning office to research zoning.

Information Found On Field Cards

The Field Card general *Property Data Section* lists the current owner's name and address, topography description, utilities available to the site, type of street or road, overall location description, the current assessed value (sometimes broken down into land value and building value), the record of ownership, and a history of previous assessments. If available, a key piece of information on the Field Card is the price paid by the current owner when the property was purchased. The field card may have a section with *Assessing Notes*. If present, they may offer helpful information on the property such as whether it is subject to water in the basement with heavy rain, if wetlands are present, if it had fire damage in its history, or other useful remarks.

The Building Permit History Section will show when a building permit was issued, a description of the work done, the owner's estimate of how much it cost, and additional comments. For example, if a new roof was installed before the current owner purchased the house, then it should not be considered a reason for a higher price now. If the house has an addition, finished basement, or finished attic, was a permit obtained and work approved by the local inspector?

The Land Section of the Field Card describes the lot size, its use (single family), and its zone (residential). The Land Section may break the lot into different classes for valuation purposes. The first class allocates the minimum lot size for this zone at the market rate. Other land use is shown next. Other land uses might include surplus, excess, wet, topography, or ledge. All of this information may be helpful in your negotiations with the property owner. For example you may be told the lot has three acres for possible expansion or sub division when in fact, most of that land may be wetlands, and not usable.

Field Card Building Description provides details on the structure. The Building Description includes the house style, number of stories, exterior finish (shingle, clapboard, vinyl, metal), type of roof (hip, gable, mansard, flat), roof covering (asphalt, slate, wood shingle), interior walls and flooring, heating-cooling system type (FHW, FWA, electric, radiant, unit heater, central air), and heating system fuel (oil, gas, electric), actual year built, effective year built, and/or year remodeled. The effective year built is the assessor's estimate of the age of the property considering improvements made. If a 100 year old house has an effective age of 40 years, this means that it would compete with other 40 year old properties. Key points here are the year the home was built, the year of any remodeling, and the assessor's estimate of its effective age.

Sketch and Photo. The Field Card often includes a sketch and photo of the building. This section provides the assessor's calculations of the building area. When reviewing the sketch of the building, it may be helpful to ask the assessor for a list of the building abbreviations included and their meaning. Building abbreviations often include the following: BAS for first floor living area, FUS for finished upper story living area, FAT for finished attic space, FOP for a framed open porch, and UBM for an unfinished basement. You can then use the building sketch and abbreviation codes to help identify the Gross Living Area (GLA) in the home. The sketch may show support areas that are not as valuable as the main GLA. The BAS and FUS are the areas that are included in the GLA. The FAT, FOP, and UBM are not included in the GLA.

Yard Items. Items listed as improvements in this section include garages, barns, sheds, pools, and tennis courts.

Prepare For the Walk Through or Inspection

You may have an MLS listing which will have some photos and descriptions, but these should be augmented with your own walk through observations.

Aerial view. It is insightful to access one of the several aerial view websites available such as [bing.com] or [maps.google.com]. These web sites provide a 360° view of the property as well an aerial view of the immediate neighborhood, and in some cases a street view. You may choose to go to a series of Open Houses, or a Real Estate Broker will set up appointments for you to walk through a series of homes in which you express interest.

Get the assessor's field card before you go. Use the sketch from the assessor's field card to make a working sketch of the property. Use a grid sheet (available at an office supply store) with 10 x 10 blocks. One block equals one foot. In your sketch, set one block equal to one foot.

As you walk through each home, take pictures with a digital camera or cell phone camera. Try to make the first photo the front of the house. This will help to organize the photos later. After viewing a dozen houses, you will not recall which house is which. The sketch and photos are helpful in recalling specific details about each residence. The front photo will tell when info for a new house starts.

Update the field card sketch as you walk through the house, pencil in the room layout. You may be able to draw in the main load bearing wall which will help in dividing up the rooms. Take careful note of where the staircase is. It will help in dividing the second floor space into rooms.

Take photos of the kitchen. Include pictures of all of the appliances, the bathrooms, the flooring and wall finishes. Take a photo of any special amenities such as fireplaces, swimming pool, porches, decks, and finished basement or attic rooms. Also take photos of utilities including heating system, hot water tank, electric box (open it to establish whether fuses or circuit breakers), water and sewer connections, and sump pumps, if any. A sump pump is a water pumping electric motor that sits in a hole or well in the basement floor. There is a float device that will turn the pump on if water rises to a certain level. If the basement is subject to flooding in heavy rain, the sump pump will keep the basement dry. A sump pump indicates a wet basement.

Environmental hazards. Look for indications of asbestos, lead paint, radon, UFFI (blown in foam insulation), mold, buried oil tank, leaking oil tank, and/or composite siding (asbestos). You cannot see some of these items, so ask the broker or owner. The home inspector should remove some of the electrical cover plates to check for the presence of UFFI. Determine what's under the vinyl siding. If you smell oil in the basement, ask where it's coming from and why. A gas odor could be dangerous. If you smell gas, leave the house until it is fixed.

Exterior walk around. Check the landscaping, driveway, garage, barns, shed, and swimming pools. Look for signs of recent updates or deferred maintenance.

Other Initial items of Preparation. It's best to meet with an attorney before you start looking at houses. Get the necessary addendum forms you will need to make or add to an offer. You may not have time to have your attorney review the offer before making it.

Be sure all parties are clear about the role and compensation of any real estate brokers involved. If you are working with a buyer's broker, be sure to notify every other broker you come across in your house search. In most cases the buyer's broker will have you sign an agreement indicating your relationship. This is important since this determines who gets paid a commission.

Since most offers are not accepted the first time, be prepared to negotiate. Since you have been studying the market, you should have a pretty good idea of the value of the property. Most properties sell below the listing price. In some markets desirable properties sell above list price. In a "seller's market" properties can sell above list price. A shortage of property for sale creates a seller's market. If a listing price is well above what you believe to be the property value, it is a "trial" listing to see if "the right" buyer will pay the high price. Skip these unless you are "the right" buyer for that particular property.

How Much Is It Worth?

Whether buying or selling a house you need to know its market value. A detail of The Valuation Process that allows you to calculate a market value for any property is available in the addendum. While The Valuation Process provided will not replace an appraisal done by a licensed Real Estate Appraiser, it can give you a close approximation of market value.

As a Real Estate Appraiser and home owner, I am firmly of the opinion that all buyers and sellers develop a good understanding of what a house is worth. They do this by looking at a number of properties. They begin to understand what the market paid for various locations, styles, quality, condition, and amenities. The looking and evaluating process sharpens your skills in estimating property value. The valuation process in the addendum is for readers who have the interest and ability to gather a large quantity of data, organize it, and then analyze it.

Some readers may like an abbreviated approach which is shown here.

Sales Comparable Grid - Qualitative							
Subject		Comparable 1		Comparable 2		Comparable 3	
Element of Comparison	Description	Item/ Desc.	Adjustment	Item/ Desc.	Adjustment	Item/ Desc.	Adjustment
List Price							
Sales Price							
Price/SF							
Days on Market							
As Of Date							
Rooms/Bedrooms AG	/ /	/ /		/ /		/ /	
GLA							
Location							
View							
Design (Style)							
Lot Size							
Quality / Appeal							
Effective Age/Cond.							
Heat/CAC							
Deck, Patio, Porch							
Garage							
Fireplace							
Finished Basement							
Finished Attic							
Net + or -							
Net Adj Total							
Adj Sales Price							

This abbreviated analysis uses a *qualitative* adjustment process. It is a series of plus [+] and minus [-] adjustments without applying a dollar amount. If the comparable sale is better than the subject it gets a [-] so the price is reduced. If the comparable sale is worse than the subject it gets a [+] so the price is increased. In the chart you are comparing the variables of the comparable sales property against the subject property.

Element of Comparison	Subject	Comparable 1	
Quality	Average	Better	Minus (-)
Condition	Average	Worse	Plus (+)

This is sometimes confusing to first time users of this concept. Your first instinct is say "The comp is **Better**, so I should **ADD**". For each adjustment complete this sentence "The comp is **Better** than my subject, so I **SUBTRACT** the adjustment to make the comp equal to my subject.

Number of Baths: Write in a [+] if the sale has fewer baths and a [-] if it has more baths.

Gross Living Area: Write in a [+] if the sales Gross Living Area (GLA) is smaller than the subject and a [-] if it is larger.

Location/View: Write in a [+] if the sales location is worse, [-] if it is better.

Design (Style): Write in a [+] if the style is worse, [-] if it is better.

Lot Size: Write in a [+] if the sales lot size is smaller and a [-] if it is bigger.

Quality / Appeal: **Don't confuse quality with condition.** Write in a [+] if the quality of the sale is worse and a [-] if it is better.

Condition: Write in a [+] if the condition is worse and a [-] if it is better.

Garage: Write in a [+] if the sales garage is worse and a [-] if it is better.

Fireplace: Write in a [+] if the sales fireplace is worse and a [-] if it is better.

Finished Basement/Attic: Write in a [+] if the sales basement or attic is worse and a [-] if it is better.

Other Items: The grid has three extra lines for you to add any particular item that may be in your market. This might be used for a pool, outbuilding, tennis courts, or anything else.

Net [+] or [-]: Add up the [+] and [-] for each sale and put the net number here.

Net Adjusted Total: Set an amount for the value of a [+] or [-]. You can start at 1-3% of the average sales prices, say $4,000. For example, if there are three pluses [+++], the adjustment is +$12,000. If there are two minus[- -], the adjustment is -$8,000.

Adjusted Sales Price: Add the *Net Adjusted Total* to the sales price for each sale. This is the indicated value of the subject based on this sale.

Reconciliation

The three comparable sales are indicators of value for the subject property. Each comparable sale has its strengths and weaknesses. From these three adjusted value indicators you will form your opinion of the market value of your subject property. The first step is to see the range of values:

Range	Value
Low	
Average	
High	
Range	
Value	

Enter the low and high values. Calculate the average and round to the closest $1,000. Calculate the range of values as the High indicator minus the Low indicator. Now select a value within the range that you conclude represents a market value for the property.

A Completed Example:

Sales Comparable Grid - Qualitative								
Subject		Comparable 1		Comparable 2		Comparable 3		
Street:								
City, State:								
Element of Comparison	Description	Item/ Desc.	Adjustment	Item/ Desc.	Adjustment	Item/ Desc.	Adjustment	
List Price	$152,000	$145,000		$152,000		$160,000		
Sales Price	$152,000	$140,000		$149,000		$155,000		
Price/SF	NA	$127		$124		$119		
Days on Market	45	20		30		50		
As Of Date	04/01/12	02/01/12		01/01/12		03/01/12		
Rooms/Bedrooms AG	6/3 /1	6/3 /1		6/3 /1.5	-	6/3 /1		
GLA	1,200	1,100	++	1,200		1,300	- -	
Location	Average	Equal		Equal		Equal		
View	Average	Equal		Equal		Equal		
Design (Style)	Ranch	Ranch		Ranch		Ranch		
Lot Size	10,000	9,000	+	10,000		11,000	-	
Quality / Appeal	Average	Average		Average		Average		
Effective Age/Cond.	Average	Worse	+	Equal		Better	- -	
Heat/CAC	FWA/No	FWA.No		FWA.No		FWA.No		
Deck, Patio, Porch	deck	deck		deck		deck		
Garage	1 Car Att	1 Car Att		1 Car Att		none	+	
Fireplace	1	1		1		1		
Finished Basement	none	none		none		none		
Finished Attic	none	none		none		none		
Net + or -		++++		-		- - - -		
Net Adj Total		$8,000		-$2,000		-$8,000		
Adj Sales Price		$148,000		$147,000		$147,000		

In this example, the subject is a small ranch house listed for sale for $152,000 which has been on the market for 45 days. The subject has 1,200 square feet of GLA with 6 rooms, 3 bedrooms, and 1 bath on a 10,000-square foot lot. It's in average condition. It has a one car attached garage and one fireplace. Location and view are both average. There is no finished basement or attic space in the subject property.

After researching the market, there are three similar recent sales in the subject's immediate neighborhood. Sale #2 has a superior half bath reflected with a [-]. I set a [+] for each 50 square feet of difference in GLA. Sale #1 is 100 square feet smaller so it gets two pluses [++]. Sale #2 is the same size, so no adjustment is recorded. Sale #3 is 100 square feet larger so it gets two minuses [- -].

The lot size is adjusted based on each 1,000 square feet of difference. Sale # 1 is one plus [+], and sale #3 is one minus [-].

Quality and appeal are the same in both the subject and comparable sales.

The condition of the comparable sales is an estimate. Sale #1 is one plus [+], #2 is equal, and #3 is two minus [- -].

Garage space is the same for both #1 and #2. It is 1 plus [+] for sale #3 since it has no garage.

The fireplace is equal for the three comparable sales and for the subject.

Net [+] or [-]: After completing the chart, add all the pluses and minuses. Sale #1 has four pluses. Sale #2 has one minus, and sale #3 has four minuses.

Adjustment is calculated based on $2,000 per plus or minus. This is an estimate and you can refine it with your own estimates. Sale #1's adjustment is plus $8,000 (4 × $2,000). Sale #2's adjustment is minus $-2,000 (-1 × $2,000). Sale #3's adjustment is minus -$8,000 (-4 × $2,000).

The adjusted sales price is now the original sales price plus or minus the adjustment.

Reconciliation

Range	Value
Low	$147,000
Average	$147,333
High	$148,000
Range	$1,000
Value	$147,000

The average value indicator is $148,333. Sale #2 had the fewest adjustments with an indicated value of $147,000. I conclude the estimated market value is $147,000.

4 BUYING THE PROPERTY

Is an Offer a Contract?

In most states a signed Offer to Purchase is a binding contract even when it is "subject to" the signing of the more comprehensive Purchase and Sale Agreement. If a seller signs and accepts an offer he or she cannot accept a higher offer while the contract is in force. Conversely, if a buyer finds another house they like better, they are still committed to the first offer while the contract is in force.

Most attorneys will advise you to have a contingency clause attached to the Offer to Purchase. At a minimum, the contingency clause covers your ability to get mortgage financing, the home inspection, and specialty inspections for radon, lead paint, pests and other hazards.

A mortgage contingency clause does not protect you in the event the appraised value of the home in question is less than the agreed upon sales price. There are situations in which a buyer is approved for a mortgage loan but the lender's appraisal is less than the purchase price.

There are many situations where you do not need 80% financing and so an appraised value less than the purchase price does not affect you qualifying for the loan.

To be clear, this clause allows you to void the offer, even though you have been approved for the mortgage.

As a buyer, you should have a specific clause that states the offer to purchase is contingent on the lender's appraisal supporting the purchase price. When you get the call from the lender that you are approved, ask what the appraised value is. **This is important!**

Real Life Example
A good friend and his wife were looking to buy a retirement home in Florida near us. They had a large down payment from the sale of their home back north. In discussing the process I advised him to have the clause added to the offer that the price was "Subject to the appraised value." The bank's appraisal came in $40,000 less than what they offered. After several more rounds of negotiating, they agreed on a price much closer to the appraised value.

In years gone by, the lenders had no obligation to share the appraisal or the appraised value with the borrower. It was considered an internal document to assist them with their loan decision. More recent laws require lenders to provide a copy of the appraisal to the borrower at least three days before the closing.

Make an offer within your budget. The offer is the first step to homeownership. Before making an offer on a house, make sure the price is within your budget. The lender is only interested in your ability to repay the loan. Your other life plans don't come into their equation but must come into yours. There are other things we want or need to do in our lives, like retiring, raising a family, putting kids through college, having enough insurance to protect our assets including health, life, disability, helping with aging parents, dealing with children with health or disability issues, etc. Take other areas of your life into consideration when you consider a budget for purchasing a home.

Things to Have in Hand in Making an Offer

The pre-approval letter. You will be in the strongest negotiating position if you have a pre-approval letter with you as you prepare to make an offer on a house. If possible, have several pre-approval letters at different mortgage levels. For example, suppose you are approved for a $200,000 mortgage, but a listed house needs a mortgage for $180,000, and you want to make an offer that needs a $170,000 mortgage. If you show the seller the $200,000 pre-approval letter, they may feel that you can afford the $180,000 mortgage and hold firm. If you include a letter at $170,000, the seller will conclude that you are at the top of your range and may be more willing to accept or negotiate at this price. Most banks provide a prospective borrower with one pre-approval letter for the full amount approved. An independent mortgage broker may be able to provide a prospective borrower with several pre-approval letters.

The deposit. You will need to make a deposit with your offer. A check for $1,000 is enough in most markets. Be sure to check with brokers as you look for houses. Local requirements may vary.

Decisions on existing home. If you own your current home, decide in advance how to handle the sale of your existing home. If you decide you want to find the new house first, then all offers you make will have to be made "subject to" your selling your existing home. This means that the offer and purchase and sales agreement must have a clause that states that the agreement is "***subject to your selling your house***." This alternative is not good for the seller and will often be rejected.

You may sell your house first and get to a solid Purchase & Sales Agreement (P&S) with the mortgage contingency clause met. This is a contract with no outstanding contingencies. This leaves little that can go wrong. Now you are free to find your next house.

Selling first, then buying. Start preparing your house for sale and at the same time start looking for the new house. List and sell your house first and try to negotiate a long closing period. This will give you time to find your new home. Once the buyer of your existing house has met all contingencies, you can move forward in purchasing the new house. Understand, however, that if your buyer defaults on the P&S contract then you may also default on your P&S contract. In this event, you will get the deposit that your buyer put on your house as liquidation damages, but you will lose your deposit on the new house because you defaulted.

Secure a bridge loan. A bridge loan may be available if you have great credit and a good relationship with your local lender. In a bridge loan, the lender gives you a short-term loan so you can close on purchasing your new house. If this occurs, you may then have two mortgage payments for a while. With your bridge loan you will be able to complete the transaction and not lose the deposit on your new home. Markets change, however, and fewer banks are now offering bridge loans. If you need a bridge loan, you should contact lenders in your area to determine if they are available.

A Sample Offer to Purchase Form

The offer to purchase. Each market area has a standardized Offer to Purchase form, which will contain items such as:

The offer is to the owner of record, the seller.

It is from you, the buyer.

The financial terms include the purchase price, the amount of the first deposit accompanying the offer, the additional deposit upon acceptance of the offer, and the balance due at closing.

Offer is subject to your obtaining a mortgage for the amount financed by an indicated date.

Offer is subject to a list of items included in the sale. This is a list of items that otherwise might be considered personal property such as the draperies, washer, dryer, refrigerator, above ground pool, and/or shed on blocks.

Special conditions. Property to appraise at offer to purchase price.

See additional addendum. The offer will have this link to other conditions that are written at the end of the offer. This allows you to include a longer addendum if needed. You may have worked out a list of conditions with your attorney in advance. The list can be attached to the end of the offer.

Date of closing. Be sure you can meet this date.

Disposition of the brokerage commission and which real estate agency gets how much of the commission. If you used a buyer's broker, make sure they are compensated.

Inspections for lead paint, termites, pests, private sewer system, private well, home inspection, radon, mold, and/or others. There will be a date by which the tests must be completed. Ten days is standard. There should be a threshold (1% of sales price) of the cost to repair deficiencies found in the inspection. Example: If the inspection finds more than $3,000 in repairs, then buyer can cancel the agreement.

Any disclosures provided on the property are listed. The seller may have completed a disclosure about the house that may include items such as the basement gets water in heavy rain, the boiler is 20 years old or the roof is 30 years old. This means you as the buyer were made aware of these items before your offer. As a result you cannot rescind the offer after your home inspector tells you the roof needs to be replaced. Read the disclosure to see if it implies that something needs to be replaced. If so, incorporate that into your offer to purchase.

Dual agency disclosure. If your buyer's real estate agent is also an agent of the seller then dual agency is created. Dual agency means your buyer's agent is no longer working for you alone. Reread the section on buyer agency above (see section on Professionals: Real Estate Broker) to be sure you understand that you may be giving up some rights. If you are not sure, check with your attorney. You should have been made aware of dual agency before you get to the point where you are ready to make an offer.

Offer time period. This is the amount of time that you allow the seller to consider your offer. This should be a short time period, one day or less. You are frozen with this offer until it expires. If a great opportunity comes up while this offer is active, you cannot proceed. Otherwise you might end up with two accepted offers.

Negotiation to a final price. Seller can accept the offer, refuse the offer, or counter the offer: If the seller *accepts* your offer, the next move is to the inspection phase. Once the inspection phase is completed the Purchase and Sales agreement is signed. If your offer is *refused*, then you are finished with the offer cycle. To begin again you must make a new offer.

In the counter offer, the seller has come back with a change in price and/or terms. Terms are negotiable as is price. The purchase price is the point of contention in most cases, but may include terms that are more favorable to the seller. For example, if the seller has a new job, he or she might agree to your price if you can close in 30 days.

In your process of looking at houses, you may come across personal property that would be valuable to you but not to the seller. If you are moving from an apartment you will need to buy lawn equipment, draperies, washer and dryer, to name a few. The seller may not need or want some of these items. You can include these items in your counter offer thus saving the cost of buying it new. Limit personal property items; don't include a car. The real estate appraiser only values the real property, not personal property.

The Purchase and Sales (P&S) Agreement. Activity speeds up as soon as an offer to purchase is signed. Contingency clauses are hated by sellers. They can stop the sale, so they schedule all of the necessary home inspections right away. The ideal P&S only has a mortgage contingency. If you have been pre-approved for a mortgage, there is little that can go wrong. The appraisal is the only thing left to complete the deal.

Be prepared to call your home inspector to have all of the inspections completed in a few days. As the inspections proceed, the P&S is prepared. If the seller's listing broker prepares the P&S it will have all of the clauses in favor of the seller. The listing broker represents the seller, and it is his or her duty to protect the seller as much as possible.

Purchase & Sales Agreement Protections

Your attorney will add an addendum to protect your interests. Here is a brief summary of things to watch out for:

Address is correct (street, lane, road, circle, terrace; north, east, west, south)

Title reference is provided, a book and page reference is usual.

The *price* is correct and allocated to deposit and balance due. You will deliver the balance due at the closing.

Closing date, time, and location is scheduled.

The extension to perfect title is a standard clause with one point of concern. In periods of rising interest rates, a borrower must lock in an interest rate that is good for a period of time, say 60 days. If the seller has a problem with the title, they will use the time allocated here to make the title clear (perfect the title). If the extension causes you to lose your rate lock, the prevailing rates may be higher than your original locked rate. This situation does not happen often, but it is a good idea for your attorney to modify this clause. The extension to perfect title clause should state that if the use of this time causes you to lose a rate lock to a higher rate, then the seller will buy down the rate to its original level. A loan rate buy-down is similar to paying points. A fee is paid to the lender in exchange for a lower interest rate.

The *insurance* clause is worded as "currently insured." This clause should be modified by your attorney so that all risk lies with the seller. If the house burns down between the agreement and the closing, the closing must still take place. However, the seller must turn over the insurance proceeds to the buyer. If the property is under-insured, you will not get enough cash to rebuild. A natural disaster such as hurricane, flood, tornado, or forest fire may raise issues about what the insurance policy covers. In any event, you will have a building project that you did not plan on since it may take months to restore the property. The insurance clause can be written with a threshold (1% of selling price). All of the options should be with the buyer not the seller. For example, let's say the threshold was $3,000 and there is fire damage amounting to $5,000 and the seller's insurance covers $4,000. The buyer should have the option to proceed with the sale.

Check the *broker's fee* to be sure it is correct and allocated between buyer's and seller's brokers as agreed.

Deposit escrow agent. Identify who is holding your deposit money.

If you can't get financing, the mortgage contingency is your escape clause. If you have a pre-approval letter this should not be an issue. However, you should add a clause indicating that the agreed price is subject to the lender's appraisal of the property supporting the purchase price. If the appraised value is less than the agreed price, further negotiations are required with an option for the buyer to terminate the contract with deposits returned.

Other Addendum Items to be Considered

Identification. Attorneys need social security numbers for IRS forms.

Assignment. Does not affect most buyers but in special cases the buyer may be representing someone else who does not want his or her identity known. Once the agreement is official, the buyer has the right to assign the sale to someone else.

Condition. Once all of the inspections are completed, the property is sold AS IS. This means the buyer cannot come back later in the process and raise an issue about anything else pertaining to the condition of the house.

Title Provisions. All buildings and improvements are within the lot boundaries with no encroachment on other lots. No encroachment on your lot from abutting lots. Lot must have access by public or private way (accepted by the town) allowing access.

Methods of *paying for items* of value such as fuel oil or gas and last utility payments.

A statement by buyer and seller that no other broker is entitled to a commission.

Title insurance documents. The seller states no one may file a mechanics lien due to unpaid bills. A lien is an encumbrance on the property as security for a debt. The lien holder is entitled to payment of the debt reducing the property value. The title search uncovers liens. However, the property may be subject to a new lien. Unpaid workers can record a lien on the property, after the title search. This could occur after closing. This affirmation by the seller makes them responsible for any such liens. The title insurance company is insuring that the title is clear and that there are no liens on the property, as of the title search date.

Additional Certificates. Seller agrees to provide, within reason, any written information the lender needs to complete the loan. This is a catch all for the lender in case they need additional information.

Insurability of Title. Ensures that the title is clear and insurable. If not, the Purchase and Sales agreement can be terminated.

Seller's closing requirements. Seller agrees to obey all laws, pay their share of fees, provide information required by the settlement agent such as non-foreign status, sign the 1099-S form and provide seller's social security number.

Notice. Provides the addresses of where notices related to the transaction must be sent to be considered notified. This prevents someone from sending an important notice to the wrong address.

Access. Allows the buyer and the buyer's agent reasonable access from P&S to closing. As soon as the P&S is signed, access must be available for any outstanding inspections. For example, the appraiser will need access for the appraisal; also the home inspector, lenders surveyor, and others may require access to complete the inspections.

Legal representation. The buyer will pay for the lender's attorney as part of the closing costs. Remember the lender's attorney represents the lender's interest. As the buyer you should retain your own attorney. In some instances a buyer may use the lender's attorney so long as he or she is comfortable that the lawyer can represent the buyer's issues as well as the lender's issues. It is rare that an attorney would have a conflict of interest between the buyer and the lender. If a conflict occurs, the attorney should advise the buyer to get additional legal representation.

Damage by fire, vandalism, or other casualty. This is further definition and expansion of the insurance clause already discussed. It is advisable to have the 1% threshold on any damage caused from any source. The option to proceed should be a buyer's decision.

Property is to be delivered free of tenants, including the current owners. Sometimes an owner will ask the buyer if they can stay after the closing for a period of time. You should never do this. If anything goes wrong during the stay, you will be responsible, including issues like the house burning down and liability issues if someone is injured. They become your tenant. Should they decide not to go after the short stay, you will have to evict them and comply with your states laws on eviction. You may be in violation of your mortgage, since you stated that you will owner-occupy the house. Conversely, do not ask to move in early. There are still many things that could go wrong, and the closing may not occur. You may have to move out again.

Additional representation of seller. These include items such as: no other party may acquire an interest in the property, seller is not in or contemplating a lawsuit including the property, there is no right of first refusal agreements with any other party, there are no municipal betterments that may cause an assessment against the property. A municipal betterment is something that the municipality has built that improved (bettered) your property. This could be public water, sewer, or sidewalks. To pay for the improvement, all of the homeowners that benefited from the improvement pay the municipality a fee on an annual basis to pay for the betterment. These statements in the P&S addendum protect the buyer from potential negative implications from agreements made by the seller with a third party.

Recording of deed. Monies are held in escrow until the deed is recorded. Most sellers want their proceeds at the closing, but they must wait for the deed to be recorded. This insures no last-minute difficulties with the title.

Condition of building systems and appliances. The seller delivers the premises in a "broom clean" condition. All the systems and appliances must still work, assuming they were working before the agreement. Broom clean means that no items are left in the house, on the land, or in the outbuildings. Once the seller's personal property is removed, the house is swept clean. The buyer may want some items left such as paint cans from recent work, left over roofing or siding materials, or removed doors stored in the basement. The buyer and seller should agree on anything that is to be left: everything else is removed.

Environmental law. The seller makes a disclaimer that all notices were given and/or all laws have been obeyed. The environmental law will vary from state to state regarding lead paint, UFFI, asbestos, private septic, private water, and others.

No violations. The seller warrants that he or she has no knowledge or notice of any federal, state, municipal, or local violations of any health, sanitary, environmental, law, statute, code, rule, regulation, or ordinance. Buyer is relying on this affirmation, and any misrepresentation is enforceable and survives delivery of the deed. This is a clause that ensures the seller is not withholding any information that could affect the property.

Hazardous substances. Seller states that he or she has no knowledge of any hazardous substance created, used, stored, or disposed of on the property.

Underground storage tanks. This will vary from state to state. The regulation ensures any buried oil or gas tank has been removed and disposed of in compliance with the law. Any current underground oil or gas storage tank must conform to state law.

Additional matters. Seller assigns warranties to the buyer. If the seller has installed something that came with a warranty, then he or she must transfer the warranty to the buyer.

The Home Inspection

As discussed earlier, you should go on the home inspection. The inspector can educate you about the condition of the house. Take a note pad and write down the inspector's feedback. In all likelihood the home inspection will result in a list of deficiencies.

Negotiating inspection issues. There is a good probability the home inspection will result in a list of items that will need attention. The offer to purchase will have a threshold which gives you an exit from the transaction based on the home inspection. For example, if your threshold was $3,000 and the inspection report identifies $5,000 in repairs, then you have the option of cancelling the offer and having your deposit returned.

Repair issues in the inspection report must be items that were not disclosed by the seller and/or the seller's agents. Example: The seller's broker stated the basement gets water in heavy rain. It's raining the day of the home inspection and the inspector notes water on the floor which is reported as a fault. The estimated cost to repair is $4,000. This exceeds the escape clause threshold of $3,000. The seller will state the buyer knew about the water issue when the offer was made. If the seller showed the buyer an owner's disclosure statement, the buyer is not in a good bargaining position regarding repairs to anything on the disclosure list. Be advised that some states may prohibit home inspectors from providing cost estimates, so you may need to find qualified estimates on your own or with the help of your agent.

The buyer can ask the seller to repair items discovered in the home inspection. The escape clause is something that you may invoke to apply pressure on the seller to make these repairs.

If the seller states that he or she can't or won't make the repair, the buyer has three choices. The buyer can accept the refusal and proceed with the transaction accepting the property "AS IS." The buyer can invoke the right to cancel the contract. The buyer can negotiate for a reduction in price or for other terms.

If negotiations get close to the offer's drop dead date, the buyer should get an extension. The responsibility is on the buyer to exercise his or her rights.

Be aware that an escape clause has a *date certain* attached. Notice to invoke your right to cancel the offer to purchase must be in writing.

If a buyer fails to notify the seller that he or she is invoking the right to cancel by the date certain, then the buyer has lost the opportunity to cancel the offer based on the findings in the home inspection.

Authors Note
I cannot stress enough the importance of paying close attention to the requirements of an escape cause.

If the negotiations drift past the date certain, the buyer will be in a gray area. The seller may take the position that the time limit for the home inspection has passed, and with no extension, the offer stands. This doesn't happen often, but its best to follow the letter of the contract to avoid gray areas that could lead to future legal actions.

Be prepared to walk away from the contract. In a true negotiation, the buyer should be prepared to walk away from the sale. After terminating an offer and thinking the process is finished, the seller may come back to the buyer's last position. As the negotiations get close to a final agreement, the seller may refuse to do something that the buyer believes to be reasonable. If the parties are at an impasse, the buyer can agree to the seller's position or walk away from the transaction. A seller may come back even a week later and ask if you are willing to complete the deal based on your requirements.

Buyer's Remorse. Buyer's remorse is a feeling of regret after a purchase. In the case of purchasing a home, buyer's remorse may occur after the offer is accepted or the Purchase and Sales agreement is signed. It can be aggravated in a market where there is a lot of interest and several buyers have been bidding on the property. A buyer may feel he or she overpaid. Maybe the property has more flaws than the buyer originally thought.

No one wants to be wrong, so as soon as you win the bid you may feel no one else wants it at that price so maybe you overpaid. Perhaps you may have gone over your original budget and may feel that the purchase is now an extravagance. You may have gotten swept up in the sales process and now feel you were persuaded to buy by the sales broker. Or, perhaps there have been some news articles discussing potential economy problems.

You can lessen your concern with thorough preparation. Having escape clauses and limits in the offer and Purchase and Sales Agreement will also give you a feeling of confidence. You won't take all of the advice coming up in the next chapters, but the more you use, the more confident you will be as you go forward.

DONALD J. GRIFFIN, MAI, SRA

5 SELLING YOUR PROPERTY

Prepare Your Property For Sale

Timing the market is important in listing and selling your home. Is there a better time to sell than others? It's possible, depending on the market and your neighborhood. Homes that are popular with families with school age children tend to turn over during the summer. However, families move due to relocation and economic reasons throughout the year. In a seasonal area, homes tend to sell during the peak season. If you're not sure, check with the brokers you talk to for the optimum time to list a house for sale in your neighborhood. You should enter the market when the number of buyers is large.

When preparing to sell your home, begin by taking a careful walk around the property and making a list of any deferred maintenance items. When something reaches the end of its useful life and is not replaced, it is called deferred maintenance. Deferred maintenance is something that should have been done earlier but has not. Talk to some brokers and ask their advice on what needs to be done to prepare your home for sale.

Repairs and maintenance. Don't replace major items if they still function and are useful. For example, this may not be the time to replace the roof and the heating system. Remember the general rule of thumb on repairs and maintenance. In the sale of the property you'll get back about 50% of costs for general updates and about 80% for kitchens and baths. The carpeting may be old but a new owner will want to choose their own color. It's better to agree to a smaller sales price than to put $20,000 into updates and only get $10,000 back in sales price.

If you know for sure that there is a functional problem that will be discovered during the home inspection, it is better to get that fixed before you list the property for sale. For example, in Massachusetts it is the seller's responsibility to have a functioning private septic system. A good friend was selling his house and he knew that the private septic would not pass state private septic system inspection. It cost $30,000 to put in a new septic system but the house could not be sold with a failed septic system.

Interior show condition. Getting a house in "show condition" may take work but will help the house sell. A house shows best when it is clean and without clutter. Buyers like a neutral color pallet on the walls. If you have a lot of belongings and furniture, consider renting a storage unit for a few months and storing the excess. Family photos send confusing signals to prospective buyers. If it looks like your house, they will not be able to envision it as their house. Take down 75% of the pictures and put them in storage.

Closets need to feel adequate. Having four seasons of clothing jammed into the closet tells buyers the closets are small. Take the off season clothes and put them in the storage locker. If the attic is full of old unused "stuff," remove the excess. Do the same with the garage and basement. Take all those half empty cans of paint to the hazardous waste dump, saving the most recent in case the buyer wants to keep them. If hardwood floors are worn but still in good condition, rent a buffer and go over them and then reseal with a fresh satin finish coat.

Kitchen and baths. The condition of the kitchen and baths is important to most buyers. Remove clutter and open up windows to let in light. Check each light bulb. If it is low wattage, replace with a brighter light. Replace any burned out lights. If a three-way light has only two elements working, replace it. Check all smoke detectors and carbon monoxide detectors. Make sure they are all up to code and working properly. Municipalities improve building codes, including requirements for smoke detectors and/or carbon monoxide detectors. If you are not sure that your detectors are in compliance with current codes, ask the brokers or call your fire department to see if yours are in compliance.

Exterior show condition. If needed, call in a landscaper to trim all the bushes and re-mulch flower and shrubbery beds. If there are any burned out areas in the lawn, have them re-seeded. If the exterior house siding is dirty, have it power washed. Wash the walkways, porches, and decks as well. Painted surfaces can be touched up as needed.

Broker's Nugget
Unless the exterior paint is worn, do not re-paint. If worn exterior paint is the first thing you see, then invest in repainting. If the windows are dirty, wash them. *The windows are the eyes of a house. Keep them open and clean.*

If there are open cracks in the driveway, apply some crack sealer. If the driveway appears old and dull, reseal it. Check all downspouts and make sure there are diverters in place to move rain water away from the house. Make sure all shrubbery is at least a foot away from the house siding. Shrubbery close to the house may hold in moisture and cause mold and mildew. Check all painted surfaces such as metal railings, porches and deck railings, lighting posts, landscape elements, fences, and trellises. Paint as needed. Make sure all exterior lighting is working with the proper wattage bulb. Check the basement window sills. If rotted, have them replaced. If it appears there may be termite damage, have it tested and treated.

Give special attention to the main entryway. Other than the overall exterior, the entryway is the first thing a prospective buyer sees. Put on a nice new full glass door if the storm door is old and/or outdated. Repaint the front door to a nice fresh, bright color. Drive around your neighborhood for ideas on front door colors. Repaint or re-stain the door's threshold. If the house numbers are old, replace them with new ones. Also replace a worn mail box. Make the front stoop as attractive as possible and remove any weeds in cracks.

The Real Estate Broker

Most real estate is sold with the help of real estate brokers. They are paid a commission for being the agent that procures the buyer for your property. They provide many valuable services to earn the sales commission. If you list the house with a real estate company, one of the key services they provide is to list the house for sale in the local Multiple Listing Service (MLS). The MLS lets every broker in the area know that your house is for sale. It also opens the door to all of the prospective buyers working with other brokers. Brokers will help with setting the list price, by handling pre-screening of potential buyers, providing advice in preparing the house for sale, running the open houses, preparing and paying for all marketing material, and handling legal paperwork in the offer and purchase and sales agreements. Brokers also assist in negotiating and delivering offers and counter offers.

Owners may decide to try and sell the house themselves. A For Sale by Owner is known as a FSBO, pronounced "Fisbo."

Estimating the Value of Your Property. Real estate brokers can provide you with a Current Market Analysis (CMA), even if you are contemplating a FSBO. Be honest with brokers by letting them know you are considering a FSBO. If you are unsuccessful in your FSBO, you will be listing it for sale with a broker. This gives brokers an incentive to help you. They know that many properties listed as a FSBO do not result in a closed sale. Most homes are sold through a broker.

You can also estimate market value by accessing Internet sites such as Realtor.com, Trulia.com, or Zillow.com. These Internet sites allow you to find listing prices and recent property sales in your area. From these you can establish a preliminary estimate of the value of your property.

Web site data or CMAs provide the foundation for estimating the current value of your property. If you're not comfortable with estimating the value of your property, you can retain a licensed real estate appraiser in your area. All states require real estate appraisers to be licensed. Appraisers can continue their education, experience, and peer review and obtain a designation with a national professional organization like The Appraisal Institute. The designation indicates additional education and experience has been completed. The Appraisal Institute's SRA designation is an expert in Residential appraising, while the MAI designation is an expert in Commercial real estate appraising.

The Appraisal Institute's web site [AppraisalInstitute.org] can help you find a local designated real estate appraiser.

If you are using data from the Internet and/or CMA data, make sure that the gross living area (GLA) of the homes you use is counted correctly. It is possible that the GLA may include finished basement or attic space. If you need to be accurate in the GLA for the subject or a comparable sale, you can check with the assessor's data. (See the section on GLA in House Styles and Living Area.)

The raw data from the Internet does not have adjustments for location, quality, house style, condition, or other property features. If there is a wide range of value in the properties you are using for comparison, drive by them and use your judgment to adjust for any differences in value. Refer to the section on Start Looking at Property.

The Sales Process in a FSBO

If you choose to sell as a FSBO, you will handle all paperwork and discussions with potential buyers yourself. This includes preparing the flyers and marketing material. You will conduct all of the showings and all of the pre-qualification of prospective buyers. You will screen all of the telephone and e-mail inquiries.

In a FSBO, the real estate attorney representing you handles the legal work. Before you begin the FSBO process, talk to your attorney and arrange to have blank offer forms available. Ask your attorney to be prepared to write the purchase and sales agreement and to act as the escrow agent. In a real estate transaction, the attorney acting as escrow agent holds the borrower's deposits until the transaction is completed. The escrow agent is an attorney working for the buyer, seller, or lender. When a property for sale is listed with a real estate broker, the broker's company may also act as escrow agent.

Your FSBO signs are placed in your yard indicating that the property is for sale and when you are running an open house.

Listing your FSBO. If you undertake a FSBO, you may be able to obtain a limited Multiple Listing Service (MLS) listing through a local real estate broker. Another option is to list your property on an online site such as ListMLSbyowner.com. ListMLSbyowner.com charges a fee to list your property for sale in your local MLS for a stated period of time. Their listing fee is based on the number of services selected. Their basic service fee includes your MLS listing and a listing in Realtor.com with one photo. Other services with increased cost include listings on real estate services offered in sites such as Google, Yahoo, and AOL. ListMLSbyowner.com will include a yard sign with phone inquiry code, forms, forwarded e-mail inquiries, and a web page. For an additional fee you can add more photos, have phone inquiries processed, fax your flyer on demand, run open house ads in the local MLS, create a virtual tour, and/or take professional photos.

Commissions still apply. With a FSBO, you still have to be concerned about real estate commissions. You may want to find the buyer yourself and pay no commission to anyone. While that is possible, be aware that no real estate company will want to participate. You will not have access to the vast majority of buyers that are using real estate brokers. You may find a buyer who is looking for just FSBO's; however, buyers want to have the price reduced by the commission or at least split the commission.

If you are co-operating with real estate brokers, you are acting as the listing company, so you must be prepared to pay a sales commission to the selling broker's company that brings in the buyer. You can check with local real estate companies to determine the prevailing commission rates in your market. Real estate commissions that are split between the listing and selling broker companies may range from 4-6%. Note: You may see offers to list your property at lower than prevailing commission rates. These are limited service offerings. Check to determine the services they provide to compare with a full service broker.

You also have to be knowledgeable about the role of buyer brokers. If an offer comes through a buyer's broker, they must also be compensated. Check with buyer brokers in your area to determine the sales commission rates for their service.

The sales commission is set by you before you subscribe to an online MLS service. It will be required to complete the listing. Do not expect a lot of activity from the real estate brokers if you offer a lower than typical commission split. A broker is not obligated to show your house to their prospective buyers. Since real estate brokers' income is based 100% on sales commission, they will be less interested in showing a prospective borrower your house if the fee split is 1% and the prevailing split is 2%.

Running an Open House in a FSBO. Now with your FSBO process in place you are ready to prepare for your first open house. Consider running a newspaper ad to let the public know the house is for sale. There are also Internet sites that allow you to advertise a home for sale. If you are using an online MLS service, follow their procedures to advertise your open house. Create a flyer with many photos that describes your house and have it available as people visit.

Be sure to create a disclosure sheet that informs the buyer of everything you know about the house that could be considered a detriment. This may seem counterproductive but these issues will be discovered on the home inspection. Better to have the detrimental issues listed up front so they are considered in the offer. Dealing with detrimental issues after the home inspection will make negotiations longer and more difficult.

Selecting a Real Estate Agent

If you decide not to try to sell your house on your own, you will need to find a real estate agent to list your property. Begin the selection process by getting a referral from a friend or relative. It's advisable to have two or three real estate companies prepare a Current Market Analysis (CMA) for you. With three CMAs you will have a high, low, and mid-range prospective list price. Don't just consider the high listing price. There is little that a real estate company can do to cause someone to over pay for a property.

A listing price is a small percentage higher than the expected purchase price. This leaves some room for negotiating. Ask the brokers how they intend to market your property. Question their approach to using newspaper ads, open houses, broker open houses, and Internet advertising.

The real estate broker may want you to commit to a long term listing of six or more months. It is in your interest to have a shorter listing period of three months. This gives you a chance to try another real estate company if the original real estate company is not satisfactory.

Handling Offers

The offer to purchase. As discussed earlier, you have three options when an offer is made on your home. You can accept the offer, reject the offer, or counter the offer. If you have multiple offers, you will need to evaluate risk vs. price. You may have one solid low-priced offer but with a large down payment and buyers who are pre-qualified for a small mortgage. Other offers may have higher offer prices but with less solid financials or a lot of contingencies. Your real estate agent can advise you, but in the end, it's your decision. If you are in a rush to sell because of other life factors, then you may want to minimize your risk and work with the strongest offer. With multiple offers you may decide to accept the highest one and reject the others.

If an offer to purchase is below the expected selling price, you may make a counter offer of a higher amount. Caution is the watch word in a counter offer since it cancels the original offer. If you change your mind later, you cannot say you will accept the original offer. The offer–counter-offer cycle continues until you reach an agreement on an offer to purchase or an impasse.

Don't forget the offer you accept may have inspection contingencies with a threshold amount that allows the offer to be cancelled if needed repairs exceed a set dollar value. This is an area where you can get some added protection if you are accepting a price below what you would like to receive on your property.

Example: The offer is $290,000 with an inspection threshold of $3,000. You were hoping to get $300,000. You could counter at $295,000 with an inspection threshold of $6,000. If the inspection results in $5,000 in repairs, the offer is still good. If you had an accepted offer at $300,000 with the $3,000 threshold, the offer could be withdrawn. In any event, you need to negotiate the $5,000 in repairs. You can also negotiate for time. It may be beneficial to you to have a shorter or longer loan closing date.

When you come to an agreement, the offer is signed and the inspection process begins. If the inspections turn up any major issues that exceed the threshold for cancellation options, you will need to re-negotiate to reach a settlement.

DONALD J. GRIFFIN, MAI, SRA

FINANCING SECTION

DONALD J. GRIFFIN, MAI, SRA

6 SAVING FOR THE DOWN PAYMENT

Real Estate Cycles – Supply and Demand

Markets—like stocks, bonds, commodities, or precious metals—fluctuate, and so does the real estate market. There is a fundamental growth pattern. Consider it the inflation rate, which works as a good illustration.

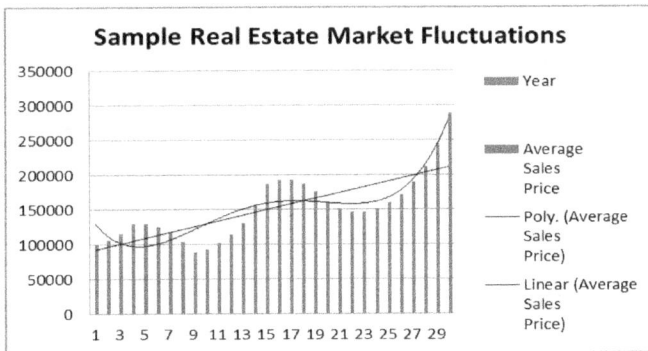

Sample Real Estate Market Fluctuations

The chart shows the Average Sales Price (ASP) for a thirty-year period. The ASP fluctuates up and down with changes in demand caused by outside forces. The straight line up reflects the overall value trend. The wavy curve is a smoothing of the changes in demand.

The areas under the average line are losses incurred due to an over-supply; the areas above the average line reflect above average gains caused by an under-supply.

Like all markets, you have an actual gain or loss if you sell. Any ups and downs are paper profits or losses while you are holding it. If you ignore the fluctuations, then overall you will realize a gain in value, assuming you can ride out any downturns. See the addendum for an explanation of the 2003-2011 real estate market influenced by Collateralized Mortgage Backed Securities (CMBS).

Own or Rent

During a lifetime there are many times when renting is preferable to owning. One main factor is the length of time you plan to be there. If your future plans are uncertain, then renting is better than owning. However, if you get to a point in your life where you are fairly certain you will be in one place for a long period of time, say five years or more, then it makes sense to consider buying a house.

Your marginal tax rate is a factor that affects the overall cost of home ownership. In my lifetime there were times when I was in the 50% marginal tax bracket. For every dollar earned, $.50 went to taxes. The higher your marginal tax rate, the more likely that home ownership is a cost-effective investment. This has to be tempered with the expectation that property values will increase during your period of ownership.

One of the major goals is to retire with no mortgage on your retirement home. That way your only housing expenses are taxes, insurance, and maintenance. This will always be less than a comparable rent payment. In the Lifetime Planning section of the book, you will find a discussion on several paths to owning homes over a lifetime, leading to the retirement home with no mortgage.

For this discussion, think of retirement as that period from age 65 to say age 80, or from the period when you are not working to the period where you may need assisted living.

Briefly, after renting for thirty years, you do not own a housing asset. If you buy a $200,000 house and pay it off with a thirty-year mortgage, and if it increases in value at a 3% inflation rate over thirty years, your house will be worth about $485,000. Therefore, the choices are no asset or a house worth $485,000. If you retire with a $485,000 asset, it gives you a lot of options.

Saving For a Down Payment

You may be able to get all or part of the down payment in the form of a gift. Gifts are regulated, but in essence, a family member can give you cash to use for the down payment. This must be a gift, not a loan, and cannot have interest expense for the gift. The donor will need to sign a gift letter as part of the mortgage application documentation.

Notes on Gifts and Estate Taxes

If the gift exceeds the $13,000 gift threshold (as of 2012), there may be tax implications for the person providing the gift. The threshold rises periodically. A person can give any amount to any relative with no tax deductions for the giver (the donor) and no income taxes owed by the recipient (the donee) of the gift. The main issue is if the gift would otherwise be taxable as part of the estate of the donor.

If the donor has a large estate that will be subject to estate tax, then a gift over the threshold is considered part of the distribution of the estate. In other words, if I had a $100 million dollar estate and was on my death bed, I cannot simply give the estate to my children to avoid the estate tax. Any gift over the threshold is considered a distribution of the estate, so the estate tax will still be owed on the amount given, when the estate is settled. To account for gifts over the limit each year, the Internal Revenue Service (IRS) requires the donor to file a gift tax form. For more information on this topic see the IRS publication 950 [irs.gov/pub/irs-pdf/p950.pdf], or consult your tax advisor.

Mortgage down payment programs are available. There are several federal and state programs available for down payment help or grants. If you would otherwise be able to make the mortgage payment, but cannot save the down payment, then consider these programs.

In addition to the down payment, you will need funds for closing costs. This will include prepaid items such as three months prepaid taxes and a one year prepaid insurance policy. Closing costs also include mortgage application costs, title insurance costs, and recording tax stamps. The seller can help with closing costs up to a usual 3% maximum, depending on the type of loan. If the seller gives you $5,000 in concessions, it is in exchange for a higher sales price. Think of a seller concession as a way for you to finance some of your closing costs, since the concession becomes part of the price and increases the mortgage amount.

To get started you need that first down payment, which comes from savings. That may not be as hard as it appears. There are first-time home buyer programs available. Mortgage lenders can lend with as little as 3.5 to 5% of the purchase price if the mortgage is insured. Lenders sell mortgage loans to a secondary market, which insures them. The two best known are the Federal National Mortgage Association (Fannie Mae), and the Federal Home Loan Mortgage Corporation (Freddie Mac). These are national investors in mortgages. Banks sell mortgages to Fannie Mae/Freddie Mac, and get the funds back to reinvest again. This makes cash available for mortgages, and does not limit the bank to the deposits they have on hand. A third organization is Government National Mortgage Association (Ginnie Mae), which adds a U.S. guarantee to the private lenders, without buying the mortgage.

An important part of a low down payment mortgage is the additional expense of Private Mortgage Insurance (PMI). A rough estimate is $65 per month for each one hundred thousand of loan value. This assumes a minimal down payment. The more you put down, the less risk the insurance has to cover and the lower the rate. You only need it until you reach an 80% Loan to Value ratio (LTV). As time moves on, the amount owed decreases and the value of the property increases.

The most difficult part of saving is that there are so many other demands on our available cash that most people wind up saving little to nothing. The following are suggestions that work, but each has certain drawbacks. To use these techniques you must have the big picture in mind, and be willing to suffer in the early days of your life to have a better quality of life later. As one wise unknown investor once said, "The first million is the hardest." When first starting out, we are at the lowest point of our earning capacity in our lifetime; therefore, only a small amount of income is allocated to savings, and the effects of compound interest don't increase it much.

Rent As Cheaply As You Can

The first basic is to minimize rent expense. If you are spending $800 a month on rent, that is $9,600 a year. If you invested $9,600 per year at 2% for 5 years you would have $50,000 in savings. One alternative, if open to you, is to live with your parents for a block of time. If you choose this route, it may impact your social life, and require you to work out living arrangements with your parents.

If you choose this option, you should pay for your own expenses. Pay for your food if you eat at home. Help with cleaning and maintenance. Remember to think long term and focus on your goal.

In some cases you may find yourself in a position where you can defer expenses. One of our nephews from Arizona was going to graduate school at a nearby college in Massachusetts. He lived rent free with us for two years, and we assigned him the task of taking out the trash. He is now a stock broker in a prestigious firm and oversees our stock investments. In the long run this was a win-win for both of us. He saved thousands of dollars in rent payments, and we have a trusted advisor for little to no cost.

Living with parents or a relative for minimal rent is not available to everyone. In that case, rent in the lowest cost apartment you can find.

Consider all neighborhoods. One of our nieces, when first married, had a goal to live in a nice community, but knew that to purchase there would require a significant down payment. They rented a small apartment in a high density inner city location. It would not be considered dangerous, but it was at the lower income level. They saved the down payment by both working, and minimizing expenses. They now live in that nice community in a very desirable neighborhood, after buying, upgrading, and selling three homes. They enjoyed their time in the inner city, and saw a part of the wider neighborhood they would never have known otherwise.

Rental agreements. If you do rent, you may have to sign a lease. If you don't have a lease you are a "Tenant at Will." If you pay rent by the month you have to give a month's notice to leave. Conversely, the landlord needs to give you a month's notice to evict you or to raise the rent. If you sign a one year lease, you and the landlord agree on rent for that period. There may be a security deposit required, and you may be required to pay the last month's rent in advance. This could amount to three month's rent to start, one month of security, the first month's rent and the last month's. If your apartment rent is $1,000, you need to have $3,000 to get the keys. Other agreements are less strict. You can sign a one year lease and start paying rent.

As a tenant you have obligations as stated in the lease. It is a contract. As with all contracts *read the lease.* When you sign a lease, you enter into a contract. The first key point is that the landlord expects you to return the property in the same good condition when leased to you. Simple enough, and with two reasonable parties, this is never an issue. You received a nice clean apartment with everything working, and you returned the same.

Some landlords can make extra income by having the tenant default on the contract. There is some deferred maintenance when you take possession. At the end of the lease the landlord states that you caused the damage and keeps your security deposit.

Take a camera with you when you are doing your walk-through and take a photo of problem areas. For example, suppose there is a stain on the carpet, one of the cabinet doors is cracked, and/or molding is broken. It does not take much for the landlord to make a case that you caused the damage, and he or she is keeping your $1,000 security deposit to make repairs.

You may be moving far away and don't want to get involved with a law suit, so you walk away. By taking the photos, making a list of deferred maintenance items, and making this part of the lease, you protect yourself from this type of abuse.

If you're single and can't live at home or with a relative, then share living quarters. Even after college you can have roommates to lower your overall housing costs. Again there are difficulties in shared living space, but it will teach you to be flexible. With your focus on your savings goal, you can endure anything for a few years.

Exchange living space for services. This requires luck and research. A friend was a police officer in a wealthy town with many high value homes. One wealthy owner was concerned about getting robbed, so he made an arrangement for the police officer to live in the guest house rent free in exchange for keeping an eye on the premises. This is an example of a win-win situation for both parties.

There are many situations where someone needs some form of service that you could provide in exchange for living space. An elderly person wants to stay at home instead of in assisted living, but needs help with shopping, driving, and household chores. Parents have a child that needs some form of tutoring in math, science, or sports such as tennis, golf, or sailing. If you are talented in a particular area, there may be someone that would exchange living arrangements for coaching their child.

Minimize Auto Expense

The next biggest expense item in your budget after rent and food is transportation. The best way is to forego a car altogether and save the cost of ownership, fuel, and insurance. The next best is some form of shared transportation.

If you seldom need transportation and live near a Zip-car or similar location, use that for a few years. If you are in a city or have short travel needs, you may be able to use public transportation or a bicycle. Another option is a motor scooter, a low-cost, high-mileage transportation alternative. If you must own a vehicle, then choose a used, small, and fuel-efficient car. Use the *Consumer Reports Buying Guide* to help you choose.

Lease vs. Buy. The short answer here is never lease, always buy. This assumes long term ownership to minimize overall cost per mile. Later in life, if having a new car every 2-3 years is important and you can afford it, then consider the lease option.

Other Auto tips. A dealership service option is always safe, but may be higher cost. A better solution is to find a skilled reputable auto mechanic, who has worked for a large dealership and is familiar with the systems and technology of modern cars. This may be someone referred to you by a family member or a good friend.

If you move into a new area, ask around among your new contacts for referrals. Don't be put off by the industrial aspect of a mechanic's shop. It means low rent, not poor service.

The single most important service is frequent oil changes. That will do more to minimize repairs and maintain long life than anything else. The conflict here is that busy people don't have time to leave the car for a day to have the oil changed on the prescribed schedule. Using oil change companies is a good alternative, but you are inundated with other "Upsells."

You need your air filter, coolant, transmission oil, etc. changed, always at high cost. With your own mechanic available, you can simply say "Just the oil and filter, please. Thanks for the tip, but my mechanic takes care of that." Now you can change your oil on schedule without losing your car for a day or paying high prices for things you may not need.

Shop Smart and Be Frugal

In every category of purchases including food, clothing, grooming, technology, phones, Internet service, you name it, there is a range of costs, from low end to high end. Take some time to research the range of price options. If you can meet your needs with a middle of the road selection, you will save money over the long run. If you always buy top of the line latest fashion, you will have less money to save. Buying the cheapest offering may not be a good solution either since it may not wear as well over time.

The best way to save money is to stop spending it. Later you will learn about making a budget. By detailing where you spend your money, you can find ways to trim areas that no longer serve you well. If you're paying for a seldom used gym membership, drop it and take up walking. Companies often tell mangers to reduce budgets by 10% in austere economic periods. This is a way to reduce expenses that build up over time. Learn from these companies and review your budget each year to see what expenses can be eliminated.

Work At a Part Time Job

After you have trimmed all of your expenses, consider increasing your income. If you have a chance to work overtime, take it. There are many part-time jobs that are available for an energetic person. It may seem draconian to think of doing additional work after you've put in a full day at your main job. You deserve a break, and everyone is entitled to a social life, right? There is a higher probability of meeting your life partner in an unplanned and unexpected environment than by traditional social gatherings or the Internet. If you get on with what you need to do to meet your long range plans, the rest will fall into place.

Later you will learn the value of having a wide range of skills to manage your home. A part-time job in a hardware store, for example, will teach you a tremendous amount about fixing and replacing a wide range of housing elements. People coming to the hardware store are looking for solutions to problems.

In the beginning you will know little, but you will learn from customers and your employer. You will learn the cost of items that you may need later when you are fixing your own home. You can learn the cost of tools, plumbing and electrical fixtures, appliances, heating and cooling systems, decks, porches, lumber, etc. This knowledge will benefit you as a home owner.

Likewise, consider a part-time job as an administrative support person for a busy real estate agent. Again, you will gain valuable skills to help once you own your own home. There are also many home maintenance companies that use temps during their busy season and seek painters, landscapers, carpenters, etc. Part time does not have to be for the full year.

7 YOUR CREDIT SCORE

Most people who buy a house will need a mortgage loan. How much you pay in loan origination fees and the interest rate on your mortgage loan will be influenced by your credit score. Your credit score may also determine if you can get a mortgage loan.

What Is Your Credit Score? Your credit score or credit rating is one of the critical factors in financing a house. FICO® is an acronym for Fair Isaac and Company who developed the software used by the three major credit reporting bureaus to calculate credit ratings on consumers. The three major credit reporting agencies and the name of their FICO based scoring product are Equifax (BEACON® Score), Experian (Experian/Fair Isaac Risk Model), and TransUnion (EMPIRICA®).

You are entitled to a free annual copy of your credit report (not your credit score), from each of these providers. You can access your report through [annualcreditreport.com], which was created to comply with the Fair and Accurate Credit Transaction Act (FACTA). There are many similar sites that offer you a wide variety of services, for a fee, to provide you your credit score. It's not necessary to pay for these services. Your goal is to make sure you have no negative or incorrect items in your report. Go to [myfico.com/crediteducation/creditscores.aspx] for additional information about the scoring system.

You can stagger getting a free copy of your report every 4 months. In January get it from Equifax, in May get it from Experian, and in September get it from Transunion. This way you can see if anything is amiss without the cost of a service.

The exact formula for calculating a FICO® score is secret; however, they have released this data:

1.　　*35%: Payment history— paying bills on time is good, late payments are bad*

2.　　*30%: Credit utilization—being maxed out is bad. Using a reasonable amount of your available credit is good. If the total available credit is $10,000 from 3 credit cards, and you get an increase from one that makes the total now $12,000, then you improve your credit utilization, since the amount owned divided by the amount available decreases. If you cancel a card, then you reduce the amount of available credit and therefore increase your credit utilization, which is bad. This may seem counter intuitive, since you are retiring your debt and that should be a good thing. However, the credit rating companies are looking at your ability to repay debt, and you are dealing with a computer program. All it sees is that you're starting to approach your maximum credit limit, and that is bad.*

3.　　*15%: Length of credit history—a longer track record of using credit is good, indicating stability.*

4.　　*10%: Types of credit used (auto, credit card, installment, and mortgage). Different types of credit add diversity to the mix, which is seen as good.*

5.　　*10%: Recent search for credit—many applications for credit is seen as a bad thing, since it indicates that you may be in financial difficulty.*

How to Get Your Free Annual Credit Report

When you go to the free site [annualcreditreport.com], you will be asked for identifying information including address and social security number. You will be offered the option to use just the last four digits of your social security number. This is a good idea. At some point in time you may discard this report and it's not a good idea to have your full social security number on it. Many people like to shred their old financial documents to reduce the likelihood of identity theft.

The request form for the free credit report will ask you questions about yourself to prevent unauthorized access. You will select one of the three reporting agencies. You can get all three once a year, but you have to go through the process three times.

What you get from this inquiry is your credit report, not your credit score. The credit report is what you want to review. The report shows all of the places that you have used credit, and your track record of payments.

Looking at your credit report. Equifax is used in the discussion here and in the next section. It's important to become familiar with your credit report. If you have been around for a while, the credit report can be lengthy. The credit report is divided into 9 sections: Credit Summary, Account Information, Inquiries, Negative information, Personal information, Dispute File information, Summary of your rights under the Fair Credit Reporting Act (FCRA), Remedying the effects of Identity Theft, and Your Rights under State Law. The credit report contains a lot of detail, but is understandable with a bit of effort.

How to Read and Correct Your Credit Report

Credit Summary. This is a summary of all of your credit uses. It shows the total number of mortgages, installment loans, revolving lines of credit, and other credit. It shows how much you owe in total, and the available credit left. The next column is the Debt to Credit ratio. It is the amount owned divided by the credit limit. Look at the bottom of this column line and see the total Debt to Credit Ratio. This percentage reports the amount of debt you are using of the total available. The closer it gets to 100%, the more maxed out you are. The rating agencies like to see a range of credit uses such as a car loan, a credit card, and an installment loan for an expensive item. Remember that variety is good.

Next the credit report lists the details for all mortgage history and then installment, revolving, and other credit. In each account class it reports open and closed accounts. The first thing to look for is that all of the reported accounts belong to you.

Check the names of the creditors. You may have known the company by one name, when the legal or parent name was something else. If you have a question, look at the amount borrowed and the date opened, and see if it jogs your memory. If any of the accounts are not yours, go to the section on how to file a dispute.

For each company that is listed as a creditor, check all the reported data for accuracy. The ideal summary line reports "Pays as agreed." There will be a Payment History Key following the last account. An * indicates paid as agreed. If you were late on a payment, it will show 30-180, indicating the number of days past due.

Each time you are past due it lowers your credit rating score. The other codes are:

(CA) collection account,
(F) foreclosure,

(VS) voluntary surrender,
(R) repossession, or
(CO) charge off amount.

Each indicates debt not paid as agreed, which negatively affects your credit rating.

If the data is correct, then accept it, and work towards better payment discipline. If it's not correct, collect your supporting evidence and follow the process to dispute the data.

If it is correct, but there were extenuating circumstances, you can request a consumer statement be added to the report. Here you can explain the circumstances. If you are a victim of identity theft, you can request a security freeze. This will prevent the consumer reporting company from releasing your data without your express consent. This is a stop gap solution to prevent someone who has stolen your identity from using your credit history to open new accounts. It will also impact you, so use with caution.

Inquiries. The next section on the report is for inquiries. When a company is considering making you a loan, they get a copy of your credit report. This section of the credit report lists all inquiries made in the last two years. These may impact your overall rating since it indicates a need for debt. Other inquiries from employers, companies qualifying you for a promotional offer, or your own inquiries are shown only to you. If you apply for a mortgage loan to several banks in a short period, that is counted as one request for debt. The same is true for a car loan.

You can ask the credit reporting bureau to not divulge your credit history to companies trying to qualify you for an unsolicited offer. The typical result of this type of inquiry is a letter stating, "Based on your good credit, you qualify for a new car: call now for special offer."

Other information. Negative information is debt that was not paid as agreed. It could be an account turned over to a collection agency, or public records for bankruptcies, liens, or judgments. These items stay on record for seven years, 10 years for bankruptcy, and up to 15 years for unpaid tax liens.

Personal information is all about you. Verify that it is correct. Items include: Other identification (such as maiden or prior name), employment history, alerts, and your consumer statement.

The last sections explain how to dispute data, your rights under the Fair Credit and Reporting Act (FCRA), remedying the effects of identity theft, and your rights under your state's laws.

Summary on How to Keep Your Credit Score High. Pay your bills on time, and have a mix of credit including credit cards, auto loans, and department store revolving credit. Keep the balanced owned less than 50% of total credit.

Get overdraft protection on your checking account. This is a safety net for those times when a bill is due but you are short of cash until next payday. Don't bounce checks. A returned check is not reported to credit reporting agencies. But, it may become a collected account if it is turned over to a collection agency.

It is a good discipline to pay the bill when due and dip into your overdraft protection, then catch up later. A better discipline is to have a savings account linked with your checking account. Keep a reserve in the savings account, and if you're short, transfer from savings to checking.

DONALD J. GRIFFIN, MAI, SRA

8 APPLYING FOR A LOAN

The Basics of a Mortgage Loan

Select a lender. As a buyer, the interest rate you pay for a mortgage is important. Banks and credit unions are your primary sources for obtaining a mortgage loan. It makes sense to begin with a lender you do business with now. Your lender knows you and may be able to offer a competitive interest rate on a mortgage loan. Remember you are shopping for a loan before you make an offer on a house. You'll need the pre-approval letter to indicate to buyers that you have the resources to purchase a home. You should also review the current interest rates to determine what you can afford.

When considering a mortgage loan you may also check with a local mortgage broker. Mortgage brokers work with many lenders and are aware of all the programs for which you may qualify. If you plan to use a mortgage broker be sure to get a referral from someone you know and trust.

Most mortgage brokers are honest and do an excellent job. However, there have been instances when a borrower has been misled and did not get the agreed upon terms. Mortgage brokers may also offer loans from lenders in other states. This could impact loan processing if the lender's employees are unfamiliar with the property types, systems, appraisal processes, or state laws in your area.

If possible, have your attorney review the mortgage documents. He or she may see something that is unusual or not in your best interest.

Loan Term and Rate. The term of the mortgage is the number of years that you will have to repay the loan. Most first-time buyers will get a thirty year mortgage term. Later in your life, you may be refinancing your mortgage. At that time you may select a twenty or fifteen year term to pay the loan off faster. Interest rates are lower with a shorter term loan, but payments will be higher.

The most common mortgage loan can be either a fixed rate or adjustable rate. The adjustable rate is also known as a variable rate. The fixed rate mortgage means that the interest rate will not change over the term of the mortgage.

The adjustable rate mortgage. The adjustable rate mortgage (ARM) means the lender will have the right to change the interest rate at some period in the overall term. Some popular loan terms are 1, 3, 5, 7, or 10 year ARM. This means that at the end of each 1, 3, 5, 7, or 10 year term, the lender may increase or decrease the interest rate.

The new rate will be set to an index. An index is an interest rate that is published on a regular basis that is easily known to the lender and the borrower but which neither controls. An example of an index is the prime interest rate as published in the Wall Street Journal. Another rate is the U.S. government one year Treasury Bill constant maturity rate. This index is published by the U.S. Federal Reserve Board. It is the average yield on United States Treasury securities adjusted to a constant maturity of 1 year.

An ARM rate is the base index rate plus a margin. The margin is a fixed interest rate that is added to the base index rate. For example, if the index for the 1 year constant treasury is 2.0%, and the margin is 3%, then the starting interest rate is 5% (2% base plus 3% margin). If the base index for the 1 year constant maturity is 3.5% when the adjustable rate is reviewed, then the new interest rate is 6.5% (3.5% base plus 3% margin)

Another index is the LIBOR rate. LIBOR is an acronym for London InterBank Offered Rate. LIBOR is compiled by the British Bankers Association (BBA) and is used as a benchmark for bank rates in many parts of the world.

ARM rate caps. The amount that the interest rate can increase is "capped" in the mortgage contract. The three caps referred are the first cap, subsequent cap, and life cap. Caps are sometime called 2/2/5. This is read as a 2% maximum first cap, a 2% cap on subsequent increases, and a 5% lifetime cap on the mortgage interest rate. A 2/5 means the first cap and subsequent caps are the same at 2%. To calculate what the highest interest rate for your mortgage might be, take the base rate 2% plus the margin 3% plus the life cap 5% which equals 10%. Over the life of this mortgage the interest rate may get as high as 10%.

Other mortgages available. In the interest only (IO) loan, you pay the interest for a period of time, then the payment changes to include the principal.

A Jumbo Loan is a loan for a single family residence above Fannie Mae conforming loan limits. The Fannie Mae/Freddie Mac loan limit varies over time and location. The conforming loan limit (at time of writing) is set at

$417,000 for single families in the continental United States and $625,500 in Alaska, Hawaii, Guam, and the U.S. Virgin Islands. The Housing and Economic Recovery Act of 2008 changed Fannie Mae's charter to expand the definition of a "conforming" loan. Two sets of limits are provided for first mortgages – general conforming loan limits, and high-cost area conforming loan limits. Honolulu, HI has the highest threshold of $721,050, while New York City is at $525,500. Check the Internet for current conventional loan limits. The threshold limits have always increased since inception in 1980. The dual limits have been in place since 2008.

Mortgage Points. There are origination points and rate discount points that may be associated with a mortgage loan. A point is 1% of the mortgage loan amount. If the mortgage loan amount was $200,000 then one point is $2,000. When you apply for a loan, the lender may charge an origination fee quoted as 1 point. You pay the lender $2,000 to process your loan. Part of this may be a commission paid to the lender's loan officer or your mortgage broker if you are using one.

You may also pay points to lower the interest rate. For example, you can get a 4.625% interest rate if you pay 1 point. The same loan with no points is 4.75%. You should consider how long it will be before you refinance this mortgage or sell the home. A general rule of thumb is that it takes about five years to break even on points paid in advance. That is the position where the monthly savings in smaller mortgage payments offsets the cost of the points.

APR vs. Interest rate. Federal Truth in Lending laws require lenders to show you both the interest rate for the loan as well as the Annual Percentage Rate (APR). The lender may charge you an application fee in addition to any origination fees. Some of your estimated closing costs are used to calculate the APR. You may see a rate quoted as APR 4.181%, rate 4.125%, fees in APR $1,340. This means they charge $1,340 in fees for the loan. The higher 4.181% reflects some of the application costs. This makes it easier for you to compare loan rates and application fees. When considering a mortgage loan, always compare the APR rates and inquire as to what fees are included in the APR, to determine the real cost of the loan.

For a fair comparison the included fees should be the same, as should the term, and type of mortgage. You cannot compare a fifteen year term APR with a thirty year term APR. Also, you cannot compare a variable rate APR with a fixed rate APR. The rate lock period must be similar. A ten day rate lock cannot be compared to a higher rate with a sixty day rate lock. If you can close in ten days, great, but most people can't. Remember apples to apples comparison.

Also consider how long you expect to keep this loan. You pay the loan costs now and they are spread out over the term of the loan. Loan costs are less important than the loan rate, if you plan to stay for a long term, say 20+

years. If you plan to refinance in less than five years, then keep the loan costs down, since once you refinance, you will pay a new set of financing costs.

Rate Lock. When a lender quotes a rate, it is good for a specific period of time. This is the period the rate is locked for or the Rate Lock period. It is quoted in 30, 45, or 60 day periods. From the lender's perspective, a short rate lock time period is better since they know what rate the secondary market (such as Fannie Mae or Freddie Mac) will pay for the mortgage. When they go to a longer period there is some risk that the secondary market rates may increase. This would mean that the loan they are selling to the secondary market will bring in less than the amount they gave to you, because your interest rate is lower than current market rates. To hedge against this, lenders quote higher rates to protect themselves in the event of a rate increase in the secondary market.

The borrower needs about 30 days to close the loan. When comparing mortgage rates be sure to consider the quoted rate lock period. You will need to close by that date. A lower rate may be appealing, but if you can't close within its rate lock period you can't use it. If you exceed the rate lock period, you have to get a new market rate which may be higher. You may be able to extend the rate lock period for a fee.

Often the lender or mortgage broker will provide you with today's rates and suggest that you lock in the rate at some future time, as you get closer to closing the transaction. When you take this path you need to keep an eye on the lender's mortgage rates. There are periods when rates are falling, and it can be prudent to hold off on locking the rate until you get close to closing and you feel the rates have hit bottom. There is a certain risk attached to this; you may lock, and interest rates continue to decline, or you may not lock and interest rates rise.

How good credit applies to loan rates and pricing fees. For mortgage brokers, when looking at competing loan rates, you will note in the fine print that the rates are based on certain credit score ratings, sometimes called the FICO® score. Remember, FICO is an acronym for Fair Isaac and Company who developed the software used by the three major credit reporting bureaus to calculate credit scores on consumers. If you are below the credit score or FICO limit then you do not qualify. You may be required to pay fees to get this rate. If you have a good credit score, you may be able to get a better rate.

For lenders, the advertised rate is the rate you will get. But, there may be some loan fees that reflect many aspects of the loan. This can include your credit score or credit rating and the loan to value (LTV) ratio. The type of transaction plays a role, too, such as whether the loan is for a first time buyer, a refinance for rate or term, a refinance with cash out, or secondary financing.

To refinance for rate or term means that you can refinance to get a better interest rate or to change the term of the loan from say thirty years to twenty years. To refinance for secondary financing can mean that you want to change the rate on an existing loan, or you want to add another loan, or simultaneous loans. All of these factors can affect the final loan cost.

To make sense of all of this, we need a way to compare the different loan rates you see in the market. To start, consider the difference between buying with cash and buying with a loan.

In the cash transaction, there are still a number of expenses you will have to pay for at the closing. These will include the fees for all of the professionals. With or without a loan, a buyer should complete the same due diligence research that a lender would including the cost of an attorney, the appraiser, the home inspection, the site plan survey, the title search, title insurance, deed recording fees, and other expenses associated with the closing.

Now consider the escrow process. The lender is collecting money from you in advance to pay for items that you have to pay anyway such as taxes, and homeowners insurance. These expenses have nothing to do with the cost of the loan. They would have to be paid by you with or without a loan. The escrow process allows the bank to collect the monies in advance to pay the bills when they come due.

Now consider the loan. Direct lenders (banks and credit unions), are required to offer a single rate to all borrowers regardless of credit worthiness with or without points, but collect additional fees based on the loan criteria reviewed earlier. Mortgage brokers are allowed to advertise loan rates, but it is based on certain factors, such as a threshold credit score for a specified transaction type, such as first time home buyer. To compare them we need to calculate the Annual Percentage Rate (APR) based on the quoted rate and the true loan costs, excluding all escrow expenses and all closing expenses. For an example assume you have three loans that you are considering, shown below. This is an example of how to calculate the true APR:

Item	Bank	Mortgage Broker 1	Mortgage Broker 2
Type	1st Time	1st Time	1st Time
PMI Insurance	None	None	None
Credit Score Threshold	None	700	700
Credit Score	750	750	750
Complies	Yes	Yes	Yes

The first items for comparison are shown above. Is the loan for first time buyers only? Will the loan rate require Private Mortgage Insurance (PMI)? It will if the amount of the down payment is less than 20%. For this example there is none. Does the loan require a threshold credit score? In the example the mortgage broker loan rates require a minimum credit score of 700. If your score exceeds the minimum required, then you qualify. For the example, the borrower qualifies for the loan based on credit score since they have a score of 750 and only need 700. Next calculate the payment you would have to make based on just the quoted rate. For the example, the borrower wants a $160,000 mortgage which will be for thirty years with a fixed interest rate.

Item	Rate	Bank	Mortgage Broker 1	Mortgage Broker 2
Price		$200,000	$200,000	$200,000
Loan Term		30	30	30
Down Payment	20%	$40,000	$40,000	$40,000
Loan LTV	80%	$160,000	$160,000	$160,000
Quoted Rate		4.125%	4.250%	4.178%
Payments based on Quoted Rate		$775.44	$787.10	$780.37

To set up the example, I have three identical loans for a first time buyer with a 20% down payment. I compare a bank rate of 4.125% with two mortgage broker quotes of 4.25% and 4.178%. We are solving for PMT, the monthly mortgage payment.

Brush up on Your Calculator Skills
If you want to follow the examples on your financial calculator, refer to the addendum for the HP-12c steps for calculating a mortgage payment.

First calculate the monthly mortgage payment for each of the three loans using the quoted rate:

Monthly Payment with 4.125%				
	n	i	PV	PMT
Variables	30 years	4.125%	$160,000	?PMT
Key	30 [g] [n]	4.125 [i]	160000	$775.44

Next for the 4.25% rate:

Monthly Payment with 4.250%			
	n	i	PV	PMT
Variables	30 years	4.250%	$160,000	**?PMT**
Key	30 [g] [n]	4.25 [i]	160000	**$787.10**

And the last one:

Monthly Payment with 4.178%			
	n	i	PV	PMT
Variables	30 years	4.178%	$160,000	**?PMT**
Key	30 [g] [n]	4.095 [i]	160000	**$780.37**

Summary of potential loan payments:

Item	Rate	Bank	Mortgage Broker 1	Mortgage Broker 2
Loan LTV	80%	$160,000	$160,000	$160,000
Quoted Rate		4.125%	4.250%	4.178%
Payments based on Quoted Rate		$775.44	$787.10	$780.37

On the surface it would appear that Bank has the better rate at 4.125%. The monthly mortgage payment is $775.44 compared to Mortgage Broker 1 of $787.10 and the other mortgage broker payment of $780.37

Now we take a closer look at the loan costs.

Item	Rate	Bank	Mortgage Broker 1	Mortgage Broker 2
Application Fee		$0	**$225**	$0
Loan Fees		**$2,600**	$0	$0
Points		$0	$0	**$1,600**
Total Fees		$2,600	$225	$1,600
APR		4.262%	4.262%	4.262%

The bank loan, after evaluating the borrowers LTV of 80%, their credit score of 750, and the first time home buyers loan product, determines that the loan fee will be $2,600. *Mortgage broker #1* has a $225 loan application fee, and nothing else. *Mortgage broker #2* requires 1 point be paid for the lower rate, which is $1,600 (1% of $160,000). As you can see, the APR is the same for all three loans. Now let's see why.

Deduct the loan cost from the mortgage amount to get the net loan then calculate the APR based on the Net Loan. This is the same calculation as above, but instead of the mortgage amount being $160,000 it is the amount you will receive. This is the Mortgage amount less the fees and points.

Item	Rate	Bank	Mortgage Broker 1	Mortgage Broker 2
Loan LTV	80%	$160,000	$160,000	$160,000
Total Fees		$2,600	$225	$1,600
Net Loan		$157,400	$159,775	$158,400
Original Payments		$775.44	$787.10	$780.37
APR		4.262%	4.262%	4.262%

You will pay the fees and points at the closing. Your total fees and points plus the mortgage amount will equal the $160,000 you need for the closing. The last step is to calculate the APR rate. Here I am calculating the interest rate based on the 30 year fixed rate loan, with the Net Loan as the borrowed amount, and the monthly payment calculated for the $160,000 loan.

Negative Cash Flows
Remember that a payment is an outflow of cash, and is always a minus (negative) number. When you enter the monthly payment in these next steps enter it as a minus number. You can also use the CHS (change sign) key to do this.

Solve for APR for Bank				
	n	i	PV	PMT
Variables	30 years		$157,400	$775.44
Key	30 [g] [n]	?i	157400	-775.44

To calculate the APR (interest rate), enter the three variables, Loan Term, PV and Monthly payment (enter as a negative number), then solve for the interest rate. Loan term is always the same 30 years fixed.

For the Bank loan the total loan amount with the fees of [157400] is entered into PV, and the monthly mortgage payment for this loan of [-775.44] is entered into PMT (the monthly payment). Last step is to press [i] to get the interest rate. This is a monthly rate so multiply it by 12 to get the annual APR. It is 4.262%.

Do this for broker number 1 loan:

Solve for APR for Mortgage Broker #1				
	n	i	PV	PMT
Variables	30 years		$159,775	**$787.10**
Key	30 [g] [n]	**?i**	159775	**-787.10**

And the last one:

Solve for APR for Mortgage Broker #1				
	n	i	PV	PMT
Variables	30 years		$158,400	**$780.37**
Key	30 [g] [n]	**?i**	158400	**-780.37**

Summary

Item	Rate	Bank	Mortgage Broker 1	Mortgage Broker 2
Loan LTV	80%	$160,000	$160,000	$160,000
Quoted Rate		4.125%	4.250%	4.178%
Payments based on Quoted Rate		$775.44	$787.10	$780.37
Application Fee		$0	**$225**	$0
Loan Fees		**$2,600**	$0	$0
Points		$0	$0	**$1,600**
Total Fees		$2,600	$225	$1,600
Net Loan		$157,400	$159,775	$158,400
Original Payments		$775.44	$787.10	$780.37
APR		4.262%	4.262%	4.262%

When looking for a loan, consider the points charged and application fees to know the true borrowing costs. The lowest rate is not always the best rate.

Consider how long you plan to hold the mortgage. If you hold the mortgage for five years or less, you should not pay a lot in loan costs, a higher rate would be better. Loan costs are expected to be amortized over a thirty year mortgage. If you sell the house or refinance in five years, you will not get the benefit of thirty years amortization of the loan costs. To get the equivalent rate again, you will have to pay loan costs once more.

Other Lending Relationship. Some lenders may offer you a better rate if you have a checking account with them and allow them to withdraw the mortgage payment directly from your checking account.

In summary, when comparing fixed term mortgage rates, consider the APR rate offered, total closing costs, the term, rate lock period, points, the credit score to qualify, and other lender discounts for above average credit and/or other lending relationships.

If you are comparing adjustable rate loans, you should also know the adjustable time period, index, margin and loan CAPS.

This chart shows how you might see interest rates quoted on financial web sites:

Product	Interest Rate	APR
Conforming [1]and FHA Loans		
30-Year Fixed	3.63%	3.80%
30-Year Fixed FHA	3.38%	4.41%
15-Year Fixed	2.88%	3.18%
5-Year ARM	2.25%	3.15%
5-Year ARM FHA	2.38%	3.04%
Larger Loan Amounts in Eligible Areas – Conforming		
30-Year Fixed	3.88%	4.00%
30-Year Fixed FHA	3.75%	4.78%
5-Year ARM	2.50%	3.20%
Jumbo1 Loans – Amounts that exceed conforming		
30-Year Fixed	4.13%	4.26%
5-Year ARM	2.88%	3.33%

If at all possible, it is best for first time home buyers to get a thirty year fixed rate loan. You may qualify to buy a more expensive house with an adjustable rate or interest only mortgage. But, this can lead to financial trouble in the future if the interest rates increase.

When a variable rate is useful. There may be occasions when you are buying a property for a fixed block of time. One example is a situation where a child is going to college for four years and the parents are in a position to buy a condominium for the student instead of paying rent for four years. In this case it would be prudent to get a five year adjustable rate mortgage since you know for sure that you will be selling the property in five years or sooner.

In your retirement years, you may want to spend much of your time in a vacation area. You don't plan on keeping the property forever, so you buy it with an adjustable rate note. You plan on staying for five years then selling when the rate is scheduled to rise. If the rate is still reasonable, you lock in for another five years. This may allow you to get a nice vacation home for a block of time with overall costs less than renting for 3-4 months a year in high season.

The Loan Application

A mortgage loan will require your income and expense data, and it is wise to get all your information organized in advance. Being prepared will speed up the loan application process. The following is a summary of the Fannie Mae/Freddie Mac Universal Residential Loan Application form (Freddie Mac Form 65). *See an example on the Internet.*

https://www.efanniemae.com/sf/formsdocs/forms/1003.jsp

If the application is made for a specific property, you will need the offer to purchase or a purchase and sales agreement, the price to be paid, the amount of your down payment, and the source of the down payment funds. Be sure to include a copy of the deposit check. If someone has given you money for the down-payment, have a copy of the gift letter included. This is a letter that states the money is a gift, not a loan, and does not have to be repaid.

There are boxes checked for type of loan (purchase, refinance, construction, construction-permanent, or other). If you are having a house built on a lot of land that you already own, then it is a construction loan. A construction loan is a short-term loan to pay for the construction of the house. It is an interest only rate during the construction phase. When the house is complete, you get permanent financing called a construction permanent loan.

If you are buying a house that will be constructed on a lot of land that is also being purchased at the same time, then it will be a traditional purchase. The lender makes the loan based on the planned house being finished. The real estate appraisal is completed based on the plans and specifications for the house. When the house is complete, the real estate appraiser does a final inspection to insure that the house was built as planned.

As a part of the loan application, you tell the lender how the title will be held. See Chapter 10: The Anatomy Of A Lot of Land—Form of Title. This describes the various ways that people can hold the title of the property.

All about you and your co-borrower. These items will be needed for both the borrower and co-borrower, if there is one. The application will require name, address telephone numbers, social security numbers, age, education level, dependents, and their ages. It will require information on whether you own or rent, how long you have lived at your current residence, and if less than two years, your prior address.

Employment. You'll provide name, address and telephone of employer, number of years at this employer, number of years in this profession, position or title, type of business. If employed less than two years, you will list prior employers.

All sources of income. This includes the base employee income, overtime, bonuses, commissions, dividends, interest income, and any net rental income from investment-owned property. List all of your other income such as Social Security Disability Income (SSDI), Supplemental Security Income (SSI), Social Security, and/or income from lottery winnings, if on an annual payout. **Alimony, child support, or separate maintenance income does not need to be revealed if you do not want it considered as income to repay the loan.**

You must provide copies of W2s for the last two years and two current pay stubs. If self-employed, you must include copies of income tax returns from the past two years. It is also good to have the current year's year to date profit and loss. If you receive child support, alimony, or separate maintenance income and you will be counting that income, then have copies of the agreement.

List all cash/investment assets. For each account asset (see list) include the institution name, address, account number, name of the account holder (yourself or co-borrower or both), and the asset value. Account assets include checking, savings, investment, all types of retirement accounts such as 401K, Individual Retirement Account (IRA), Roth IRA, Simple Plans, and Self-Employment Plans (SEP).

List all tangible assets. Identify each tangible asset, list the year acquired, and estimate current market value. Tangible assets include stocks, automobiles (copy of title if paid off), life insurance net cash value, and net worth of any businesses owned (with financial statements).

List all real estate owned. List the address, type (single, multi-family, or commercial), market value, mortgage amount, mortgage payments, real estate taxes, and property insurance. Caution: Take care not to double count taxes and insurance. If your taxes and insurance are included in your mortgage payment as escrow payments, then deduct them from the monthly mortgage payment, so that it just shows the principal and interest amounts. If it is a rental property, list the gross rental income, maintenance expenses, and net rental income. Include copies of mortgage statements or rent payments for the last three months.

List all liabilities. Liabilities are debts. For each account include the institution name, address, account number and account holder (yourself, co-borrower or both). List monthly payment, number of months remaining, and total amount owed for a fixed loan such as an auto loan. Some lenders may exclude debt (liability) if there is less than one year of payments remaining. List the monthly payment and outstanding balance for revolving credit such as credit cards and department store loans. List all court ordered alimony, child support, or separate maintenance agreements. Attach copies of the last three months of all major credit card accounts, department store, student, and auto loans. Provide copies of child support, alimony, or separate maintenance agreements you pay.

The lender will want you to make several declarations such as:

Are there any outstanding judgments against you?

In the last seven years, have you had a bankruptcy, foreclosure, title or deed in lieu of foreclosure?

Are you a party to a law suit?

Have you been obligated on any loan which resulted in foreclosure, transfer of title in lieu of foreclosure, or judgment? These include loans such as mortgage, Small Business Administration (SBA), home improvement, educational, manufactured, financial obligation, bond, or loan guarantee. *More simply put, have you ever defaulted on a loan to any government agency?*

Are you delinquent or in default on any federal debt or any other loan, mortgage, financial obligation, bond or loan guarantee.

Are you obligated to pay alimony, child support or separate maintenance?

Is any of the down-payment borrowed?

Are you a co-maker or endorser on a note?

Are you a U.S. Citizen?

Are you a permanent resident alien?

Do you intend to occupy the property as your primary residence?

Have you had an ownership position in a property in the last three years?

If yes, was it principal residence, second home, or investment property?

If yes is title held by yourself, with spouse, or other person.

Background Loan Activity

The real estate appraisal. Once the loan application is in process, the lender will retain a real estate appraiser to determine the market value of the property. Once the value is determined, the appraiser sends the appraisal report to their client, the lender. As the borrower, you may ask for a copy of the appraisal report.

When talking with the lender about the appraisal, make sure to get the actual dollar value of the property as determined by the appraiser.

If the appraised value is less than your offer price, you will want to renegotiate the sales contract. This assumes you put that clause into the offer and/or P&S.

The appraiser is not allowed to discuss the appraisal report with anyone other than his or her client, the lender. While the appraiser is not allowed to provide a copy of the appraisal report to the borrower, the lender is required to give you a copy of the appraisal if requested. Some lenders do it as a matter of routine; some release it on written request. Some states have time limits on how long you have to request it, say 90 days. The lender may charge a fee for a copy of the appraisal. The fee should not be onerous, but enough to cover copy and postage charges.

The site or plot plan. The lender also retains a surveyor who completes the site plan. The site plan insures that all of the improvements lie within the subject plot. The site plan becomes a discussion point only if there is a problem.

The Credit Report. The lender will request a current copy of your credit report from one or more of the credit reporting agencies.

Tax report. If you are self-employed, the lender may request copies of your actual tax returns from the IRS.

Environmental survey. If there is some indication that an environmental risk is present, the lender may order an environmental survey.

Your Duties During the Final Steps to the Closing

Managing the closing process. As the borrower, remember to watch the dates as defined in the contracts, both offer and Purchase and Sales Agreement (P&S). The offer and P&S have many tasks that must be completed by certain dates.

Date certain items include inspections, the mortgage contingency date, and the closing date. Caution: Do not let a scheduled due date go by without it being completed or getting an extension.

If a date goes by, the contingency has been met. This is true of the mortgage contingency. If the mortgage contingency must be met by the 15th and you don't have the lender's commitment in writing by the 13th, **you must get an extension.** Other parties might say it's not an issue, don't worry about it. **But, you must worry about it.**

Delays happen all the time due to schedules, weather, or high volume periods. If the mortgage contingency date slips by and the lender does not approve the loan, you may lose your deposit. If you put 5% down on a $300,000 house, you may lose the $15,000. Once all required items are completed, the lender schedules the closing.

Getting ready to move. With your lender's commitment letter in hand, you are ready to begin planning your move. Your move-in plan involves notifying everyone affected by your move. Those affected include your current landlord, utility companies, post office, and newspapers. Find and schedule a moving company.

Be aware that you may not get the keys to your new home on the day of closing. You don't own the house until the deed is recorded. In some instances the closing takes place at the registry of deeds so keys can be provided there. In other instances the closing takes place in one of the attorney's offices.

The best case for you as the borrower is an early morning closing. This allows the lender's attorney or its designated escrow agent to have the deed recorded that day. Then you can receive the keys later that afternoon. The seller is just as interested in a quick recording since they don't get their money until the deed is recorded.

In preparation for the closing, you will get a copy of the HUD-1 settlement form discussed in the addendum. The HUD-1 statement provides the exact amount the borrower must bring to the closing. Your attorney will advise you on the form of the payment. A certified check is typical. If the amount is small, your check may suffice. Be sure to bring along your checkbook. There may be some minor last minute items that were not included in the HUD-1 sheet. Note: See the Addendum section on HUD-1 to get a box-by-box description of the report.

Schedule a final walk through of the property just before the closing. This is your last chance to ensure the seller left all items of personal property listed in the P&S. Check for any significant damage that the sellers caused as they moved. Make sure all other personal property including trash has been taken. The Purchase and Sales Agreement calls for the seller to leave the property in broom clean condition.

At the closing, you will be doing most of the signing. The seller just signs the deed over to you. You have to sign the mortgage and all the loan documents. You will need picture ID and a credit card for identification. Be sure to bring everything the lender requires.

9 LIFETIME PLANNING

This Chapter will show you the many potential paths to reach your goal of retiring with no mortgage.

Once you reach age thirty-five, you have thirty years until you are sixty-five. If you get a new thirty year mortgage every 5-7 years it will be difficult to have the mortgage paid when you retire. A better plan is to always structure the length of your mortgage payments so that the loan is paid off when you retire. This assumes your plan is to retire and live in your current primary residence.

Assume you're refinancing your mortgage loan when you're forty-five years old, and mortgage rates have dropped. You can get a twenty year loan term so the mortgage is paid up at age sixty-five. A better plan is to refinance with the standard thirty year fixed rate and then recalculate your mortgage payment for twenty years:

	Loan	Payment
Mortgage	$200,000	$200,000
Term	30	20
rate	4.50%	4.50%
Payment	$1,013	$1,265

Using the model you pay the bank the $1,265 each month instead of the $1,013 called for in the loan. Your loan will be paid off in twenty years. This gives you more flexibility. Part of your monthly payment may be for an escrow account to pay for taxes and home insurance. You increase the payment by the difference in the two loans: i.e., one at thirty years and one at twenty years. The escrow amount will remain the same. Check with your lender to make sure that excess payments will go against the principal and are not added to the escrow account.

Some people plan on staying in their home until they die. Others plan to sell the house when they retire and move to something smaller. If the latter is your plan, then you have to be sure there is enough equity in the original house to pay for the smaller home at a later date. Be sure to factor in all of the selling expenses such as final improvements or repairs before the sale, as well as any sales commission, seller closing costs, and moving expenses.

Real Estate Market Compared to the Stock Markets

It is the intent of this book to help you manage your real estate purchases so your home is paid off when you retire. Buying your first house will be the most difficult.

Over time, the equity in your first home will increase and, as your income increases, you may decide to purchase a more expensive home. Under normal circumstances the value of real estate increases at a rate faster than inflation and at a more stable rate than the stock and bond markets.

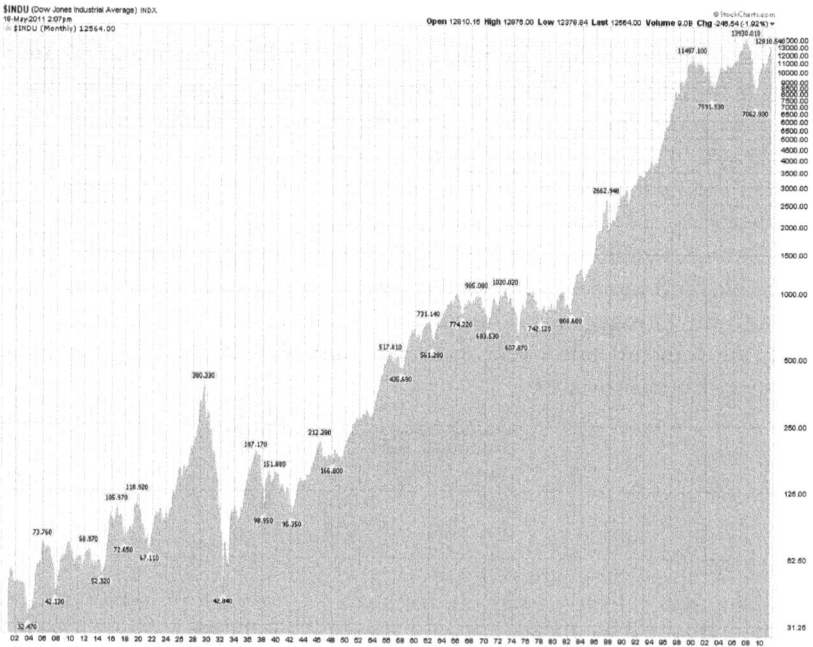

Data provided by: Thompson Reuters and IDC/Comstock
© 1999-2011 Stock Charts.com all rights reserved
Chart Courtesy of StockCharts.com

This is a chart of stock prices since 1900. Overall the trend has been up with many wide fluctuations.

Some people do not relate to charts and the mathematics that goes into analyzing trends. For those that want to skip over the details, here is the quick summary.

For thirty years, the average sales price for a single family home in the United States increased at a rate higher than inflation. Due to unusual outside forces, real estate values increased at a high rate from 2003-2006. From 2006 to 2010, values declined.

The real estate market corrected itself and returned to a normal growth pattern of the prior thirty years. Going forward, the single-family real estate market should behave in a fashion similar to the prior thirty-year period.

While there are no guarantee's in life, I do not expect there will be a recurrence in the market of rapid increase followed by rapid decrease in values. There will of course be some overall minor fluctuations in the market, as there are in all markets.

This should not prevent someone from buying a home, due to a fear that the value will plummet. The fundamental need for housing caused by growth in population needing access to employment, shopping, education and entertainment will be the driving force for new homes.

Now the Details:

The following chart shows the national median home prices as they occurred (dark curve) and then adjusted for inflation (gray curve). The lowest dark curve is the unadjusted median sales prices of homes in the United States reported by the National Association of Realtors ® (NAR).

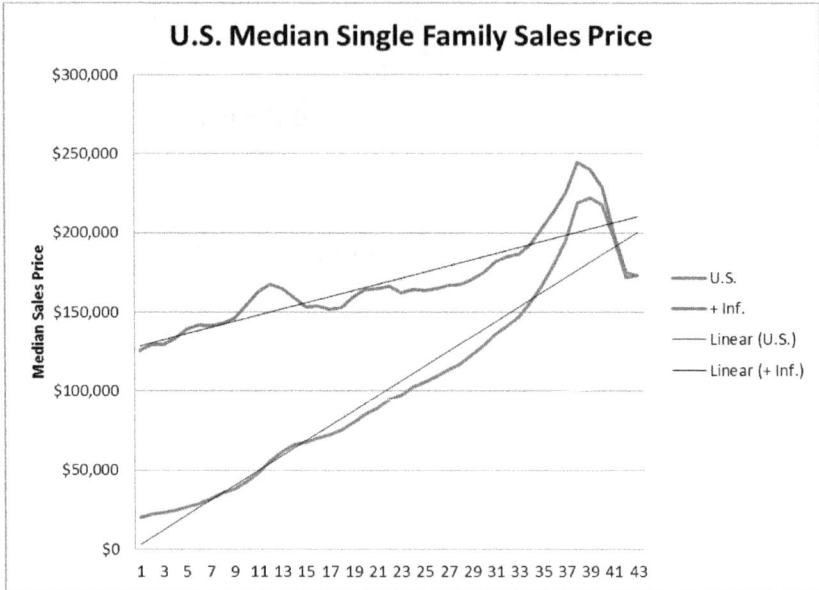

U.S. Median Single Family Sales Price

Raw data source is from the National Association of Realtors ® (NAR)
Single Family Median Price

The top curve line in gray shows the same sales data after adjusting for inflation. The median sales price of $20,100 in 1968 would be $126,000 if adjusted for inflation. The straight line through the two actual curves is the trend line. The trend line smooth's out the ups and downs of the market and shows the overall upward trend of sales prices.

In this chart, the trend line shows that the unadjusted sales price (the lower straight line) is a steep line indicating fast growth. Now compare it to the upper trend line after the sales are adjusted for inflation.

This is the higher straight line in the chart. The inflation-adjusted trend line is still increasing but not as fast as the unadjusted sales line. In this chart, the median sales prices of homes in the United States increased at a faster rate than inflation. The growth above inflation is a key reason that owning real estate is a good long term investment.

This is a summary of the changes from 1968 to 2001 (the beginning of the rapid rise in real estate values).

Value Growth	Total	1968-2001 Years	Annually
Unadjusted	679%	33	20.6%
Adjusted	61%	33	1.9%

The first row (Unadjusted) shows that the median single family sales price increased about 20% each year over this thirty-three year period. This increase included inflation.

The second row (Adjusted) shows that the median price increased about 1.9% (say 2%) per year over inflation. This is a good value increase over inflation, and the overall history shows a stable growth trend.

Broker's Nugget
This is strong support for real estate as not only shelter but as an investment and a hedge against inflation.

Now look at the right side of the chart from 2001 to 2010. This is a blowup of that section:

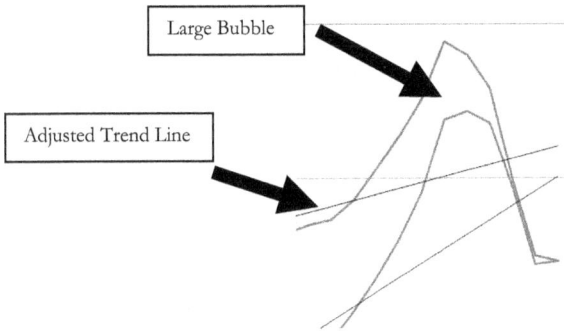

The large bubble above the Adjusted Trend Line is the result of the artificially created demand caused by the Collateralized Mortgage Backed Securities (CMBS) debacle. See the addendum for more detail on CMBS.

Buy low sell high. This adage is more appropriate to the stock and bond markets than real estate. If the market is low, you will have to sell your existing home in the same low market.

If you sell your home at the top of the market, you will also buy your next home at the top of the market. On average, the value of a home increased 4% annually from 1900 to 2000. This can be summarized as about 2% growth due to inflation and 2% growth in overall value.

Having Your Home Paid Off by Retirement

Your goal is to have no mortgage when you are retired. The simplest approach is to buy a house and pay off the mortgage in thirty years. This assumes you will not take out an equity loan or refinance during that period. I will discuss techniques on how to refinance and still be paid off in thirty years.

Primary Residence Paid Off When You Retire. Another approach is to shorten the length of a mortgage if you purchase more than one home during your working life. For example, a thirty-year-old gets a thirty year mortgage in order to retire mortgage-free at age sixty. A forty-year-old gets a twenty year mortgage and also retires mortgage-free at sixty. Some retirees use the equity in their homes to downsize into a smaller retirement home, which enables them to pay cash. (The purchase price is less than or equal to the equity in their current home.) There are a few choices for ensuring your primary retirement residence is mortgage-free.

Buy a fixer upper and apply sweat equity. If you have the skills, time, and patience to modernize a home, you can gain additional equity in the house through your own hard work.

There is the concept of "flipping" where you buy a worn property, make some repairs, and then resell for a profit. This is not the process I am outlining. In this approach, you are buying a property that you want to live in for 5-7 years, at a minimum.

A property may have three types of depreciation. These are *functional, physical* and *economic depreciation*. You have some control over physical and functional problems. Economic depreciation is caused by a change in the economy which you cannot control.

Physical depreciation describes worn property. Deferred maintenance is a replacement or repair that should have been made, but was not. Using the roof as an example, it may have a useful life of twenty years, and is then replaced. If the roof reaches the end of its useful life and is not replaced, it is called "deferred maintenance."

Functional depreciation describes items that do not function in a manner accepted in modern design. Earlier, a description of the "box cars" was provided. Remember, a box car exists when you have to pass from one bedroom through another to get to a hallway.

Another example of a functional problem is an older kitchen compared to a modern one. Modern kitchens have an efficient work triangle integrating the sink, stove and refrigerator. Modern kitchens have a large number of upper and lower storage cabinets, and plenty of countertop work space.

Older kitchens have more open space with area for a kitchen table. The sink was often in a small area off the main kitchen known as a pantry and there were few storage cabinets. The kitchen range stood against a wall as did the refrigerator. They were not integrated into the work triangle. This older kitchen layout is no longer considered functional in modern design.

When looking at a potential "fixer upper" try to envision how it could be brought up to date. There are two types of worn properties to consider.

The first is one that has been vandalized, poorly constructed, or one with functional problems. In this instance, the entire neighborhood is run down, not just this house. The property may be a bank sale or in foreclosure. In these sales the property may be sold "AS IS" with a limited opportunity for inspections. Take care in considering this type of property as you really can't tell what you are buying.

The second type of a fixer upper is a normal house consistent in design with the neighborhood but it is just worn. There may be an unkempt lawn with overgrown bushes or the property may have old siding or need exterior painting.

The interior hardwood or carpeted flooring in this type of fixer upper may be worn and stained, with walls and ceilings that need painting. The kitchen is older style with minimal appliances. Baths are older style with some cracked tile. It is in an overall good location and other properties in the neighborhood sell for more and are well maintained.

If, over the next 5-7 years, you can bring this property back to life, you will increase your equity. Called sweat equity, your work in fixing up this type of property will pay off in the increase in value of your home.

How Equity Builds Up Over a Lifetime

In order to prepare for having a mortgage-free retirement, it's important to understand how equity in real estate builds up over a lifetime. This section describes the building of equity in your home over a lifetime of ownership. The example provided is based on data collected nationally.

Your first house. At this time, the National Association of Realtors® (NAR) data reports the median value of a home in the United States is about $170,000. First-time home buyers purchase at the lower end of the median price. For this reason, our example uses a $150,000 sales price for a single family home. Examples of condominium ownership are discussed in another section of this book. Here is the calculation of equity build-up for a single family home:

	First
Years	1-7
Price	$150,000
Down Payment /DP	$30,000
Mortgage	$120,000
Term	30
Rate	5%
Pmt (Principal & interest)	$644.19
Taxes (Monthly)	$125
Insurance (Monthly)	$31
PITI Monthly	$800.19
PITI Annually	$9,602
Needed Income 28%	$34,000

Example: You buy your home for $150,000 with a $30,000 down payment and a 30-year fixed rate mortgage at 5%. The principal and interest payment is $644.19 per month. Add in $125 for taxes and $31 for home insurance. Remember that basic housing costs include the Principal and Interest for the Mortgage, Property Taxes and Homeowners Insurance, often called PITI (principal, interest, taxes, and insurance).

Total monthly PITI is $800.19, total annual PITI is $9,602 ($800.19 × 12). You need an estimated income of $34,000(rounded), which allows for 28% of your income for paying PITI ($9,602 / .28).

Historically, residential real estate property increased 4% per year. Compound interest is used in calculating the estimate of growth over time.

Compound interest is the continuous and systematic additions to a principal sum over a series of successive time periods so that prior earned interest itself earns interest.

If the growth estimate is 4% for one year, the overall increase is 4%. For two years it is 8.16%, not 8%. Note: 8% would not reflect the increase in value from the previous year's interest.

The calculation is 1.04 times 1.04. For three years it is 12.49% or 1.04 × 1.04 × 1.04. Note that for decimals you put a 1 in front of the decimal: 1.04 not .04. When you complete the calculation you drop the 1.

The result shown in the calculator for the above example is 1.124864. After dropping the 1 and rounding to two decimal places it is 12.49%. This process is repeated for as many years as you are forecasting.

This is tedious for long holding periods such as seven years. You would complete six calculations of 1.04 × 1.04 × 1.04 × 1.04 × 1.04 × 1.04 × 1.04 to get the compounded growth rate of 31.6% for 4% growth for seven years.

Compound Interest on the HP-12c financial calculator

In math terms, this is known as exponentiation or exponents. It is also known as raising a number to a power. For example, 2 squared is raising the number 2 to the power of 2 or multiplying it by itself 2×2. So, 2 cubed raises it to the power of 3 or $2 \times 2 \times 2$. This is written as 2^2 for 2 squared or 2^3 for two cubed or 2 raised to the third power. The financial calculator has this calculation available shown as Y^X. This is read as Y raised to the X power. Y is your interest rate with a 1 in front of it 1.04. X is the number of years you want it compounded, in this case 7. After clearing the calculator, press 1.04 and enter, then 7 Y^X. The result is 1.315931. Now remove the 1 and round to 31.6%.

Holding Period	7
Growth Rate	4.0%
Compounded 7 Years	31.6%
Remaining Years	23
Remaining Mortgage	$105,534

After living in the property for seven years, you may decide to buy a new house. There are still 23 years left on the mortgage. The mortgage balance will decline over these 7 years to $105,534.

First, estimate how much of a remaining mortgage is owed after seven years. This is done in two steps on the financial calculator.

Calculate the original monthly payment. The interest rate is 5% for a term of 30 years with a $120,000 loan. This calculates to $644.19 monthly.

Calculate Mortgage Payment					
	n	i	PV	PMT	FV
Variables	30 years	5%	$120,000	????	not used
Key	30 [g] [n]	5 [g] [i]	120000	**PMT**	
Answer				-644.19	

Don't clear the registers for the next step.

After this calculation all of the registers have the correct values. You only have to change the number of years left on the mortgage.

Calculate Remaining Mortgage Balance					
	n	i	PV	PMT	FV
Variables	23 years	5%	120000	-644.19	not used
Key	**23 [g] [n]**		**PV**		
Answer			105534		

The second step calculates the remaining mortgage after seven years. Change the term from 30 years (360 months) to 23 years (276 months). This is the remaining term of the loan after paying for seven years, solve for the Present Value (PV). The remaining mortgage is $105,534.

The property will have increased in value at the rate of 4% compounded for seven years, or 31.6%. Property value is $197,000 ($150,000 × 1.316).

Value in 7 Years	$197,000
Selling Expense 5%	$9,850
Net Proceeds From Sale	$187,150
Pay off Existing Mortgage	$105,534
Proceeds Rounded	$81,600
New Buying Power	$408,000

Sales commission is 5% or $9,850 ($197,000 × .05), so your net proceeds from the sale are $187,150. After you pay off the mortgage you have $81,600 (rounded). This is your new down payment for purchasing your next house. Your buying power is $408,000 ($81,600 / .20).

Capital Gains Tax Law
Under current tax law, a single person can exclude the first $250,000 of capital gain in the sale of their principal residence. A married couple can exclude the first $500,000 of gain. You must have owned and resided in the house for 2 of the previous 5 years. In this example the house was purchased for $150,000 and sold 7 years later for $197,000. This is a capital gain of $47,000 ($197,000 - $150,000). For most transactions the capital gains tax will not be an issue. If you live in one home for a long time, then capital gains may be a factor.

Your second house. If things are going well, you may decide to sell the first house and buy a more expensive home.

Example of second real estate purchase. With the proceeds of the sale of your first home of $81,600, you purchase your second home for $408,000 with an $81,600 down payment and a mortgage of $326,400. It is a 30 year fixed rate mortgage at 5%.

Payments are $1,752.19 per month. Taxes are $340 per month and home insurance is $85 per month. Total monthly PITI is $2,177.19 or $26,126 per year. You roughly need an income of $93,000 allowing 28% of your income for PITI ($26,126 / .28). This second property will also increase in value at 4% annually.

Here is a breakdown comparing first and second home purchases:

	First	Second
Years	1-7	**8-14**
Price	$150,000	**$408,000**
Down Payment /DP	$30,000	**$81,600**
Mortgage	$120,000	**$326,400**
Term	30	**30**
Rate	5%	**5%**
Pmt (Principal & interest)	$644.19	**$1,752.19**
Taxes (Monthly)	$125	**$340**
Insurance (Monthly)	$31	**$85**
PITI Monthly	$800.19	**$2,177.19**
PITI Annually	$9,602	**$26,126**
Needed Income 28%	$34,000	**$93,000**
Holding Period	7	**7**
Growth Rate	4.0%	**4.0%**
Compounded 7 Years	31.6%	**31.6%**
Remaining Years	23	**23**
Remaining Mortgage	$105,534	**$287,053**
Value in 7 Years	$197,000	**$537,000**
Selling Expense 5%	$9,850	**$26,850**
Net Proceeds From Sale	$187,150	**$510,150**
Pay off Existing Mortgage	$105,534	**$287,053**
Proceeds Rounded	$81,600	**$223,100**
New Buying Power	$408,000	**$1,116,000**

When is it OK to mortgage more than 28% of income? The guide of allocating 28% of your income to the housing costs (PITI) is designed for most income earners, but especially first time buyers. As you get older and your income increases, the ratio of 28% to housing may not hold.

Example: As your household income rises from $50,000 to $100,000 to $150,000 to $200,000 the proportionate share that is spent on other debt, utilities, food, clothing, entertainment, vacations, car payments, insurance, gas, car maintenance, home repairs and maintenance does not increase at the same rate. You may be able to allocate 35-40% of your income to the PITI, and thereby afford a more expensive house.

Outgrowing Your Home — Options

When a house no longer fits, sell it and buy what you need. There is a strong temptation to modify the footprint of a home you're living in now to meet your needs for expansion. You may love the neighborhood and local schools and have a lot of friends and family nearby.

Broker's Nugget
Before you begin an expansion, hire a good architect.

It is difficult to maintain the functional integrity of a house with an addition. The architect will insure it is done properly. Without a proper design, an expansion may decrease the value of your home.

Example: Let's say you decide to add a second story to your ranch style home. In theory this doubles the GLA and makes it a colonial. This assumption is incorrect.

The first floor bedrooms are difficult to retrofit into the classic colonial layout. The result may be a first floor with three small rooms that were once bedrooms but are now trying to serve as a front-to-back living room. The dining room is the former living room and may now have a fireplace. The kitchen/dining area may not have the right layout for a larger colonial style kitchen. The second floor is the same footprint as the elongated ranch and the bedrooms are difficult to size properly.

Another example is you begin with a Cape Cod style home and want to bump out the back to create a family room. At the same time you decide to build a second story to create a large master bedroom.

The family room on the first floor is fine, but the second floor master bedroom is now oversized compared with the other bedrooms. For buyers interested in a colonial house, the large master with its walk-in closet and large bath are great. However, you still have two small bedrooms.

The exterior of the home is also now out of character and may not appeal to either the colonial buyer or the buyer interested in a Cape Cod style house. Instead of renovating, consider selling this house and buying the sized house you really need.

The Vacation Home Alternative

Instead of buying a larger second house, some people opt to buy a vacation home. This can be a simple cottage in the woods, on a lake, at the beach, or in ski country. Some people purchase a vacation home in a southern climate. It can be a condominium or a single family home. Decisions about vacation homes are mainly ownership vs. rental. If you don't plan to use it much, it is more cost effective to rent a vacation home.

You can get a lot of use from a nearby vacation home. In New England, for example, a large number of lakes, beaches, and mountains are within a two hour drive. It is easy to drive up Friday evening, spend a nice relaxing weekend and drive back Sunday night. It is not so easy to drive 1,500 miles to Florida.

The chart below offers a return on investment analysis to determine if it is cheaper to rent or to buy. If you have reached a point in your life where you want to spend three months in the vacation area you love, then it may be more cost effective to own a cottage or condominium.

Here's an example of the calculations for purchasing a vacation home:

Purchase Price	$250,000	
Down Payment	$50,000	
Mortgage	$200,000	
Furnishings	$10,000	
Down payment plus furnishings	$60,000	
Term	30	
Rate	5%	
Cost	Monthly	Annual
Payment	$1,074	$12,884
Taxes	$150	$1,800
Condo Fees/ maintenance	$250	$3,000
Insurance	$50	$600
Total Initial Costs	$1,524	$18,284

Assume you have reached a point in your life where you can spend three months vacationing. You may purchase a condominium for $250,000 or rent a similar unit for $3,000 a month in high season. If you decide to buy, you put $50,000 down (we'll discuss this after the main analysis) and will spend about $10,000 in furnishings.

You take out a 30 year fixed rate mortgage at 5% which is a monthly mortgage payment of $1,074 or annual cost of $12,884. Taxes are $1,800 a year and the annual condominium fee is $3,000. Property insurance is $600. Your total annual costs so far are $18,284.

On the surface, this seems that renting for $9,000 a year is better than buying at $18,284 a year. However I need to factor in some other things: *The interest expense and taxes on a second home are tax deductible.* Estimate 95% of the mortgage payment is deductible interest expense or $12,240 ($12,884 ×.95). The interest expense and property taxes provide $14,040 in tax deductions ($12,240 in interest + $1,800 in taxes).

TAX DEDUCTIONS

Tax Deductible Item	Cost	Deductible
- Interest 95% deductible	$12,884	$12,240
- Property Tax	$1,800	$1,800
Total tax deductions		$14,040

If you are a married couple earning $69,000+ as of 2011, the marginal tax rate is 25%. Every dollar earned over $69,000 is taxed at the 25% rate. Most people live in a state with a state income tax. This varies by state; however, for this example I use a 5% state income tax.

We also assume that mortgage interest is deductible for state income taxes. Total marginal tax rate is 30%, (25% federal and 5% state). At a 30% marginal tax rate (state and federal), the tax savings from the $14,040 deduction is $4,212, ($14,040 × .30).

Total tax deductions		$14,040
Marginal tax rate / tax savings	30%	$4,212

The $4,212 is a savings that will reduce your total overall costs:

Cost	Monthly	Annual
Payment	$1,074	$12,884
Taxes	$150	$1,800
Condo Fees/ maintenance	$250	$3,000
Insurance	$50	$600
Total Initial Costs	$1,524	$18,284
Tax Savings		$4,212
Net Cost after tax savings		$14,072

The initial costs were $18,284. Now subtract the $4,212 in tax savings for an adjusted total cost after tax savings of $14,072. This is still higher than the $9,000 rent option.

One last step. This model assumes your new vacation property appreciates in value over the expected seven year holding period and the mortgage balance will decline. So, just like your primary residence, you can calculate the growth.

First, estimate how much of a remaining mortgage is owed after seven years. This is done in two steps on the financial calculator.

Calculate the original monthly payment. The interest rate is 5% for a term of 30 years with a $200,000 loan. This calculates to $1,073.64 monthly.

Calculate Mortgage Payment

	n	i	PV	PMT	FV
Variables	30 years	5%	$200,000	????	not used
Key	30 [g] [n]	5 [g] [i]	200000	**PMT**	
Answer				-1,073.64	

Don't clear the registers for the next step.

After this calculation all of the registers have the correct values. You only have to change the number of years left on the mortgage.

Calculate Remaining Mortgage Balance

	n	i	PV	PMT	FV
Variables	23 years	5%	200000	-1,073.64	not used
Key	23 [g] [n]		**PV**		
Answer			175890.03		

The second step calculates the remaining mortgage after seven years. Change the term from 30 years (360 months) to 23 years (276 months). This is the remaining term of the loan after paying for seven years, solve for the Present Value (PV). The outstanding mortgage balance after seven years is $175,890.

Next calculate the estimated value of the house in seven years. The projected average annual increase is 4% for seven years which is the overall growth of 31.6%. Remember for compounded growth use the Y^X calculator function to raise 1.04 to the power of 7, as discussed earlier.

Original Loan	$200,000
Compounded 7 years	31.6%
Value in 7 Years Rounded	$329,000

Value in 7 Years Rounded	$329,000
Selling Expense 5% Rounded	$16,500
Net Proceeds From Sale	$312,500
Pay off Existing Mortgage	$175,890
Proceeds Rounded	$136,600

The rounded property value is forecasted to be $329,000 ($250,000 × 1.316), based on 4% compounded growth. Selling expense is 5% (rounded). Net proceeds are $312,500 ($329,000 - $16,500).

After you pay the mortgage balance you have $136,600 ($312,500 - $175,890). Capital gains would be $62,500 (net proceeds of $312,500 less $250,000 purchase price).

Capital Gains Tax Law—Vacation Homes
The capital gains exclusion available for your principal residence does not apply to a vacation home. In a vacation home 100% of the capital gain is taxable.
This comparison is a rent vs. buy decision, so the tax on capital gain is not considered. You may keep the property as a vacation home forever, you may sell it for a profit, or you could turn it into a rental property.

You invested $50,000 as a down payment and spent $10,000 for furnishings. In this model you will need to return the $60,000 at an interest rate equivalent to the mortgage or 5%. The future value of $60,000 invested at 5% for seven years is about $85,100, which is repayment of the investment.

Calculate Future Value					
	n	i	PV	PMT	FV
Variables	7 years	5%	$60,000	not used	????
Key	7 [g] [n]	5 [g] [i]	60000		FV
Answer					-85,082.16

On the financial calculator present value (PV) is $60,000, interest rate is 5%. The number of years is seven. Solve for future value which is $85,082, rounded to $85,100. This can also be calculated in Excel with the Future Value formula [=FV(.05/12,7*12,,60000)].

Proceeds Rounded	$136,600
Return Down Payment + Interest	$85,100
Net growth	$51,500

Net growth in value in this model is $51,500 ($136,600 - $85,100). In summary you will have netted $51,500 in profits after holding the vacation home for seven years, after repaying the $50,000 for the down payment and the $10,000 used to furnish it.

Now, it is interesting to determine how much you would need to save each month to accumulate $51,500 at 5% interest for seven years. On the financial calculator future value (FV) is $51,500, interest rate is 5%, number of years is seven, solve for payment (PMT). The monthly payment is $513.

Calculate Sinking Fund to reach a Future Value

	n	i	PV	PMT	FV
Variables	7 years	5%	not used	????	$51,500
Key	7 [g] [n]	5 [g] [i]		**PMT**	51500
Answer				-513.31	

This means that you would need to save $513 monthly in a savings account that pays 5% for seven years to accumulate $51,500. This can also be calculated in excel with the payment (PMT) formula [=PMT(.05/12,7*12,,51500)]. If you are not familiar with the concept of a sinking fund, see the addendum on this topic.

We now deduct the $6,160 ($513.31 × 12) which is the annual sinking fund amount needed to match the $51,500 in profits:

Cost	Monthly	Annual
Payment	$1,074	$12,884
Taxes	$150	$1,800
Condo Fees/ maintenance	$250	$3,000
Insurance	$50	$600
Total Initial Costs	$1,524	$18,284
Tax Savings		$4,212
Net Cost after tax savings		$14,072
Equity Growth	$513	$6,160
Final Projected Cost		$7,912
Rent 3 Months	$3,000	$9,000

The net cost after tax savings was $14,072. The monthly equity growth is $513 or $6,160 annually. After deducting the equity growth, total final estimated costs are $7,912, compared to the cost of rental which is $9,000 annually. In summary, if you can commit to a three month vacation in the same location for seven years, with these assumptions, then buying is a good alternative to renting.

The vacation home down payment. If you do not have the $50,000 saved to purchase the vacation home, you may be able to get it from the equity in your second home.

Assuming you purchased the second primary residence after holding your first one for seven years, you will start to build up equity in the second home as you pay down the mortgage and as value increases as shown in the following table:

Year	Value (A)	Mortgage (B)	Equity (C) (A- B)	20% LTV (D) (A × .20)	Over 20% (C - D)
0	$408,000	$326,400	$81,600	$81,600	$0
1	$424,320	$321,584	$102,736	$84,864	$17,872
2	$441,293	$316,522	$124,770	$88,259	$36,512
3	$458,945	$311,201	$147,743	$91,789	$55,954
4	$477,302	$305,608	$171,694	$95,460	$76,234
5	$496,394	$299,729	$196,665	$99,279	$97,387
6	$516,250	$293,549	$222,701	$103,250	$119,451
7	$536,900	$287,053	$249,848	$107,380	$142,468

At the end of the first year in your second home, you have increased your equity over the required 20% Loan to Value (LTV) ratio by $17,872. The new value is $424,320, mortgage balance of $321,584, and total equity of $102,736 ($424,320 - $321,584).

You need 20% to maintain the LTV or $84,864 ($424,320 × .2). The equity over the LTV is $17,872 ($102,736 - $84,864).

In summary, at the end of year one you could borrow $17,872 as an equity loan without changing the primary mortgage. You can see by the end of year three you have over $50,000 in usable equity in your second home.

Key Point
If you want to have your home paid off when you retire, do not think of using the equity in your primary home to buy a new car or take a vacation.

Your equity should only be used to place you in the position of having your retirement home paid off at the time you retire. Your vacation home should be considered a part of your primary home investment.

Your Retirement Home

As you approach retirement, it's important to have a lot of flexibility. If you plan to stay in your primary home, then you should have no mortgage.

If you plan to move to a different home for retirement, you should plan to have enough equity in your primary residence to purchase the new home outright without a mortgage. If you have a vacation home, and plan on keeping that along with your primary retirement residence, then that property should also have no mortgage.

Aging in place. As you get older, several new housing issues may arise. For example, your retirement assets may be partly depleted and inflation could have taken a toll on your budget.

As you proceed through your retirement, you may find your taxes become a larger percentage of your budget. Food, clothing, medical, and transportation costs will likely increase with inflation.

An eighty year old male has a life expectancy of 7.9 years. A woman of the same age can expect to live 9.43 years. In later retirement you may reach a point where you need additional income.

Some people purchase a *life annuity* if they need more income in their old age.

A life annuity turns an asset into income.

There are many types of annuity products offered to suit a wide range of purposes; this is specifically about the *life annuity*.

A life annuity is a financial instrument in which you invest capital such as cash, stocks, bonds, real estate, or a paid-up whole life insurance policy.

The life annuity has an expected rate of return over the holding period. The holding period is your expected remaining life. With a life annuity, you receive periodic fixed payments, usually monthly.

The fixed payment is partially a portion of your investment and partially interest earned at the interest rate quoted. Only the interest portion is taxable income. When you die, the asset is gone.

At the end of your life, any remaining value in the annuity reverts to the insurance company that provides the annuity. This is done to guarantee that the income continues for life for both you and the large pool of other investors in the life annuity product.

The insurance company relies on a concept called cross-subsidy or the "law of large numbers." The distribution of funds from the annuity is based on the average lifespan of all of the people buying that product. People that die early will not use all of their investment. Those that live longer will use more than they invested. Thus it is a form of longevity insurance.

Example: Assume you have $150,000 to invest. This is the future value (FV) from the provider's perspective. The rate of return is 3%. Your life expectancy is ten years. The payment to you is $1,073 per month [=PMT(rate,term,,FV)] in Excel. Calculate with the HP-12c:

	n	i	PV	PMT	FV
Variables	10 years	3%	not used	????	$150,000
Key	10 [g] [n]	3 [g] [i]		**PMT**	
Answer				-1,073.41	

Alternatively, think of the $150,000 in a savings account that earns 3% annually. This would provide an annual income of $4,500 ($150,000 × .03) or $375 monthly.

In a simple savings account, the principal is untouched and you get just the interest. In a life annuity you get the interest *plus a portion of the investment.*

The comparison then is $1,073 monthly for the rest of your life, with no asset remaining, or $375 a month for the rest of your life with your $150,000 base asset left to your estate. At the end of ten years with a savings account, you still have the $150,000 base investment. With a life annuity, upon death, the asset is gone.

Downsizing. Think of your home as an asset. When you die, the asset will go into your estate. You have many choices of what to do with the house as you age. If costs exceed income in your retirement home, you can sell it, buy something smaller and use the surplus cash to augment your income.

As an example your home may be worth $500,000. You can buy a small comfortable condominium for $250,000. This will leave you with $250,000 in cash (excluding selling expense and other costs). If you invest this in a safe investment vehicle paying 3% annually, it will provide $625 monthly income.

If you need more than that, you can use the $250,000 to buy a life annuity described above that would pay you about $1,789 monthly assuming a ten year life expectancy.

Calculate Annuity Payment					
	n	i	PV	PMT	FV
Variables	10 years	3%	not used	????	$250,000
Key	10 [g] [n]	3 [g] [i]		**PMT**	
Answer				-1,789.02	

Keep an eye on the tax consequences when you buy something smaller. You can exclude up to $250,000 in capital gains if single or $500,000 if married. Talk to your tax accountant for help here.

Your maintenance costs will decrease as well. If you add up all of the expenses of maintaining the exterior of a $500,000 single family home, it is likely to be more than the condominium fee. Your utility expenses are likely to be smaller since it costs less to heat/cool a small condominium than a large single family dwelling.

The Reverse Mortgage

Another alternative is the reverse mortgage. If you stay in your home and you need additional cash, the reverse mortgage may help. When considering this product, you should talk with your trusted advisors including your attorney, banker, and tax consultant.

At this point in your life you may want the services of an attorney who specializes in elder law with skills in estate planning, long term care planning, probate administration, asset protection and estate tax planning.

If you consider a reverse mortgage you will need to meet with a HUD approved counseling agency that will teach you about the reverse mortgage and answer any questions you may have.

Because of the upfront loan costs, the reverse mortgage is not cost effective if you plan to move in a short time.

There are several rules you need to meet to qualify for a reverse mortgage. Your primary home must be mostly paid for and all owners of the property must be at least 62 years of age or older.

You must live in the home which can be a single family, condominium or 2-4 family home. If you quality for a reverse mortgage any existing mortgage loan on the property is paid off by the proceeds from the new reverse mortgage.

Most reverse mortgages are Home Equity Conversion Mortgages (HECM), and are insured by the federal government through the Federal Housing Administration (FHA), a part of the U.S. Department of Housing and Urban Development.

The maximum loan limit is $625,000 or the appraised value of the house, whichever is lower. If you have to move from the home for any reason, then the loan becomes due and payable. Typical reasons are the need for assisted living or nursing home. There is another product called the HECM Saver that may be useful for short term use or for small loan amounts.

The lender will determine what portion of the home's value is available to you for a loan. Let's say $250,000 is available to you on your home with a market value of $500,000. Also assume there is no existing mortgage on your home.

Upon approval, you can take the $250,000 in a lump sum, use it as a line of credit and take it as you need it, or the lender will calculate a monthly payment similar to a life annuity. The monthly payment might be $1,789 based on a ten-year expected life, 3% rate of return, with a $250,000 investment.

The upside of a reverse mortgage is that you can get out of it at any time by repaying the balance owed. If you live longer than expected and the amount you owe exceeds the value of the house, you will still get your monthly payments.

The following are summary details about a reverse mortgage:

You will never make a payment with a reverse mortgage.

Your income has no bearing on how you qualify.

The loan is based on the value of your house.

You can use income from the loan to qualify in other credit applications such as a car loan or credit card.

You do not pay income tax on the amount you receive.

This is a loan to you so it is not taxable.

The income you receive will not affect your Social Security, Medicare, or retirement packages. (However, if you take a large lump sum and leave it in a liquid cash account, it could affect some Medicaid programs which look at liquid assets.)

You will never have to move out of your home based on the amount that you owe.

All reverse mortgages are non-recourse loans. This means that you will never owe more than the appraised value of the home at the time it is sold.

On the other hand, you are still responsible for taxes, insurance and maintenance.

You still own the house and can sell it anytime you wish.

You will of course have to repay the loan at the time of the sale.

Upon your death, the property is in your estate.

Your estate will have the option to pay the outstanding loan balance either from the sale of the house or from other assets.

The variable interest rate the bank is charging for the loan will not affect the amount you receive, if taken on a fixed monthly income for life.

The variable rate will affect the accumulated interest being charged for the loan, and in effect how much of the home's value is being depleted each year.

There is little to no costs at closing, since all loan costs and closing costs can be incorporated into the loan. You don't escape these charges. You are borrowing from the equity in the home to pay them.

The downside factors of the reverse mortgage. The first cost is the origination fee paid to process the loan. This is 2% of the first $200,000 and 1% after that up to a maximum cost of $6,000.

In our example, the loan origination fee would be $4,500. You will also have all of the other closing costs associated with any traditional mortgage.

Next is the Mortgage Insurance Premium (MIP). This is 2% of the maximum loan plus 1.25% of the loan balance. This was raised from 0.5% in 2010. In our example, $4,000 is paid for the first MIP and 1.25% is added to the interest rate.

The service fee set-aside (SFSA) is a fee that is typically charged for servicing the loan. It does not apply to all HECM loans, so check with your lender. It can range from $20-$35 monthly. It affects the loan in two ways.

The lender calculates the total expected costs to service the loan over the expected life of the loan. Lenders typically use one hundred years as the expected life of the borrower, not the actual expected life of the borrower, which is used in other calculations. In our example, assume the borrower was seventy years old and they used $30 as the monthly service fee. The set aside amount will be $10,800 ($30.00 × 12 months × 30 years).

This amount is deducted from the amount of money available. In our example the $250,000 available for borrowing is decreased by $10,800 to $239,200. The actual amount charged is taken when the loan is paid. If it was paid off in ten years, the actual charge for servicing the loan over the ten years would be $3,600, and would be deducted from the sale proceeds.

Another alternative is the HECM Saver. There is a new product called the HECM saver. In this product the upfront MIP is lower at 0.01% compared to 2%, however the total amount available to borrow is reduced 10-18%. This is useful for people who want to borrow a small amount, or do not plan to stay in the house for a long period.

The interest rate on a reverse mortgage may be fixed, however the total expected loan must be taken in a lump sum. In our example, if a fixed loan rate is used, then the $250,000 is taken all at once.

This means that the interest charges start right away on the total $250,000 loan.

For comparison purposes, see where you could invest the $250,000 and get the same rate of return in a safe investment.

Most reverse mortgage interest rates are variable. The borrower takes the loan in amounts when needed and only pays interest on the amount owed. The downside is that the payment due on the variable interest rate may increase over time.

Most interest rates are based on the LIBOR rate and are adjusted monthly. LIBOR is an acronym for London InterBank Offered Rate. The rate starts with the current LIBOR rate and then the lender adds on a percentage for their margin, then the 1.25% MIP is added. Say the current LIBOR rate is 2.0% and the lender's margin is 1.5%.

Total variable interest rate is 4.75%. (2.0% + 1.5% + 1.25%). In the last 32 years the twelve month LIBOR rate ranged from 0.7% to 9.4% with an average of 4.4%. It tracks inflation and in 2006 it averaged 5.3%. If interest rates rise, LIBOR could go to 4.0%. This would calculate your variable rate to be 7.25% (4.0% +1.5% + 1.25%).

Most reverse mortgage loans are offered through the U.S. Department of Housing and Urban Development (HUD). The loan is made through a participating bank and insured by the federal government.

For more information, visit the HUD.gov Internet site and click on "Learn about Reverse Mortgage for seniors." The amount HUD will insure for a reverse mortgage is limited. There are other non-HUD insured lenders available for high value properties.

The Life Estate Deed/Trust

Key Point
It is best not to use this feature of home ownership until you have talked with an estate planning attorney.

In a life estate deed/trust, the owner gifts the home to someone else like a son, daughter, or life partner. This person is known as the remainder-man.

The owner, now the donor, retains the life estate and becomes a tenant in the home. The donor can live in the home for the rest of his or her life and the remainder-man cannot sell or force the donor to move.

There is a deed transferring the property to those receiving the gift (donee). The owner/tenant/donor is still responsible for taxes, insurance, and maintenance.

This is often used in estate planning and is seen in law practices which specialize in working with senior citizens.

The Age Restricted Condominium Model

A condominium project that has an age restriction for owners is often called a 55+ condominium. If you get to a point in your life where maintaining the large old home is undesirable, you might consider a 55+ community. This is different from a traditional condominium.

Most cities and towns have 55+ condominiums available. For this example, I assume you have enough equity in your existing home to net enough cash to buy a condominium outright. It also assumes you have enough income to pay the association fees, taxes, insurance, and utilities.

The original and best 55+ condominium model is designed to meet the needs of an active senior citizen in retirement. The 55+ development should be located near desirable amenities such as beaches, golf courses, and colleges or universities.

Most have features such as swimming pools, tennis courts, and walking trails. A 55+ development will have a clubhouse that offers desirable amenities such as an exercise room, crafts, library, pool room, function hall that includes a food preparation area, and a dance floor area. There may be a media room for watching movies and group events.

Some 55+ communities offer fewer amenities. The main reason is a confluence of benefits for the town and the developer. Town's like 55+ communities because they add to the tax base without adding to the school base.

Every time a new home is built, there is a probability that it will be occupied by a family with children. For a town this may eventually mean that new schools will be built, teachers added, and educational programs offered.

The taxes added from any single new house are not enough to pay for the immediate needs of school age children living in the house. Some states allow for impact fees to help offset these expenses.

In a 55+ development, the town gets the tax revenue with no additional children added to the school system. In exchange, the town may vote to offer the developer a higher density of development in a 55+.

For example, if zoning calls for one acre per unit, and the developer has a twenty acre parcel, this would allow for 20 new houses. It is to the developer's advantage to increase the density. The town and the developer agree to build a 55+ complex in exchange for the rights to build thirty units on the developer's twenty acres.

This is a win-win for both the developer and the town. The developer earns profit on thirty sales compared to twenty. The town increases its tax revenue with thirty new homes on the tax role, with no additional demand on the school system.

But is it a win for the buyer? If the only thing the condominium complex offers is an age restriction, you may be better off in a non-regulated condominium.

Complications with age restrictions. Having the age restriction limits the market from all potential buyers to those who are 55+ years of age. Regulations may create unintended consequences. For example, a 58-year-old man is married to a 52-year-old woman. She may not be allowed to stay in the unit without her husband, since she is not 55+. In another situation, parents die, and their 50-year-old daughter cannot occupy the unit until she turns 55.

Another potential issue in the 55+ condominium is grand-children. Children are usually allowed for some minimal stay, but not for a long period and certainly not long enough to be enrolled in school.

This could prevent you from helping your son or daughter with childcare in the event of an overseas military deployment, divorce, death, or disability.

Note: 55+ associations have varying rules. Before purchasing in a 55+ development, be sure to read all condominium documents and have them reviewed by your attorney.

The Assisted Living Model

There are a wide variety of assisted living facilities offering a variety of options. The basic choice comes down to the decision whether to rent or buy.

You may *rent* a small assisted living apartment and pay a monthly fee that covers the cost of the unit, all utilities, meals, and a base level of help. For an additional fee you may buy services to help you with particular health needs.

Instead you can *buy* an assisted living unit. The upfront fee covers your stay until you die. Like an annuity, your invested capital is not returned at your death.

There are many variations of this model. Some assisted living complexes may have three levels of service. These are adult living, assisted living, and skilled nursing. *Adult living*, sometimes referred to by the facility as "independent living," has no additional services and is much like the 55+ condominium option. The *assisted living model* is often described as a hotel which offers a variety of food and cleaning services. In a *skilled nursing unit*, medical services are provided as needed.

Protecting your home. Although the majority of people choose to stay in their home as long as possible, there are times when an owner may need to enter a nursing home.

In Massachusetts, Masshealth (Massachusetts' Medicaid program) will pay for nursing home care. You have to qualify for the benefit under the Masshealth regulations. Each state has its version of support for Medicaid assistance.

As beneficial as Masshealth is, the state may put a lien on your home, or force you to sell it in order to qualify for Masshealth benefits.

Be aware that the current look-back period is five years. Gifts less than five years old are counted when qualifying for Medicaid benefits.

Different ways to protect your home include, but are not limited to, irrevocable trusts, gifting your home, life estate deeds, long-term care insurance, and/or having a care-taker child living in the home with you for an extended period.

Again, these are not the only ways to protect your home from a Masshealth lien or a forced sale, and not all of these remedies are available to everyone. However, by planning in advance, your chances of protecting your home in the event you need future nursing home care are much greater. An elder law attorney may help protect your home for your loved ones.

THE HOUSE SECTION

DONALD J. GRIFFIN, MAI, SRA

10 THE ANATOMY OF A LOT OF LAND

Personal Property vs. Real Estate (Real Property)

This is not intended to be a legal course on real estate law; however, it will help for you to understand a few of the terms you'll hear when talking with real estate professionals and lenders.

When buying a piece of residential real estate, you purchase the land, the house that sits on the land, and everything attached to the land. The legal term for this is "*Real Estate.*" In addition to purchasing the land, house, and anything attached to the land, you have also purchased any "*Real Property*" involved. Real Property is often called the "Bundle of Rights." A simple example of Real Property is the right to occupy the house.

As an example of the difference, 100 Main Street is the Real Estate. If 100 Main Street is leased, the Real Property is 100 Main Street Plus the lease. If you buy 100 Main Street you get the Real Estate plus the Real Property. But, you do not have the right to occupy the property since the properties bundle of rights has been encumbered with a lease.

Note: The terms Real Estate and Real Property are sometimes used interchangeably. For the purposes of this discussion I will use the term Real Property, since this is used most often. Remember that in this case, our definition of Real Property is Real Estate. I assume the property is not leased.

You own the land in fee simple (a fee simple estate). There is a lot of history to this term going back to English law. It is the complete ownership of the Real Estate. It means that you have the right to occupy the land, to use it, and dispose of it in any legal fashion you choose.

The definition used in appraising from the dictionary of real estate appraising published by the Appraisal Institute is "fee simple estate: Absolute ownership unencumbered by any other interest or estate, subject only to the limitations imposed by the governmental powers of taxation, eminent domain, police power, and escheat."

Real property is attached to the land, and personal property sits on the land. Real property is conveyed in the sale. Personal property is not conveyed in the sale. The seller's furniture is their personal property and they will take it with them when they leave. The garage, driveway, walkways, trees shrubs, and grass are real property (attached to the land) and are included in the sale.

As owner, if you lease the property to someone else, this person becomes the tenant. In the lease, you have conveyed some of your ownership rights to the tenant. Although you still own the real estate, the tenant now has the right to occupy the house. As owner, you have the right to sell the house. However, if there is a lease in place, the lease is stronger than the sale and the new owner must honor the lease terms.

As the sale of a house proceeds, many questions may arise. For example, are the refrigerator, washer, and dryer included in the sale? Are the bookcases in the living room built in (real property) or sitting on the floor (personal property)?

Get these questions resolved before signing an Offer to Purchase or Purchase and Sales Agreement. The Offer to Purchase is a contract where a buyer documents an offer to purchase a piece of real estate. The Purchase and Sale Agreement is the contract that follows an accepted offer to purchase, and outlines the steps needed to complete the purchase. These two contracts are discussed in great detail in Chapter 4 on Buying The Property.

If you are the seller, your broker may ask you if there is anything that might be considered real property that you will want to take with you. A list of these items should be included in the Multiple Listing Service listing of your home. An example might be "excludes bookcase in living room," or "does not include chandelier in foyer." Make sure these exclusions make it to the Offer to Purchase and the final Purchase and Sales Agreement.

Legal Definition of the Land

Legal description. The legal description of a property is the metes and bounds description which is recorded in a deed in a registry book starting on a defined page. Each state has a process of recording ownership of real property in its registry of deeds. Recording the deed can be handled at the municipal or county level, often in the courthouse.

Metes and bounds. When you buy a house, you are buying the land with a house on it. The land is described by measurements and /or boundaries that can be physically recreated on the land. A simple description for a lot of land might be, "from the iron rod north 100' then east 100', then south 100', then west 100' to the point of beginning (POB)." The lot would be described as a 10,000 square foot piece of land. Metes and Bound descriptions are typical of measurements found in the northeastern part of the country. In the middle and western part of the United States, the Public Land Survey System (PLSS) is used. The PLSS is also known as the rectangular survey system. It divides most of the United States into a grid, with base lines running east and west and meridians running north and south.

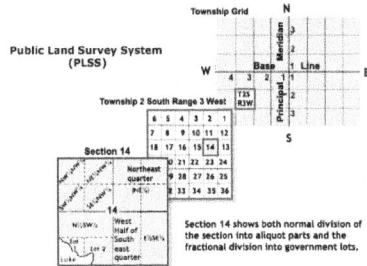

Source: http://nationalatlas.gov/articles/boundaries/IMAGES/plssinfo.gif

A quadrangle range is twenty-four square miles, divided into sixteen townships of six square miles each. The township is further divided into thirty-six sections which are one mile square. Each section is 640 acres (5,280 feet in 1 mile $\times$ 5,280 $\div$ 43,560 square feet in 1 acre). A parcel of land is described by its metes and bounds within the appropriate base and principal meridian, range, township, and section.

It's not important for you to understand all the ins and outs of the PLSS measuring system. It is important to know that when you purchase a home, you are buying a piece of land that is described in its deed by metes and bounds. Errors that occur in a deed can be difficult to fix. Later I will discuss the need for an attorney and title insurance. However, identifying and fixing potential errors is the fundamental reason to have experts that work for you during the purchase of a house.

What do you own? When the deed has been recorded you own from the center of the earth through the four corners of your parcel and through the stratosphere. This definition is important. Unless otherwise limited, you own the mineral rights below the surface of your land, and you own the air rights over your land. This definition holds for most New England States.

In some states with oil, gas, and coal deposits, you may not own the mineral rights. In high density inner city locations, air rights can be valuable. The city might have a highway that can have commercial development on top of it. The federal and state government has an easement in your air rights for air travel so long as it does not interfere with your right to the use and possession of the land. An easement is a certain right to use the real property of another without possessing it. You will learn more on easements in the deed restriction section. A more practical definition of air rights is that space above the land that may reasonably be developed.

When you purchase real property, a deed is created that shows the transfer of ownership from the prior owner (the grantor) to you (the grantee). The deed will at a minimum have the description of the land by its metes and bounds. In some states the deed will show the price paid for the property. The deed may show the tax stamps which can be converted back to the selling price.

The deed is recorded at the Registry of Deeds and becomes the permanent record of ownership. The deed is recorded in the current book of recordings, on the next available page. This is often called the "Book and Page." From the moment it is recorded, you are the owner of record until you transfer ownership to someone else.

If you borrowed money to purchase the property, the mortgage is the next recorded document. Under the law, no one can take your land without your permission (with few exceptions). The only way a lender could take your property in foreclosure (without a trial) is for you to grant them permission. This is often seen as the Power of Sale clause in the mortgage. In the Power of Sale clause, you grant the lender the power to sell the property if you default on the loan. Not all states use this language. If you are in a state that uses trust deeds, the process is different. See the description of trust deeds in the addendum.

Identifying Land with Maps

Plat plan, plot or site plan, and assessor's maps. A **plat** is a map intended to show the division of land into lots or parcels. The plat may include features such as soils, building locations, vegetation, and topography. To record the subdivision of land, a plat plan must be recorded at the registry of deeds showing the layout of the subdivided land.

A simple example is a 10 acre parcel of land that is subdivided into 10 lots with a new road accessing the lots. Each lot is drawn on the plat plan with its own metes and bounds. The legal description will often refer to the plat as further definition of the lot, or in some cases refer only to the lot number on the plat. For example "refer to plat 1123 lot 3, recorded in 1995, plan book 424, page 16."

A **plot or site plan** is similar to the plat plan except it is for a single lot. It will show the metes and bounds of the lot as well as its building improvements, driveways, parking areas, landscaping, and other features. When you apply for a mortgage, the lender engages a surveyor to draw a site plan of the house. The main purpose of the mortgage site plan is to insure that the house and all of its improvements including garages, sheds, and driveways actually sit on the lot of land as described by the metes and bounds.

In most cases this is a background activity. However, should there be an encroachment onto another lot, you have a problem. An encroachment is something on another's land. If part of your driveway is on the neighbor's lot, then it is encroaching. If part of the neighbor's fence wanders and is on your lot, it is encroaching on your property.

Assessor maps. I have discussed several descriptions of the property. First, the street address and the lot number as recorded on the plat plan. Second, the actual metes and bounds description on the plot or site plan. The assessor's office of the city, town, county, or parish assesses the property for tax purposes. The assessing office uses a separate system of identification known as the map, block, and lot. Your municipality may call it something else, such as STRAP number in some Florida counties. It is the municipality's identification numbering system for property being assessed and taxed.

Each municipality establishes a map grid for the area of land that it covers. Each map is then divided into blocks. Each block is divided into lots. An assessor's map might include the block and lot number as 30-6-03, indicating map 30, block 6, and lot 3. If you went to the municipal assessor's office you could look up the parcel of land by getting map 30, finding block 6, and then lot 3. A parcel is a piece of land of any size held in single ownership.

Types of Deeds and Ownership Forms

Types of deeds. There are many types of deeds. Based on its history and local legislation, each state has a preference for one type of deed or another. Deed types include quitclaim, warranty (general and special), grant, tax, gift, in lieu of foreclosure, trustee, fiduciary, and others. You can research the definitions of deeds further; however, the type used will be specified by your attorney, based on your needs.

Form of title. When the deed is created, the new owner or owners must select the form of ownership title. Your attorney will advise you on definitions in your state and the best form of title to meet your needs. The forms of title vary from state to state. You have sole ownership of the property, or joint ownership if there is more than one person involved in the purchase.

Joint Tenancy ownership is the title held for two or more, often related, people. Each joint tenant has an undivided interest in the property including the right of survivorship. Right of survivorship means when one tenant dies their interest is extinguished and the remaining owner(s) inherit the deceased's interest in the property.

An owner with a joint tenant may not sell their interest or leave it to another in their own estate. This may be envisioned when mom and dad die and leave the family home to their four children. It starts out with four joint tenants, then three, two and the last surviving child has sole ownership and can dispose of the property as he or she wishes.

Tenancy in Common ownership is also for two or more owners. Each person owns a varying share of the property. Like a share of stock, it can be sold or disposed of according to a will. This may be envisioned as a syndication, partnership, or corporation. For example, several people buy an apartment building and own shares based on their investment.

Tenancy by the Entirety is not available in all states. Tenant by the Entirety is an estate between husband and wife with equal right of possession and enjoyment with the right of survivorship. When one owner dies, ownership goes to the surviving tenant.

Community Property is not available in all states. Both parties own equal shares of the assets of the marriage. Assets owned before the marriage and inherited assets are not community property.

Trust form of ownership title puts ownership in a trusted third party (trustee) by a grantor (trustor). The trustee holds the property for the benefit of another (beneficiary).

Be sure to check with your attorney before deciding how to hold title.

Deed Restrictions—Limiting Your Use of the Land

Easements. The deed may give away some rights in the form of easements. A common inner city easement is a driveway easement. Example: Two houses (A and B) sit side by side and there is one driveway to access the rear of both yards. The boundary line runs the center of the driveway. Each lot owner has an easement granting the other the right to use the driveway in common. "A" has a dominant easement on "B's" lot and "B" is the servient easement to "A," and vice versa. In other words "A" can use "B's" land and "B" can use "A's" land.

An easement is a certain right to use the real property of another without possessing it. An easement involves two parties: the party granting the easement or right to use, and the party receiving the benefit of the easement. A dominant easement is held by the party receiving the benefit of the easement. A servient easement is held by the party granting the easement.

Several years ago, my wife and I were purchasing a house. We got a call from the lender bank saying the site plan showed a portion of the driveway of the house we were purchasing was located on the neighbor's lot.

The broker representing the seller wanted us to close as planned, stating that we could negotiate later with the neighbor to fix the problem. To be fair to the broker, she was doing her job representing the current owner. After discussing it with our attorney, we choose not to close but to wait for the current owner to get an easement from the neighbor for the portion of the driveway on their land.

The easement was the right that was to be granted by the neighbor to the current owner for use of the land without buying it. As it turned out, the neighbor charged the current owner several thousand dollars for the easement. We completed the purchase, but it was a lesson in not closing on a transaction until all items for clear ownership are resolved.

Utility easements allow water, sewer, gas, or electric lines to cross through a property to reach other parts of the neighborhood. If a parcel of land has an easement for utility lines, the owner cannot put anything permanent on top of the easement. For example, if a gas line runs through the back yard, the utility has the right to repair the line. If the owner has built a garage on top of the easement, the utility has the right to tear down the garage to access the gas line for repairs.

Deed restrictions. A deed may have restrictions that limit use of the land. The most common are neighborhood association restrictions. When a developer creates a new subdivision, a set of association rules may be incorporated to assure homogeneity in the neighborhood. Restrictions often include the way the exterior of the properties are used and maintained.

Property restrictions may exclude parking of commercial vehicles, boats, or unregistered vehicles. Restrictions may also exclude the use of clothes lines and may prohibit toys or bicycles from remaining unattended on lawns and driveways. There may be association rules on how long the grass can be allowed to grow before it must be cut. Pooper scooper laws may also be a part of the rules, requiring pet owners to remove pet waste. There may be restrictions on the exterior paint colors. Rules may prevent the installation of fences or satellite reception dishes. Some buyers welcome these restrictions since they create homogeneity in the neighborhood and increase value. However, association rules may restrict you from something you thought you could do. It is always wise to read and understand all of the deed restrictions.

Limitations by the Four Powers of Government

Real estate Fee Simple ownership is limited by four powers of government. These limitations include taxation, eminent domain, police powers, and escheat.

Taxes. The government has the power to tax land and improvements. A property is assessed by the municipality, and taxes are calculated based on a pre-established tax rate. This is done in the assessor's office. The assessor maintains a record of each parcel of land in its jurisdiction and the owner associated with each. The assessor's maps identify the parcels of land. The field card documents the improvements. The assessor visits each parcel on a periodic basis and updates the field card data. Each tax office has its own format, and field cards vary quite a bit. This is a description of a typical field card:

There is a photo of the property and a sketch showing the measurement of the improvements. There is a description of the construction materials, an assessment of quality and condition, and an accounting of main features, such as number of rooms, baths, bedrooms, fireplaces, garage, pool and/or shed, etc.

The assessor uses a process known as Mass Appraisal. A Mass Appraisal system is based on a sampling of properties in the community. From the sample, a computer program calculates a value for each property based on the sample data. The Mass Appraisal establishes a baseline of values by Gross Living Area (GLA). GLA is the total amount of living area. Living area is finished space that is heated or cooled. Municipalities may include finished basements and/or finished attic areas. Later discussions will expand on the definition of GLA.

When major improvements are made to a house, the owner or contractor must get a building permit from the municipality. The building permit insures safety, since all work must be inspected by the municipality before being completed. The building permit is used by the municipality to schedule inspections for electrical, plumbing and construction projects to ensure compliance with applicable building codes. A copy of the building permit is given to the Assessor who uses it to update the records.

Eminent domain. Eminent domain is the government's right to take your property for a public use. The Fifth Amendment of the Constitution requires "just compensation" for that taking. Just compensation is "the market value of the property at the time of the taking contemporaneously paid in money," according to *Olson v. United States*, 292 U.S. 246 (1934). The area of eminent domain is complex, and the valuation of rights of property taken is a complete specialty area for real estate appraisers. Condemnation is the process the government uses in the taking of land. Eminent domain is the right to take it.

Most homeowners will never be involved in a condemnation process. It often occurs when a new highway is built or widened. It can also occur if a public utility is installing new lines. The government may only take the portion of the land necessary to install cables or pipes. Under eminent domain, when the government takes a portion of the land for an easement, the owner is entitled to just compensation.

If this occurs, retain an attorney to ensure you get "just compensation". An easement "taking" on the surface may not seem like much, but it may prevent you from doing something that could improve your property value. As an example, consider an easement through your backyard. This may prevent you from installing a swimming pool or garage that could improve the property value.

Police Powers. The use of land is also regulated by powers granted to the government. Police Powers are the right to regulate property to promote safety, health, morals, and general welfare of the community. Police powers include zoning ordinances, building codes, traffic regulation, and other restrictions such as fair housing laws.

Escheat. This is the power of the government to take property that has been left with no heirs. If an owner dies without a will and there are no ascertainable heirs, then the property reverts back to the state through the power of escheat.

Accessing and Using the Land

Public and private utilities. To some degree, the value of a property is impacted by the utilities available to it. The property needs electricity, and most sites in developed areas will have public water and sewer, gas, telephone, and/or cable service. A parcel of land 100 miles from the nearest power line is less valuable due to the lack of access to utilities. Utilities not provided by a municipality are often available privately. The owner may retain a private company to install a private sewer system, private well water and/or private gas tanks.

Public and private road access. A parcel of land is located on a public or private roadway. When a new subdivision is created, the developer builds the roads to current zoning laws. Upon completion, the road is returned to the municipality which maintains it going forward. On a public roadway, the property owners along the road (the abutters) own to the edge of the sidewalk or street. The municipality owns from the property line on the left to the property line on the right which includes the street and perhaps sidewalks, curbs, and berm. The grassed area between the sidewalk and the curb or street is the berm area.

In some cases roads are designed to be private ways. On a private way the abutters own to the center of the road and they own the road. The deed will have a clause indicating that the abutting lots have granted an easement in the road to others with the right to pass and re-pass.

The abutters are responsible for maintaining the private way. This could turn into an unexpected expense if the majority of abutters determine that the road needs to be repaved. If the municipality does not provide snow plowing and sanding services, the abutters share the expense.

Zoning. "Allowed uses" and "bulk requirements" are the two main categories of zoning requirements for single family residential purposes. For a property to conform to zoning, it must be an "allowed use" and meet the "bulk requirements."

Allowed uses are those land uses established by the municipality for each zone. Bulk requirements define minimum and/or maximum thresholds for a lot to be in compliance with the zoning law. The property must be in a single family zone or a zone that allows single family use. The bulk requirements will vary from municipality to municipality and state to state. Bulk requirements are a minimum lot size and minimum frontage. For example, a lot must be at least 40,000 square feet with 200' frontage. If the lot meets this threshold, it complies, otherwise it does not.

Other zoning requirements may include a minimum width of the lot at the building line, a minimum depth of the lot, and a maximum height requirement for the number of stories or height of the building. Setbacks define how close the improvement can be to the property lines. Zoning requirements may also include the minimum amounts of open space, parking, or maximum percent of lot coverage.

If the lot does not comply with current zoning requirements, it should have a pre-existing zoning approval status. A pre-existing or grandfathered zoning status means that the house was in compliance at the time it was built. If the property does not comply with current zoning requirements and is not grandfathered, then it may have been granted a special permit.

In some zones, the zoning code may allow for a special permit. For example, an inner city lot is land locked and does not have frontage. The lot complies in all other respects except frontage. There is an existing driveway easement to access the lot when it was used as a garage. In this instance, the zoning board could grant a special permit since it would not harm or otherwise injure the ambiance of the neighborhood and meets the general goals of land use in this zone. If the lot is illegal for the zone, it should not be purchased.

Flood Plain— Need for Flood Insurance. The Federal Emergency Management Association (FEMA) publishes flood maps for the United

States. In the appraisal report, the real estate appraiser retained by the lender will report whether the property is or is not in a flood zone, within the accuracy limits of the flood maps. The key factor that determines if you need to purchase flood insurance is if the improvement is in the flood zone. **The improvement** must be in the flood zone, not just a portion of the lot.

If **the improvement** is in a flood zone, the borrower must purchase flood insurance, assuming the mortgage lender will require it. If you own land outright with no mortgage, there is no requirement that you purchase flood insurance, just as there is no requirement that you purchase property insurance. While there are benefits to being located on a river, ocean, or lake, borrowers should be aware of the potential for property damage resulting from a flood.

Protecting Your Ownership Through Title Insurance

Title insurance. When purchasing a property, a title search is completed. A title search is a search of the Registry of Deeds back at least 50 years and sometimes longer. The intent of the title search is to insure the current owner owns the property free and clear of any encumbrances or mortgages. The title search will identify any other owners that may have signed the deed transferring ownership.

On occasion a title search identifies an active mortgage. Through an oversight, the correct discharge of the mortgage was not recorded. The correct discharge of an earlier mortgage can be made in most cases.

Title can be flawed or clouded for one reason or another. A title might be flawed or clouded because of an incorrect recording of a metes and bounds description or because a partial owner was overlooked in the title search. The summary statement used when this occurs is, "There is a cloud on the title."

Title insurance protects against future claims against a property due to a faulty title. Lenders always get title insurance in the amount of the mortgage, to protect the loan. Your attorney should ask you about purchasing title insurance covering your share of ownership. When purchasing a property, it is a good idea to buy title insurance.

DONALD J. GRIFFIN, MAI, SRA

11 HOUSE STYLES AND LIVING AREA

This section describes the most typical house styles. In addition, it defines the living area of a house as the Gross Living Area (GLA). Not all sections of a house are considered living area. The correct knowledge of GLA will help you to compare different properties for sale.

As a foundation rule of thumb, the GLA is defined as the area of the house that is above ground, referred to as grade level on the first and second story. The following is the description of GLA provided by Fannie Mae and Freddie Mac. Appraisers use the following Fannie Mae definition in almost all cases.

Per the Fannie Mae selling guide dated July 26, 2011 page 551: *"Appraisers must be consistent when calculating and reporting finished above-grade room count and square footage for the gross living area above-grade. A level is considered below-grade if any portion of it is below-grade—regardless of the quality of its finish or the window area of any room. A walk-out basement with finished rooms would not be included in the above-grade room count."*

Grade level refers to the contour of the land. If you had a flat piece of land, and placed a rectangular ranch style home on the land, then all of the GLA is above grade. If you have a split level with part of the lower level below grade, then only the finished upper level is considered GLA.

GLA does not include finished basement or finished attic areas. The finished basement or attic area has some value but not to the same degree as first and second floor GLA.

Construction notes. When constructing a house, the builder places a load-bearing wall down the center of the house. The load-bearing wall carries the weight of the center wall and second story walls to the foundation structure in the basement or slab.

A load-bearing wall cannot be removed. It would cause the upper floors to collapse. Envision a ranch style house 24' wide by 50' long. If there were no load-bearing wall in the center, the support beams (joists) from front-to-back would have to be 24' long. In order to support the weight of the entire floor, the support beams would have to be extra thick.

A load-bearing wall is run down the length of the house in the center dividing it in two. Now the joists or support beams can be 12' long from the edge of the front wall to the center load bearing wall.

Types of Roofs. The gable roof is the simplest. Think of two playing cards tilted into each other at an angle. This forms the roof. The gable is the triangular section at either end of the house. The slope of the roof is the angle created by the two playing cards. It can also be thought of as the height at the center where the cards meet. On a small ranch you will see a slight slope with a center height of 4-6'. The attic area is for storage; it is not high enough to have finished area.

The Cape style house will have a steep slope in its roof with a 12-15' center height. This allows room to have finished area on the second floor.

The Colonial roof will vary in slope angle with smaller simple garrison models with a slight slope more like a ranch, to the larger traditional colonial with a steep slope creating a full attic level that has some potential for finishing.

The mansard roof has a roof section rising from the four sides on a steep slope. It rises about 9' and is then flat in the center. There is no attic area in houses with a mansard roof.

The Hip roof is similar to the mansard except the four roof sections rise to a peak, with less slope than the mansard. It is designed to be the roof of a colonial style with a full attic.

Single-Story House Designs

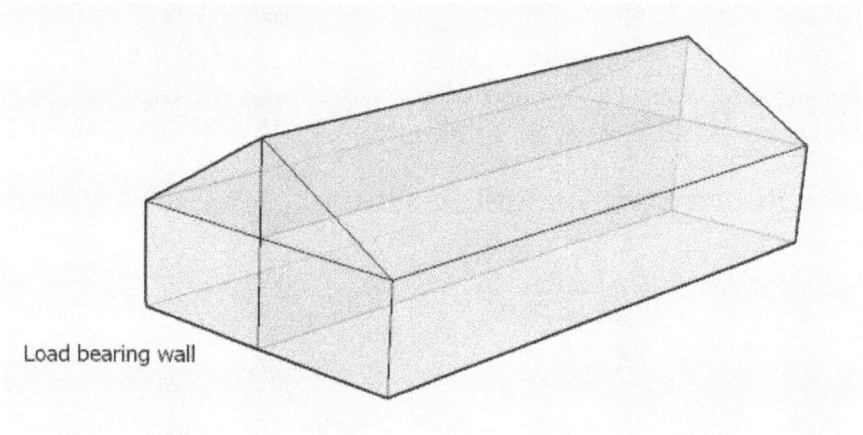

Load bearing wall

Slab Ranch House Layout

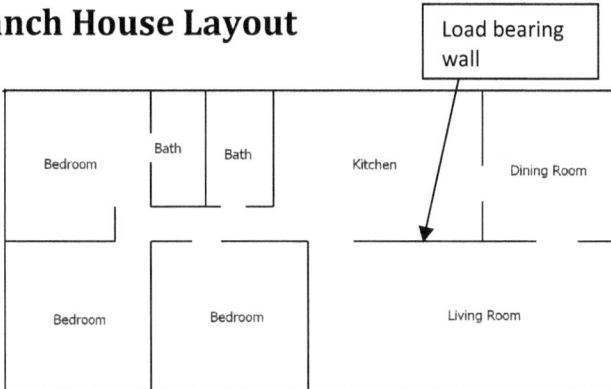

Load bearing wall

Bedroom | Bath | Bath | Kitchen | Dining Room

Bedroom | Bedroom | Living Room

Example of a Ranch Style House Design

A house is divided into the eating, sleeping, and entertainment areas. One side of the house is allocated for sleeping while the other side is for eating and entertainment. A hallway accesses the left side bedrooms. The 3' access hallway is located on one side of the load-bearing wall. Bathrooms are located on this side of the hall. Bathrooms in this design will be 9' deep as determined by the load bearing wall. The house must have a minimum of one bathroom and a master bath is desirable.

The left side is divided into three bedrooms and two bathrooms. The right side of the house is divided into the kitchen, dining room, and living room. The main entry of the house is to the living room, with kitchen and dining rooms to the rear.

Most plumbing is located in one area of the house, to minimize cost. Pipes are on inside walls if freezing is an issue.

The calculation of GLA for the most common house styles is outlined next. The design of each style of house dictates how the GLA is calculated. Any finished space below grade level is not included in the GLA. The GLA of the second floor space is calculated based on the usable floor area.

The Ranch Style on Full Basement

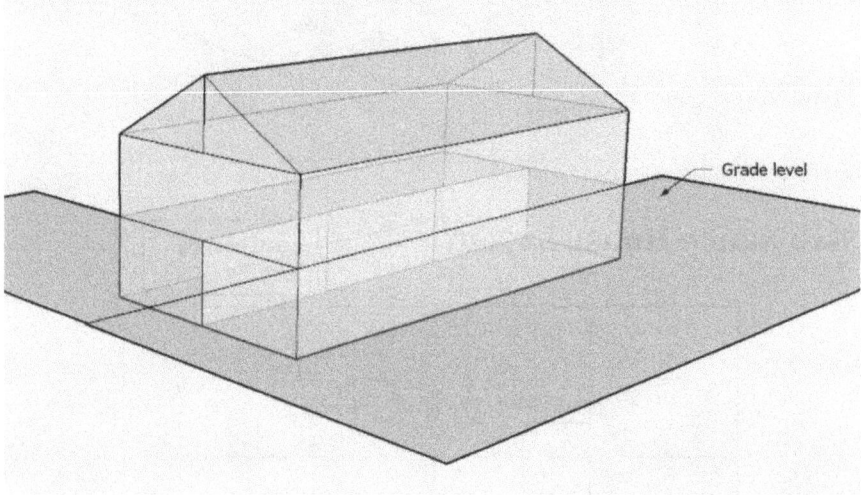

The Ranch House Style: This one story layout can be on a slab or on a full or partial basement. A slab is a poured slab of concrete, used when no basement area is built. All of its living area is above grade.

Split Level Ranch

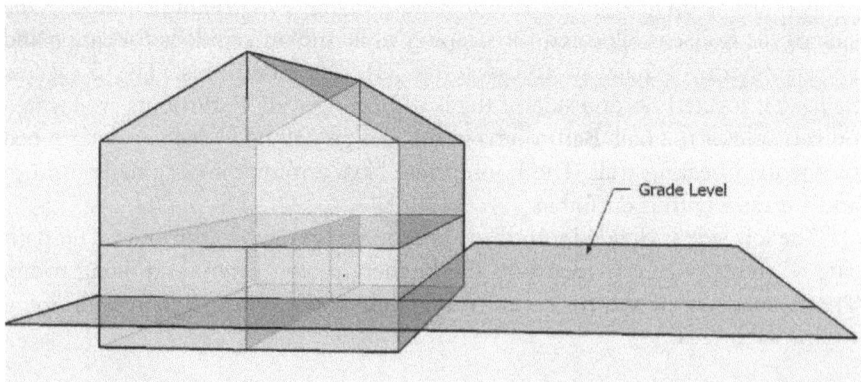

Spilt Level House Style: Envision a ranch style house sitting on a full 8' tall basement. Now envision that the basement is raised up 4'. From the foyer, you walk up six steps to the first floor which is identical to a ranch style house in design. However, in a split level design from the foyer, you walk down six steps to the lower level. One half of the lower level is finished living area below grade and is often finished as a play room or bedroom. Assuming the ranch and split level have the same exterior dimensions, then they have the same GLA. In a split level house the finished lower level is not considered GLA. The lower level finishes add some value but not to the same degree as the living area that is above grade.

Multi-Level Design

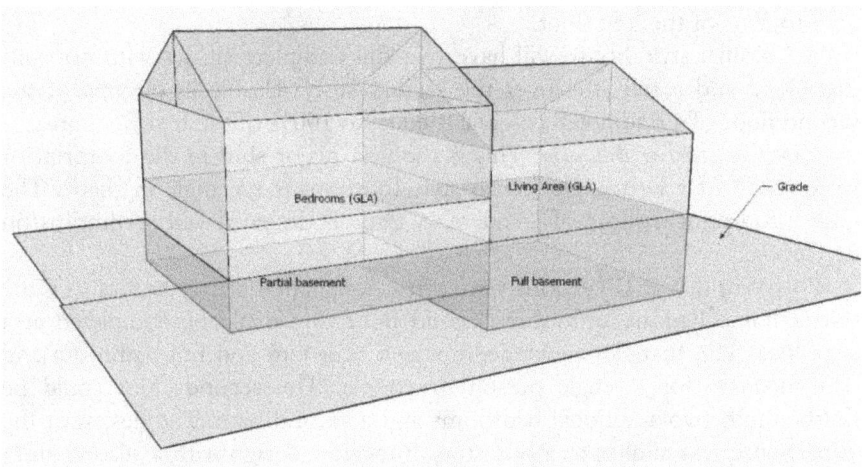

Multi-Level House Style: This style is an alternative version of a ranch style design. Again envision the ranch style house on a full basement. Divide the house in half with bedrooms on the left and living area on the right. Now *shift the left side up 4'*.

From the first floor, six stairs lead up to the bedrooms. From the first floor, six stairs lead down to a lower level (partial basement) which may be finished similar to a split level, or it may be a garage. From the lower level, another six stairs lead to the full basement section. Again, only the living area above grade and the bedrooms are considered in calculating the GLA. If the exterior dimensions of a multi-level house design are the same as the dimensions of a ranch style design, then GLA is the same. Part of the lower level and basement are below grade and therefore are not included in the GLA.

Two-Story House Designs

Two-story houses include the following styles: Bungalow, Cape Cod, Village Colonial, Dutch Colonial, Gambrel Colonial, Garrison Colonial and traditional Colonial. This list is not all inclusive by any means. There are as many house style names as parts of the country and time periods. However the key to the functionality of the two-story house is the amount of usable living space (GLA) located on the second floor. Depending on the slope of the walls or roof, the second story living area may range from 25% to 100% of the GLA of first floor area.

Think of the Bungalow or Cape Cod style as a single-story house with finished attic area. The roof line has a steep slope. Depending on the footprint and roof slope, the second floor usable living area may be equal to 25% to 50% of the first floor.

A Colonial style house will have two full complete stories with no walls that slope and a full attic over the second story. Usable living area of the second floor of a traditional colonial is equal to 100% of the first floor area.

Cape Cod(cape) or Bungalow: This is the first major shift in the footprint or basic shape of a home. The ranch style footprint is rectangle in shape. The Cape's footprint is more of a square. A Cape is designed with bedrooms on two levels.

Post World War II versions were often designed as starter homes. A Cape starter home had an unfinished second floor that could be completed at a later date. The first floor included a single bedroom and full bathroom and was adequate for a single person or couple. The second floor could be finished into two additional bedrooms and a second bath. The design of the Cape house was similar to a one story Bungalow design with a second story added. There are other names for houses like this, but the common thread is a one-and-a-half story building.

Cape Style with Eye Windows and Rear Dormer

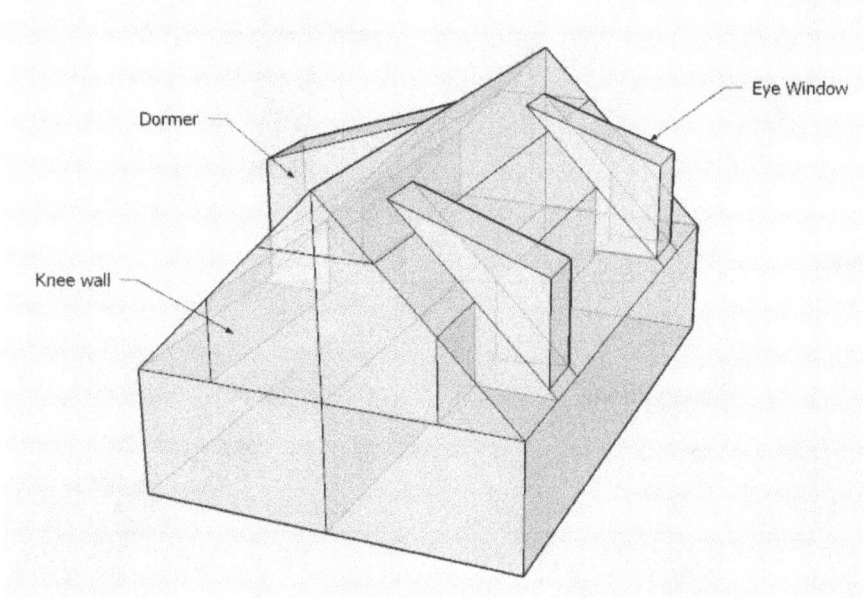

The second floor of a Cape Cod style house is technically finished attic area. It has a steep roof slope. The center height of the room directly under the gable peak is at least 6-7'. At the edge of the room, a knee wall is installed approximately 6' in from the roof edge. A knee wall is a short wall 3-4' in height from the floor to the sloped roof line (see building sketch). To provide more headroom, dormers or eye windows may be added. A dormer or eye window is a section of the roof lifted to add headroom and space.

The Cape Layout

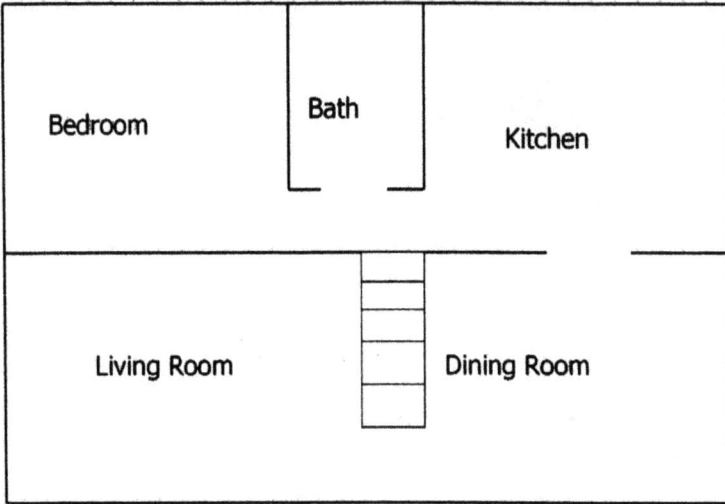

First Floor

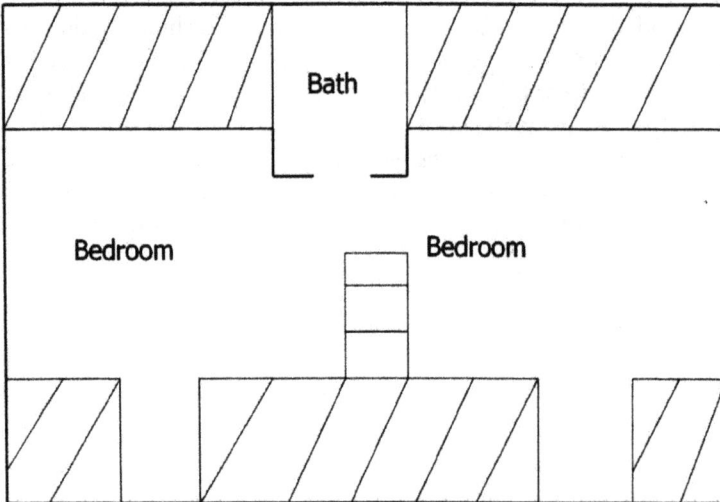

Second Floor

The Village Colonial (1-½ Story)

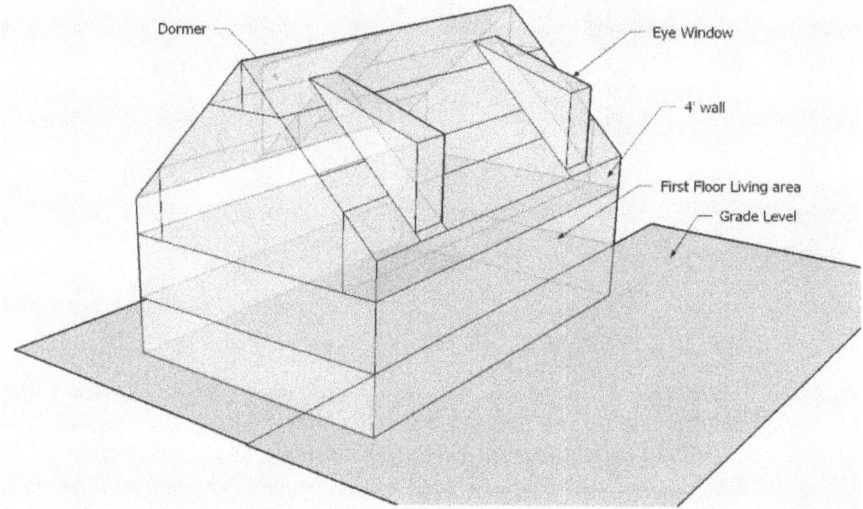

Village Colonial: The Village Colonial is a style often found in older communities. The second floor is less functional due to the sloping that begins half way up the wall because the second floor has a half wall and then the traditional gable roof. (See illustration.) The half wall is 4' high around the perimeter of the house. I contrast this with the Cape style which has no raised wall at the second story perimeter. The Colonial has a full 8' wall around the perimeter of the second story. The Village Colonial often has dormers to raise the wall to 8'.

Gambrel and Dutch Colonial Styles

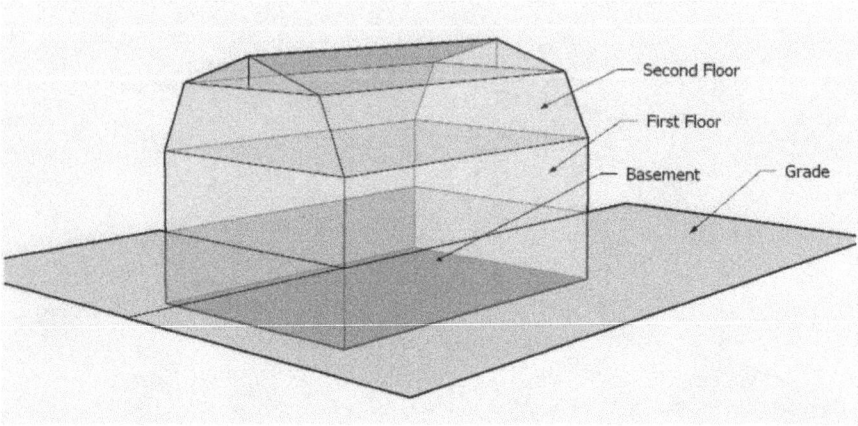

Gambrel and Dutch Colonial Styles: The *Gambrel Style Colonial* has two sloping roof pitches (compared to the straight triangle of the gable style roof). It has full GLA on the second floor but the side walls still have a modest slant to them.

The *Dutch Colonial* has full front and rear dormers. The only remnant of the Gambrel style is the Gambrel shape on the left and right side.

The second floor of a Gambrel or Dutch style colonial has a full 8' second story wall that tilts in, causing an angled perimeter wall. The slopping walls are less functional, since it prevents the placement of furniture against these walls. Often this is a negative factor and the design is improved by building dormers to make full straight walls in portions of the front and/or rear of the second story.

Colonial Style

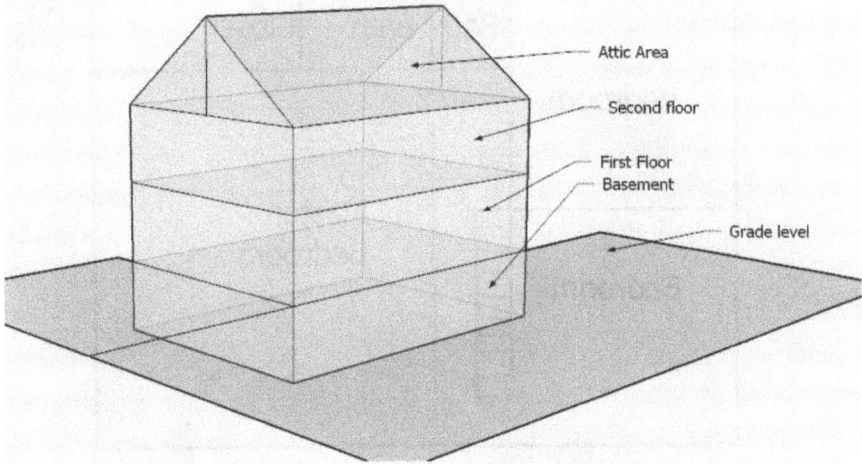

Colonial style: The traditional Colonial style home has two full stories with full height walls. All the bedrooms are on the second floor. Center entrance colonials are often designed with a front-to-back living room and a front-to-back master bedroom on the second floor that includes a master bath and large walk-in closet.

Variations of the colonial include a side entry as opposed to center entry. Some will have four smaller bedrooms. As the width of the colonial house increases, it allows for the design of four bedrooms that include a front-to-back master bedroom.

A colonial is a 2-½ story design. A garrison colonial will have 1-2' overhang in the front and/or back of the second story. This overhang allows the bedrooms to be larger.

The term Garrison comes from the colonial era in New England, when the militia army of the new republic needed a place to sleep while preparing for its next battle.

The name Garrison is a surname deriving from the location name "Garriston" in North Yorkshire, England. The name means "protection," "stronghold," "fortification," or "spear-fortified town."

New England owners of homes and taverns added a second story to their building so troops could be "garrisoned" there. The overhang was a feature to create more sleeping room for the troops.

Colonial Layout

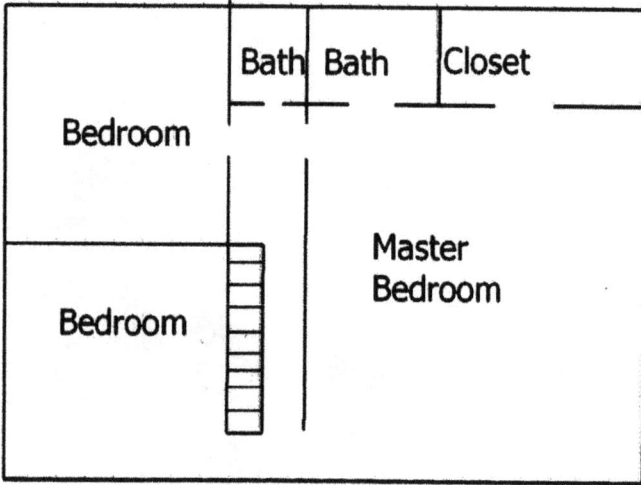

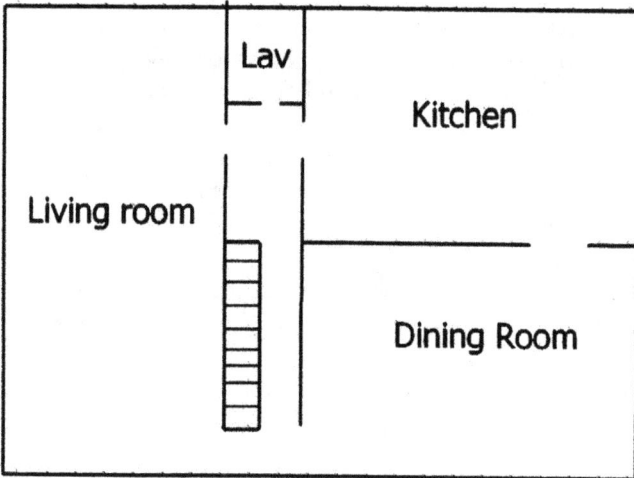

Bath | Bath | Closet

Bedroom

Bedroom

Master
Bedroom

Lav

Kitchen

Living room

Dining Room

Saltbox Colonial

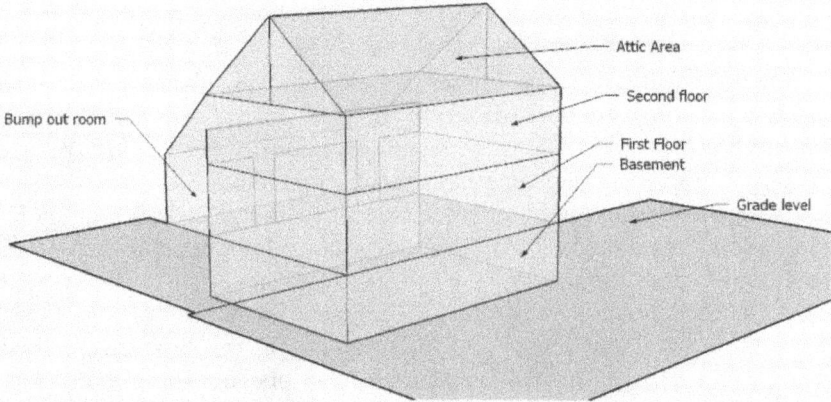

The saltbox colonial also has a twist to its roof line. There is a bump out to the rear of the house and the rear roof line is continuous to the first floor. This creates an open area in the section labeled the "bump out" room. The saltbox colonial has a half wall on the second floor that overlooks into the bump out room. The bump out room is a breakfast area attached to the kitchen, and a den or library attached to the living room area. The area over the bump out room is considered a cathedral ceiling and is not included in GLA.

Other Styles

Contemporary Style. A contemporary house has an open floor plan with one or more sections open to the second story ceiling. Contemporary homes are often set in wooded areas. They have larger windows designed to bring the natural world into the home. Contemporaries have multiple roof lines allowing for cathedral ceilings with jogs and curved design elements.

Manufactured or Modular Home. Modern manufactured houses are almost indistinguishable from homes built on a building site. Manufactured homes are built in a factory and then shipped on a trailer to the home site. These homes may have a single-story or multi-story design. They are installed on a slab or on a foundation.

Example: To create a ranch style, two sections of the home are built in the factory and then shipped to the site where they are lowered by crane onto the previously poured slab or foundation. The two sections are joined together and utility lines are connected. Modern manufacturing techniques result in the building of a quality home since the two sections are built in a covered temperature-controlled environment and are protected from the elements during construction. Manufactured homes must meet the stringent building codes of each community they serve. Once the house is assembled on the site, the house becomes real property.

Mobile Homes. These houses are distinguished from manufactured homes in that they are not attached to the land and are considered personal property. The most mobile of these are the modern Recreational Vehicles (RV's) that stop at mobile home parks for short periods.

Older versions of mobile home trailers are found in trailer or mobile home parks. The trailer still has its wheels so it could be attached to a vehicle and removed from the site.

On inspection you may find that the wheels of a mobile home have been removed. It is still considered personal property. In this instance the trailer sits on a concrete pad that the mobile home park operator leases to the trailer owner. The park owner provides access to all of the necessary utilities just like a home.

A critical point in purchasing a mobile home or trailer is that you cannot get a traditional mortgage. You may be able to get a loan. But these loans are similar to an auto loan.

Gross Living Area

Now that we have a good idea on how to identify different types of property styles, we can estimate the Gross Living Area (GLA). Remember, the GLA is the total square feet of finished area above grade on the first and second levels.

One of the value indicators of a home is the value per square foot of GLA. For example, if a property has 2,000 square feet of GLA, and the market is paying about $100.00 per square foot, you can then calculate a preliminary value of $200,000 (2,000 × $100.00).

You can see how you might incorrectly calculate the value if the home includes 400 square feet of finished basement space. The preliminary value should have been $160,000 (1,600 × $100.00). Later I will discuss valuing other features of a home, but for now I will concentrate on the GLA which is the main value driver in determining price.

GLA is important when you are comparing two or more houses. If you have one property with 1,600 square feet and another with 2,000 square feet, you can use the GLA of the second property to estimate the value of the first. Later I will discuss the use of GLA in estimating a value.

For now you will learn how to get the correct GLA for both the house you are interested in, and for any comparable sales used to support its value. *A comparable sale is a recent sale of a similar property.*

Understanding how these calculations are derived may seem like a lot of work. However the knowledge you will gain will make you a smarter buyer. Knowledge of how the calculations work may also help you when negotiating the selling price of a property.

Not everyone will care to know this level of detail, and that's fine. Just remember two key points.

First, always know what the broker, owner, or assessor has included in their estimate of GLA. Second if two houses with reported similar GLA sold or are listed for much different prices; the reported GLA is most often not calculated the same.

Compare your GLA calculations against those provided in the listing of the home for sale. If the GLA figure in the listing was taken from the assessor's office, it may include items that the market does not count as GLA.

Some assessing systems list all enclosed areas such as porches, garages, and finished basement or attic and then apply a percentage of utility such as 30% for the garage. This all adds into their total GLA. In this instance the assessor's GLA will not help you to compare the value of the property you are considering to other similar properties.

The first time you see the GLA in writing is likely to be in a Multiple Listing data sheet. Real estate brokers often provide these when a property is open for public inspection at an "open house." The GLA provided on the listing was entered by the real estate broker. There may be notes on what the GLA includes and the source of the GLA figure.

> Approx. Living Area: **1445 sq. ft.**
> Living Area Includes: **Finished Basement**
> Living Area Source: **Other**
> Living Area Disclosures: **+/-570 sq/ft in finished basement**

In the sample shown above the GLA is listed as 1,445 square feet, when in fact the GLA is 875 square feet above grade with 570+- square feet in finished basement space.

The very best way to measure GLA is to measure the house itself. This is not possible in most cases.

The next best source for measuring the GLA is the property field card. See the addendum on finding information on the Internet for a detailed explanation on how to find assessors data online.

Sample sketch from a property field card from an assessing office

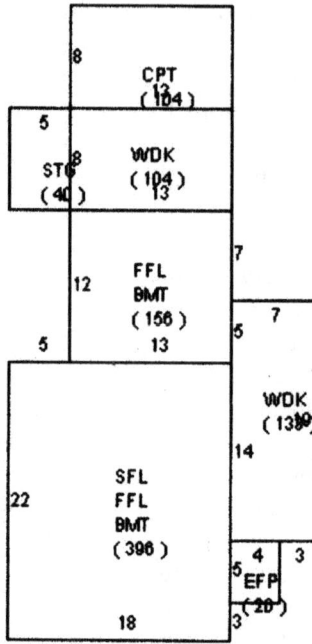

A discussion with the staff in the community assessor's office will help you interpret the codes shown on the property sketch. In this design we see the first floor living space (FFL), the second floor living space (SFL), the basement (BMT), the wood deck (WDK), an enclosed framed porch (EFP), storage (STG), and a carport (CPT).

In the design above, the largest square shows the size of this space as 18' by 22' or 396 square feet (18 × 22 = 396). This calculation tells us that this section of the house has 396 square feet of living space based on dimensions of 18' × 22'.

Since the 18' by 22' area includes the first and second floor living areas, the total calculation of GLA in this area is doubled and now equals 792 square feet (396 x 2 floors). The area in the design listed as 12' x 13' is classified as Finished First Floor (FFL) with 156 square feet of additional living space (12' × 13' = 156). The total GLA listed by the assessor is 948 square feet (396 + 396 + 156).

The rest of the sketch shows the size of the enclosed porch (EFP), wood deck (WDK), Storage area (STG), and carport (CPT).

Note: In the assessor's report the description of how the GLA is calculated is usually found in a separate section of the document, as shown here:

SUB AREA

Code	Description	Area - SQ	Rate - AV	Undepr Value
EFP	Enclos Porch	20	75.71	1,514
STG	Storage	40	0	0
CPT	Carport	104	19.502	2,030
WDK	Deck	237	50.47	11,962
SFL	Second Floor	396	100.94	39,973
BMT	Basement	552	41.18	22,734
FFL	First Floor	552	100.94	55,720
Net Sketched Area		1,901	Total	133,933
Gross Living Area		948		

SUB AREA DETAIL

Sub Area	% Usable	Description	% Type	Qu
BMT	100	RRM	90	F

In addition to the GLA calculation, the assessor's report also provides a summary of the size of any sub areas. In the SUB AREA DETAIL, the report lists the basement as 100% usable as an RRM (rumpus room) at 90% efficiency. Total basement area is 552 square feet, with 90% used as finished rumpus room or about 496 square feet in finished basement, per the assessor.

The listing showed 1,445 square feet of GLA which included 570 square feet of finished basement space. This calculates to 870 square feet of above grade GLA (1,445 – 570). The assessor's report shows the living area of 948 square feet with 496 square foot of finished basement.

There is a discrepancy between the listing which shows 870 square feet and the assessor which shows 948 square feet. This is 78 square feet or about an 8% variance.

The MLS listing sheets may have incorrect data, so it is helpful to confirm the data with another source, such as the property field card. If they agree, then you can feel confident in using those numbers. If they do not agree, more research is needed.

12 THE CONDOMINIUM

What Is A Condominium?

The Appraisal Institute's Dictionary of Real Estate Appraisal defines condominiums as follows. *"A condominium is a multiunit structure or property in which persons own fee simple title to a unit and an undivided interest in common areas."*

As you learned earlier, fee simple title is unencumbered absolute ownership, excepting limitations of government powers. A condominium differs from a single family dwelling in that the owner owns a unit with portions of the property owned in common with others.

The Co-operative Apartment. There are a few key differences between a condominium and cooperative apartment. Condominium owners have a fee simple ownership of a unit and a percentage ownership of the common land and elements.

Co-operative apartment owners do not have fee simple ownership. They own shares of stock that the cooperative apartment corporation allocates to their unit. Buying a co-operative apartment involves approval by the co-op management, which entails both financial and personal review.

The condominium form of ownership affords the owner more flexibility since the owner does not have to consult with anyone before purchasing or selling a unit. However, some condominium associations in some states do require a review of buyers to insure compliance with declaration requirements. Items that may cause rejection include violent felony convictions, convictions regarding illegal drugs, and financial irresponsibility demonstrated by bankruptcy, foreclosure or bad debts.

Creating the Condominium. A side-by-side duplex style two-family consists of two units, left side and right side. As a two family, one person owns the building. As in a single family, the owner owns all the land and all of the real property improvements.

Separate unit ownership makes it a condominium. The land and parts of the house are in common ownership. Envision drawing a dividing line down the center of the duplex. The left side is unit 1; the right side is unit 2. Unit owners own their unit in fee simple and they own the land in common. In this example, the only piece of the house they own in common is the central wall, which divides the two units. Each owner is responsible for the siding around their unit and the roof over their unit. Each unit owner may have their own full basement for their utilities.

Now envision a three-story apartment building with identical apartments on floors 1, 2 and 3. When converted into condominiums much more of the building is common area. The front and rear staircases are common to the building. The roof, siding and basement now belong to all three units. The land is also common to all three units

The Condominium Master Deed. The master deed is the legal entity that converts total ownership as seen in the fee simple ownership of a building into a condominium form of ownership. The master deed starts by naming the condominium; it defines what land is controlled by the condominium (its metes and bounds) and then provides the master list of units in the condominium, their sizes, and the percentage of common area they own.

The master deed creates the mechanisms by which the condominium will be managed by the unit owners. This is the creation of the condominium Homeowners Association (HOA) or trust. The HOA is the body that will oversee the management of the condominium, the budget, the association rules and bylaws, and the common areas.

The HOA is the main enforcement arm for the rules and bylaws. The number of HOA board members is defined as are their terms and the election process. More information concerning the HOA is available later in this section. Following are a few exceptions to a condominium owning the land and real property.

Ground rent. Ground rent is land that is leased. There is additional risk involved in leased land. If a condominium development or co-operative apartment in downtown Manhattan, NY, sits on leased land, there is risk involved when the lease expires. Depending on the terms of the lease, the land owner could take back the entire building, if the lease is not renewed, or at a minimum can increase the land rent. Land rent increases will result in a higher expense to the condominium or co-operative association and in fees to the unit or apartment owner.

Leased common elements. In the past, developers built condominium complexes while retaining ownership of the development's clubhouse and swimming pool. The developer then leased the use of the clubhouse and swimming pool back to the condominium association, in a 99-year lease. This allowed the developer to keep the unit price down and have a

99-year rental income. When considering purchasing a condominium, a lender will need to know if there are any leased common elements.

Identifying a Unit and Its Boundaries

Much like owning a piece of land where ownership is defined by its metes and bounds, a condominium unit is defined by the plans that layout the condominium building, where each unit is identified by a building number and unit number. When a unit is sold, a unit deed is recorded which identifies the unit and refers back to the master deed that created it.

You can think of this as a chain of title. Metes and bounds define the land in the deed. The land has a twelve-unit apartment building on it, owned by one person. A master condominium deed converts the apartment building to a condominium use.

It starts with the original land and building. The master deed divides the real estate into twelve units along with the common parts of the building and the common land. Twelve unit deeds now comprise the condominium. Twelve units are now available for sale.

The master deed defines in detail where each unit ends and the common area begins. One way to envision this is to think of the apartment as a rectangular box. The inside perimeter walls starting at the surface of the drywall on the walls and ceilings and the surface of the subfloor forming the base of the box are the beginning point of the unit. Everything inside the box is part of the unit. Everything else is part of the common area. Another way to visualize this is to think of a chest of drawers. You can pull out a drawer. The inside area of the drawer is like a condominium unit. The chest itself and the frame of the drawer is all part of the common area.

Unit deeds. A new owner receives a unit deed that describes the unit and refers back to the master deed. When buying a new unit, the lender will want to know if all of the common area improvements are complete and if all the planned recreational facilities are complete, as well as if there is an additional charge for using the recreational facilities. Developers do not want to spend money any sooner than is necessary so they tend to push off the building of pools and clubhouses until later in the construction process. Ever watchful of risk, the lender will be concerned that if the developer fails, the common elements will not be completed, which may affect the value of the unit.

Who pays for what if the building burns to the ground? Refer to the section on homeowners insurance for more detailed information. The master condominium insurance policy pays to restore the main or common portion of the building, while the unit owner's insurance policy covers repairs to the interior finishes. The unit owner is also responsible for exclusive use areas. Exclusive areas may include repairs to decks, patios, or yard areas.

Large condominium complexes. Large complexes often have several hundred condominium units placed on a large expanse of land. There are many common elements such as swimming pools, tennis courts, clubhouse, and walking trails to name a few. The basic concepts are the same. The unit owner owns a unit and the rest of the complex is owned in common with other owners.

Large condominium complexes are often built in phases. For example, a project of 300 units may be built in six phases of 50 units each. Large complexes may create several smaller condominium associations and one master association. In this manner it is easier to oversee the management of 50 units in one phase compared to 300 units in total.

In large condominium projects, unit owners may have to pay two association fees. These include the master association fee and the fee for the smaller association that manages a group of units. The master condominium association will typically be responsible for the main road system, guard gates, clubhouse, swimming pool, and recreation facilities used by all units.

The several smaller associations would be responsible for their 50+- units just as if that was the entire complex. If parts of the common elements include a golf course, then unit owners may have the ability to purchase a golf membership and pay master golf association fees to support the golf course.

Homeowners / Condominium Association. A homeowners association (HOA) is created in the master deed and its board of directors is elected by the rules established for that purpose. Some states delineate between a single family style home with common elements (HOA), and a condominium building with common elements (Condominium). The primary function of the HOA is to collect the condominium fees and pay bills.

They select the necessary service providers to maintain the common areas of the property. The HOA board deals with violations of the condominium association or master deed bylaws, processes complaints from unit owners, and enacts new rules as needed. In some cases, unit owners vote on changes to the master deed and association bylaws. It is a community where unit owners vote and the majority rules in most cases. Some items of change may require a higher percentage of vote, such as 2/3'rds vote. These are spelled out in the documents.

If the complex is large, the developer and the HOA may hire a management company to oversee the day-to-day operations of the development.

Rules on how long a developer can retain control vary by state. The buyer should know the percentage of units owned by the developer. The buyer should know when control of the master association will come to the unit owners.

When purchasing a condominium unit, the new owner is buying into a small community, and it is helpful to know as much as possible about the community.

If the condominium is well established and has been completed for some time, the owner is joining the HOA, its leadership and its philosophy of homeownership. Before purchasing, it is a good idea to meet with a few members of the board to determine their management strategies and any potential difficulties in managing the association.

Rules and Regulations. The buyer's attorney should review the rules and regulations found in the master deed and/or in the condominium rules and bylaws. In these documents, restrictions such as the following are often found.

Renting the unit, pet ownership and pooper scooper rules, vehicles allowed or disallowed (no commercial vans), use of common areas by unit owners and their renters or guests, the minimum unit temperature to prevent freezing, residential use only (no commercial uses), modifications to common areas, homogeneous look to front facing windows, satellite antennas, and your belongings left in common areas.

The regulations may also include a section on foreclosures and requirements to send copies of budgets and plans to Fannie Mae or Freddie Mac if they have a mortgage on one of the units. This is a brief listing of the more common items included in the HOA rules and regulations and there is no end to the things that can be outlined or restricted. The older complexes tend to have more extensive rules and regulations.

If the HOA allows units to be rented, new owners should know what percentage is rented. A high percentage of renters in a complex may result in more rule violations. If renters are allowed, there may be additional rules regarding minimal stays and/or number of tenants allowed in one year.

In a desirable tourist area with a defined summer and/or winter season, an owner might like to rent the unit out by the week. The association rules may say the minimum period is a month with no more than three tenants per year.

If a person owns more than 10% of the condominium complex, a block vote could be created that influences decisions regarding rules. If there is commercial space in the condominium complex, this is known as a mixed use development. Commercial uses may have a negative impact on the otherwise residential nature of the project.

Condominium GLA Calculations. As discussed in the section on single family dwellings, the determination of Gross Living Area (GLA) is important in comparing condominium properties for sale. The GLA in a condominium is established by the developer. In most cases it is the interior measurements of the unit. However, it is at the discretion of the developer to determine what is included in the GLA.

Gray areas that often arise include garages, finished basements, finished attics, loft areas, and enclosed porches. The assessor takes the calculation of the GLA from the master deed and uses it for assessing purposes. Buyers should take care when comparing condominium complexes and units of various developers. The rules on how the GLA was calculated may differ.

Condominium styles include the single family stand-alone house, the duplex style, and the row house. The duplex or townhouse is a two story building with a unit on each side. It functions much like the colonial style house with living area on the first floor and bedrooms on the second. If a building has 3+ units in a row it becomes a row house.

Another popular condominium style is the quarter style or coach house. Four units are built in a square. Think of a square with an X through it and build out space from each quadrant. These can be single story ranch style or two story units. Any apartment building can be converted to a condominium style of ownership. A high rise apartment building can also be built or converted into condominiums.

The Homeowners Association (HOA) structure. The HOA is created by the master deed. Board members are elected by the unit owners. The board members choose a president, treasurer, secretary, and other positions as needed. The board meets at a minimum of once a year. A HOA board should have a governance procedure. Robert's Rules of Procedures is often used. It is a set of procedures for running meetings. A copy of Robert's Rules of Procedures is available on the Internet.

The HOA deals with all of the issues that arise, authorizes the selection of vendors to provide needed goods and services, and reviews and processes complaints from unit owners.

The treasurer handles the association's checking account where all condominium fees are deposited. The treasurer provides a budget and set of financial reports at the end of year such as an income and expense report. The treasurer tracks past due association dues and follows the associations rules on collecting past due accounts. If necessary the board will engage legal counsel to help with past due accounts and any legal issues that may arise.

The bylaws are first created by the master deed, and then modified by the HOA as needed. The process for changing the bylaws is set in the master deed. As stated in the master deed, some bylaws can be changed by the association board and some changes require the approval of unit owners.

Some changes may require more than a simple majority. Each unit owner is entitled to one vote. The association may use a simple concept like the voting stick or paddle. This is a distinctive piece of wood or something like a ping pong paddle. Each unit owner gets a paddle when attending a meeting. When it comes time to vote unit owners raise their paddle to vote yes or no on questions.

The HOA budget is something that prospective buyers should review. Last year's budget and this year's plan or year-to-date should available for prospective unit buyers. The budget will include the cost of the master insurance, grounds maintenance, landscaping, water & sewer, common electric, and maintenance of common area facilities such as pools, clubhouse, and tennis courts.

Based on the percentage of ownership as stated in the master deed, the total expenses are then allocated to each unit owner. In the duplex example, each unit owner owns 50% of the common area and pays 50% of the planned budget expenses as condominium fees. In a larger complex, the percentage of ownership may be some small number like 2.34%. In this case the condominium fees for this unit is the budget times .0234.

There is a slight variation between a true HOA that is overseeing a group of otherwise single family homes and a true condominium with multiple units in one or more buildings.

In most single family complexes under a HOA, the common areas are owned by the HOA and each unit owner must belong to the HOA. In this arrangement the assessment of common charges is done by unit, sometimes referred to as "by door assessment." In this arrangement the total budget is divided by the total number of units to arrive at the cost per unit.

In the Condominium form of ownership there are usually a range of unit sizes from a small studio to a large penthouse. In this form of ownership the common elements are owned by the unit owners on a percentage basis, and the budget is allocated on a percentage basis. The small studio unit pays less than the larger penthouse.

The HOA plan vs. actual report shows the actual income and variance to plan. If there is a shortfall in income it is usually due to past due association fees. If this percentage is high due to a high rate of foreclosure or a high number of investor owned units that are not performing well, then this is a problem for the other unit owners.

In the end the bills must be paid. You may be charged a special assessment to cover a shortfall in revenue. This will not seem fair but the association has no choice but to pay the master insurance expense and other bills. It is possible that the association may collect the past due amounts through legal action or when the unit sells.

A prospective buyer should also determine if there are any recent or planned special assessments. If the association has not set aside a budget to replace some component of the common area and the HOA votes on a repair or replacement, then each unit owner must pay their proportionate share of the cost. For example, the association votes to install a new tennis court, since the old one is in disrepair. A special assessment is charged to each owner to cover the cost of the installation.

Reserves for replacement. This is a portion of the budget set aside for repairs or replacements to common areas. A reserve is often called a "sinking" fund.

Broker's Nugget
A well-managed association will have a sophisticated reserve system where each item of the common area is listed with its cost to replace, its life, and the annual amount needed to be set aside to replace it.

See the addendum on the calculation steps for a sinking fund.

A reserve function is an important protection against future special assessments. If a roof with a 20 year life will cost $10,000 to replace, the two owners of a duplex should each be setting aside $250 a year to cover the future cost ($250 × 2 owners × 20 years). Not having reserves is risky since future expenses for common areas must be paid by unit owners through a special assessment.

13 THE ANATOMY OF A HOUSE

The Bones of the House: Foundation and Framing

The foundation is the structure's solid connection to the ground. If you have a slab style home, with no basement, the foundation is the perimeter footing which is poured before the final concrete slab is poured. The foundation is placed 1-4' deep in the earth. This prevents the foundation from buckling with freezing and thawing cycles The foundation must be set deeper than the frost line for the local climate zone.

When a basement is involved, the basement hole is excavated first and then the foundation footing is poured with a key.

A key is a small channel molded into the foundation footing. The key becomes a locking mechanism for the poured foundation wall. The poured foundation wall fills in the key. When the concrete hardens the key-lock prevents the wall from moving off the footing. Reinforced steel bar (rebar) is used to strengthen the footing.

The supports for the center bearing wall are also poured with the perimeter footing. These supports hold the Lally columns in place that support the main load-bearing wall.

In a slab foundation all of the piping for the plumbing is laid in place before the slab is poured.

The foundation walls in older homes may be built from interlocking stones that were pulled from the neighboring fields when land was cleared for farming (a field stone foundation). In a split or multi-level design, the foundation wall is poured four feet deep, and a four foot partition is built on top of the foundation. If the land is hilly, the below grade foundation may have varying heights.

Frame-Wood framed house.

The frame of the house is the wooden construction that is built on top of the foundation. A 2 x 6 inch or larger board (sill plate) anchors the frame to the top of the foundation with bolts. A Styrofoam sealer is placed between the sill plate and the top of the concrete foundation. The frame bolts were set into the foundation concrete while it was still wet.

The load-bearing beam (usually three 2 x 10s nailed together) is placed on the Lally columns to create the center load bearing wall. This beam size is based on the span and the load it has to carry depending on it being a 1, 2 or 3 story house.

The first floor is built with 2 × 8, 10 or 12 inch joists running from the perimeter sill plate to the center bearing wall. Also used, is an engineered product known as Laminated Veneer Lumber (LVL). It is also shorten to LAM beams for *Lam*inated Veneer Lumber.

The floor joists are usually 16 inches on center with cross bracing and joist hangers. This means the support beams are set 16 inches apart. Cross bracing is a small 1 x 3 inch board running from the top of one joist to the bottom of the next one with an opposite piece next to it forming an X. This adds additional support to the joists and support for the floor. Joist hangers are metal brackets that attach the joists to the center beam. In some less expensive construction the floor joists are set 24 inches apart. This provides less strength and results in a "springy floor." Sub flooring (4 x 8 foot plywood sheathing) is nailed to the joists. This creates the first floor. The finished plywood floor is sometimes called the sub-floor.

The perimeter first floor walls are erected with appropriate openings for doors and windows. The first floor is 7-8 feet high, and 9 feet in more expensive homes. The second floor is 7-8' feet high. An exterior sheathing of plywood or particle board is nailed around the outside of the frame. Interior partition walls are installed. The center line partition wall is the load bearing wall and it is topped with a beam that will support the second floor. The center support beam carries the weight of the second floor through to the basement.

The second floor is built in a fashion similar to the first floor. Once the frame of the second floor is in place, the roof rafters are installed and connected with hurricane brackets. The roof sheathing is then nailed down, and the roofing finish is attached, typically asphalt shingles. Perimeter vapor permeable membrane (wind insulation) is applied to the exterior and the windows and doors are installed. The house is now considered to be weather tight.

Rough plumbing & electric, insulation and drywall. Water lines, sewer lines and electrical wiring that will be in the wall cavities is installed next. Fiberglass insulation is installed into the interior perimeter wall cavities between the studs, and the drywall is nailed in place.

Exterior finish.

A home's exterior finish is a factor in its cost to maintain. On the broad spectrum, the exterior finishes of a home include wood, vinyl, metal, masonry, or composite products. Wood and composite product finishes require periodic painting. Clapboard siding is more expensive to maintain because it requires painting every 5-8 years. Vinyl siding has a lower cost of maintenance but can be damaged and may not be as appealing. A low maintenance brick finish adds a high quality appeal to a house.

A more expensive vinyl siding such as "Cedar Impressions" or "Everlast" provides the look of painted wood but with a lower maintenance cost. Aluminum siding is low maintenance but may fade over time.

A stucco finish is a concrete and plaster finish which is hard and durable. A stucco finish can be applied on top of concrete block or masonry walls. Stucco color is permanent, although it may be painted. Stucco can also be applied over traditional wood with the addition of structural support in a lathe framework. There are exterior finish products that have a mix of stucco and a thin stone veneer. Stucco finish is more prevalent in the hot southern climates where concrete block is the predominant construction choice.

Roof. While a roof is designed to keep water out, it may also add to the appeal of a house. Lower cost asphalt or fiberglass shingles are adequate to achieve the primary purpose of keeping the house water tight. However, a more appealing look for the roof can be achieved by applying an architectural shingle. In either case, roof shingles last about 20-30 years with some up to 50 years.

When an asphalt roof needs replacing, it is possible to add a second layer of roof shingles over the existing shingles. Second layer shingles are applied to reduce the cost of replacing the roof. If two layers of shingles are already on the house, a third layer of shingles cannot be applied.

Preformed metal, wood or shake shingles, concrete tile, clay tile, and slate roof finishes all provide a higher quality roof. Higher quality roofing products have a greater cost and longer life expectancy.

As a general rule of thumb, take into consideration the surrounding neighborhood and replace your roof with similar quality roofing materials. A high cost slate roof may not be a good investment if other homes in a neighborhood have asphalt shingle roofs.

Interior Room Design and Living Areas

A home is separated into sleeping, living/social, and working areas. The ranch style home has three bedrooms (sleeping) on one side of the house and the living and dining room (living/social) on the other side. The kitchen (working area) is placed to the rear center of the house. The areas are connected by a central hallway for circulation. A home needs storage, found in basements, attics, garages or other out buildings.

Each bedroom must access a hall to a bathroom, without crossing a living, working, or other sleeping area. I use the term "box cars" (from the railroad train definition) which is essentially two rooms linked together. A functional problem is created with "box cars."

The colonial home has the sleeping area on the second floor with living and working areas located on the first floor.

In a cape style house, second floor bedrooms need a bath on that floor. No one should have to walk down a flight of stairs to reach a bathroom. Basement bedrooms also need their own bathroom on that level.

The definition of a bedroom varies from state to state. However, the main elements of a bedroom are a room large enough to hold a single bed and a chest of drawers. Each bedroom should include a closet and a window.

Insulation. In modern construction the exterior walls, floor joists, and attic flooring are insulated with fiberglass. Older homes had no insulation or might have had some form of rock wool. Some older homes may have been updated with some form of blown in insulation or UFFI.

An insulated house is less expensive to operate since it has lower heating and cooling costs. Insulation is measured with an "R" value or resistance to heat loss. The area of the country sets the recommended "R" factor for walls, floors and attics. More detailed information on the "R" factor is available on the Internet at [energystar.gov].

Interior walls & ceilings. Modern construction includes painted drywall for walls and ceilings. Older houses used lathe and plaster walls. Behind an old plaster wall in an older home, there are ¼ inch by 1 inch strips of wood (lathes) nailed to the 2 x 4 studs. The plaster was mixed with horse hair to strengthen it, and then applied to the lathes. The plaster oozed through the lathes and dried, creating a strong bond.

Room ceilings are flat. For a more dramatic effect a ceiling can be raised 8-10 inches in the center with sloping walls known as a tray ceiling since it resembles an inverted tray pushed into the ceiling. Tray ceilings are often found in a second floor master bedroom. The tray ceiling uses space above the main ceiling joists, allowing the ceiling to be raised. A cathedral ceiling is open to the roof rafters.

Interior Finishes

Millwork. Millwork refers to the wood moldings seen at the top and bottom of walls, also around window and door openings. More elaborate millwork adds quality and value to a house. Wood moldings and doors are manufactured in a wood mill hence the name "millwork."

Interior doors are an important part of the quality and appeal of a house. The simplest luan finished hollow core door is found at the low end of quality. Luan is a thin wood veneer glued to a wood frame. The finished door has a flat smooth finish similar to an "A" grade plywood finish. The veneer is thin and easy to puncture. They are lightweight and can be trimmed top and bottom to fit varying opening sizes.

Vinyl doors simulate a traditional wood door and can be solid or part hollow. The highest quality door is a solid six panel wood door. There are an infinite number of door styles, from sliding, folding, bi-fold, French, glassed, V-grooved, Dutch, mirrored, café, and raised panel to name a few.

Millwork is used for the baseboard trim along floors, walls, doors, and windows. The lowest quality millwork is Medium Density Fiberboard (MDF). MDF is sawdust and glue, fused together under pressure and heat. It varies in color from tan to chocolate brown.

Painted pine board is often found in modest housing. Maple and oak wood millwork is found in higher quality homes. There are a wide variety of styles and woods used in finished millwork here is a small list of definitions.

Baseboard: a board applied at the floor of a wall. It is a transition from the floor to the wall. In comes in many sizes often 1 by 3-6 inches.

Baseboard Cap: a small wood strip applied to the top of the baseboard, referred to as a quarter round. The name comes from its being 1/4 of a round piece of wood. It adds additional detail.

Window and door casing:
boards that trim the window or door.

Molding: a piece of wood that covers an intersecting corner. Most often seen at the top of the wall where it meets the ceiling. It is sometimes called a crown molding or dentil molding. Dentil molding has staggered regular cuts that create a molding resembling square teeth.

Chair rail: decorative and protective board that runs along a wall about a third of the way up from the floor. It is designed to protect a wall when a chair is pushed against it. It is most often seen in dining rooms.

Wainscot Panel: a decorative assemblage of wood. In its simplest form it is a square or rectangular frame around a sheet of wood panel. It is often seen in a dining room under the chair rail adding to the finished quality of the room. It is also seen as a complete finish system in libraries or as decorative finish on staircase walls. The degree of potential detail is almost limitless using varying finish styles of casings and moldings.

Architrave: This is the area over a doorway opening with an arch. Think of it as the decorative millwork around an arched opening to a foyer or formal room. It may include columns and other decorative finishes.

Fluting and mill designs: The mill can enhance the appeal of a board by adding additional design finishes. For the flute, the mill removes a channel of wood leaving 3-4 parallel channels along the facing of the board. Crown molding designs vary from simple to elaborate to enhance the top of the wall adding a formal look to the room.

Very simple installed millwork will have corner boards that butt up against each other. Simple door casings have a board with no additional features or a simple curved surface.

Mitered corners are an indicator of a higher quality of carpentry. A mitered corner is a joint where the intersecting boards are cut at a 45° angle. As the quality of millwork carpentry increases there will be a baseboard and base cap.

Floor Coverings

There are many floor covering products to choose from. They come in a range of quality. This discussion is low to high cost. However, there are a wide range of quality within a family of products and prices do overlap.

Asphalt tile is the lowest cost, has limited color section, is more rigid than linoleum or vinyl, is susceptible to cracking, but performs well in low temperature and/or moist environments.

Vinyl floors have a wide color selection and wear well in general home installations. Vinyl flooring comes in rolls or in squares. Vinyl is shiny and does not need to be waxed. It is sealed. It may need resealing in high traffic areas.

That said, be aware that it comes in varying degrees of gloss finishes that can wear over time. The image on the vinyl surface is printed or applied as opposed to solid color through the product. It is susceptible to direct sunlight and bright colors can fade. The product has a range of dent recovery and cushioning.

Dent recovery is how long it takes to have a dent bounce back if hit with a heavy object, or after having a heavy piece of furniture in place. Cushioning is the amount of material in the product to make walking on it easier on the feet.

Linoleum flooring has been around for over 100 years. It is the precursor of vinyl flooring. It comes in rolls and in squares. It is made from linseed oil and ground cork, wood, or other fillers. It comes in a variety of colors. It's waxed to have a shiny surface. It is less susceptible to direct sunlight. The color is through the product so it wears better over time. Linoleum is sensitive to water and acidic chemicals like vinegar. Dents can be repaired. It is a resilient material with a good cushion factor.

Carpeting is a popular flooring product for most rooms, often found in bedrooms and many living areas. The type of carpet fiber determines the overall life of the carpet and its resistance to stains. Three popular choices are nylon, polyester, and wool.

Nylon is popular and a lower cost choice. Polyester is less durable than nylon or wool. Wool is the gold standard and most expensive. Carpeting pad provides the cushioning. Choices include felt, rubberized felt, foam rubber, sponge rubber, or urethane. The combination of pad and rug determines the overall cushioning sensed when walking on carpet.

Hardwood flooring is popular in formal rooms. It is an oak board 1" x 3" with a tongue and groove. It can also be cherry, birch, hickory or maple. When installed the tongue is butted into the groove for a tight fit. It is finished in varying stain colors and sealed with a polyurethane finish. Hardwoods are from slow growing trees and are durable and resistant to dents. Hardwood trees have leaves.

Softwood flooring is from pine, spruce, fir, or juniper trees. The board width may vary and it may be tongue and groove or simple planks. It can also be stained and is sealed with a polyurethane finish. Softwoods are from fast growing trees and are less durable and resistant to dents than hardwoods. Softwood trees are conifers and have needles and cones like pine trees.

Bamboo flooring is a manufactured product from the bamboo plant. It can have varying degrees of hardness and softness depending on the manufacturing process. In comes in a wide range of finished colors. It comes in a range of thickness from 9-16 millimeters. It can be nailed down, glued down or floated on the subfloor. Bamboo is a grass and not a tree. It can have a beautiful wood finish similar to hardwood flooring. It comes from Asia where bamboo is native.

Parquet wood flooring contains a pattern or mosaic puzzle using multiple types of woods including oak, maple, and pine with deeper shades of mahogany, cherry, or hickory added to create depth. They come in square pieces of varying sizes with tongue and grove and are glued to the floor.

Ceramic tile flooring is a red or white clay tile fired in a kiln with a durable glaze to form the color and pattern. It is often seen in bathrooms in older homes as the 4" x 4" tiles on the floor and around the tub. It is also used as a wainscot wall finish around the remaining bathroom walls.

Ceramic tile is selected because of its ability to repel water. In modern construction the ceramic tiles are much larger with 12, 18, and 24 inch square tiles used as decorative flooring in kitchens and baths. In warmer southern climates it can be seen as the flooring of choice for any room.

Porcelain tile is a dense, fine grained and smooth product made by the dust pressed method from porcelain clays. Glazed porcelain tiles are harder and more resistant to wear than ceramic tiles (non-porcelain). Full body porcelain tiles carry the color and pattern through the entire thickness of the tile making them impervious to most wear. Porcelain tiles are available in matte, unglazed or a high polished finish.

Terrazzo tile is used for floors and walls. It is a composite material poured in place or precast with bits of marble, quartz, granite, glass, or other suitable chips. Terrazzo is cured, ground, and polished to a smooth finish. It is a decorative old-world product used in abundance in Venice, Italy.

Cork flooring is made from the bark of the cork oak tree, a renewable resource. The tree doesn't have to be cut down in order to harvest the cork. Cork has a soft, comfortable feel for your feet, back and legs. Cork flooring comes in a wide variety of color with many designs. Cork is a natural sound deadener, reducing noise and vibration. It is durable and long lasting. While protected with several coats of polyurethane, it is not water repellant, and spills can be absorbed into the cork and could compromise the tiles with warping and peeling.

Flagstone flooring can also be used on the interior of a house, as well as the exterior. Flagstone has the key characteristic that it can be split with ease. It was formed in layers millions of years ago. The flagstone can be ground to make an even surface, or left rough. It comes in a range of colors including gray, blue-green, brown, red, yellow, and cream. Flagstone is irregular in shape. But, it can be processed to regular shapes for easy installation. Flagstone is set in grout and is sealed after drying. Care includes sweeping and warm water mopping.

Slate flooring is a fine-grained, homogeneous rock composed of many elementary components such as shale, base rock, clay and volcanic ash. Slates will form smooth flat sheets of stone when quarried. They are often used for roofing and floor tiles.

Slate is often gray in color, but comes in a variety of colors. It is good for high traffic areas and wears well over time. Slate is irregular in shape. But, it can be processed to regular shapes for easy installation. Slate is set in grout, but not sealed. It is easy to care for, no waxes or finishes. Regular cleaning with a mild cleaning agent is all the maintenance needed.

Marble flooring is a natural quarried stone of many color variations. Its beauty is offset by its cost and high maintenance. It is long lasting, hard and cold to the touch. It can be glazed or left natural. Marble does not hold up well in heavy traffic. It needs regular polish to maintain its beautiful sheen. It does not tolerate cleaning products with chlorine which will ruin its shiny finish.

Granite flooring is a natural quarried stone. Granite has a very hard, durable surface and is scratchproof. It is second in line after diamond for strength and hardness and is resistant to heat. It is long lasting and is easy to clean. Granite is irregular in shape. But, it can be processed to regular shapes for easy installation. Granite flooring is set in grout and is easy to care for, no waxes or finishes.

Fireplaces

A traditional wood burning fireplace is present in many older homes. A simple to majestic wood burning fireplace may also be present in good quality modern construction. Fireplace construction is often brick but can be fieldstone, marble, travertine, sandstone, slate, granite, or limestone over concrete block.

The traditional fireplace has a hearth area where the wood is burned. Above the hearth is a damper which opens and closes, allowing the burnt gases to escape up the chimney flue. Below the hearth area is an ash pit. The ashes collected in the pit are later removed.

The traditional wood burning chimney is constructed from brick or stone. The interior of the chimney creates the draft that exhausts the hot burned gases from the fire. In modern construction the flue is lined inside the chimney; older chimneys were not lined. The intent of the flue lining is to insulate the high temperature of the flue gases from the house structure and to provide a smoother draft.

Burning wood in the open hearth area consumes oxygen (air) from the interior of the house. In modern homes, the interior air is already heated by the main home heating system. The warmer air is replaced by colder air from the outside which is drawn in through any small opening in the house. The heat generated in the room with the fire is offset by a slight cooling of the rest of the house.

In more recent construction, a gas fire log is installed in a hearth instead of the traditional brick hearth. A gas log fireplace is less expensive to construct, cleaner to operate, and more energy efficient, with a glass covered opening.

The flue in a gas fireplace is made of a galvanized metal or stainless steel. The design is similar to a wood burning fireplace, except there is no damper. The metal flue is cooler than a traditional fireplace flue so it can be encased with wood similar to the exterior of the house.

The cost of operating a gas fireplace tends to be less than that of a wood burning fireplace. A wood burning fireplace can be converted to a gas log fireplace, but the damper must be locked open or removed from the damper frame. A closed damper can allow carbon monoxide to enter the living space.

A carbon monoxide detector should be located in the living areas whenever a fireplace or combustible appliance is to be operated.

Kitchens and Baths

Broker's Nugget
The kitchen is an important factor in the value of a home. A well designed, modern kitchen has a contemporary set of appliances, a good quantity of quality cabinets, and counter space with a good work flow. Other than location, a modern kitchen will do more to sell a house than any other single factor.

Kitchen appliances. At a minimum the kitchen must have a cooking range with oven. The cooking range and oven are what makes this room a kitchen. The refrigerator is considered personal property and does not go with the house in most cases.

A built in refrigerator is real property and is sold with the house. Modern homes will have the range with a hood and fan. Other kitchen appliances include the dishwasher, built in microwave, garbage disposal, and trash compactor. As kitchens get larger they often have center islands sometimes with sinks, cook tops, and other built in appliances.

Kitchen plumbing. A sink is required for food preparation. In old houses the sink may be located in a pantry area. In average housing, the sink is stainless steel set in a laminate counter top.

If a solid surface countertop material such as Corian or Wilson Art is used, the sink becomes an integral part of the countertop. The sink can be single or double bowl.

The faucet has hot and cold on and off handles. Modern faucet design has a single handle that mixes hot and cold water to the desired temperature. There may be a separate sprayer hose that pulls out and is used to rinse food off plates.

The hose feature is now often incorporated into the main faucet which serves both functions. A high quality kitchen may have an instant hot water dispenser for hot beverages. The dishwasher is located next to the sink for access to hot and cold water and the waste drain.

The garbage disposal sits just below the sink drain and drains into the waste system. If the community allows a garbage disposal with a septic system you should be aware that it may increase the frequency of pumping out the storage tank.

Regardless of the frequency of pumping, use of the disposal should be minimized to prevent small particulates from entering the leaching field, also known as the soil absorption system. There was a period of time in New York City where garbage disposals were banned for fear of impacting the city's sewer systems. A study showed that it was not true and the ban was lifted.

There is also a garbage disposal which is designed for use with a septic system. The septic system garbage disposal liquefies waste food before discharging it into the system. An additive may be used to encourage breakdown of food particles in the system.

Kitchen cabinets. The upper and lower kitchen cabinets provide storage for dishware, eating utensils, pots and pans, and dry food goods. The kitchen should have enough cabinets for the size of the home.

Kitchen Cabinets

Cabinets are available in a wide range of quality and appeal. Lower quality cabinets are made of particle board construction with painted or laminate surfaces. These cabinet doors will have a smooth laminate finish over particle board. Drawer components will be butt joints using laminate particle board components. Drawer pulls will be plastic. Drawer slides are light weight metal or plastic and not self-closing and with no drawer stops. Cabinet door hinges will be simple and un-adjustable.

Mid-range cabinets will include some grade "A" plywood finish. Cabinet doors may include some pre-molded plastic simulating high quality millwork. Drawer components will be dovetailed using plywood or laminate particle board components. Drawer pulls are metal. Drawer slides may come with self-closing capability and drawer stops. Cabinet door hinges will have some adjustable capability.

High end cabinets are made from natural hardwoods such as oak, maple, or cherry. The box cabinet may still have some plywood or particle board. In general, higher quality cabinets will be constructed of natural wood such as cherry and have milled cabinet doors and wood stain finishes. Drawer components will be a natural wood such as birch and will have dovetail joints. Drawer pulls and drawer slides will be high quality metal self-closing. High end drawer slide stops prevent pulling out the drawer. Cabinet door hinges will be spring loaded and adjustable.

Definitions of cabinet components. A hardwood board is cut from a tree and is sanded smooth. Hardwood boards come in varying thickness from ¼" to 1". Hardwood boards are subject to moisture which may result in shrinking and expansion. Hardwood boards can split. All antique furniture and cabinets were made from wood boards. In today's construction, only the most expensive homes will have kitchen cabinets made from natural hardwood boards, such as oak, cherry, maple, walnut, and mahogany.

Plywood is a man-made product constructed from a number of thin strips of wood veneer that are laid in altering directions and glued together to form a strong stable sheet. The veneer strips are cut from a tree using a long sharp knife blade. The tree is mounted on a rotating lathe type device and the knife blade is set to remove a thin layer of about 1/10 of an inch. The result is a long wide sheet used to make plywood.

In plywood construction, some of the veneer strips will have a near perfect finish with no holes or knots. Other strips will have holes and knot holes that require repair.

The plywood finish is graded A, B, C, or D based on the finished sides. The best "A" grade plywood has an almost perfect finish with minimal repair. The sanded surface is suitable for painting or staining and is considered a good finish for an exposed cabinet. It will be the most expensive of the grades.

"B" grade plywood is a smooth sanded surface with some repairs to the surface as well as small knot holes up to ¼" wide.

"C" grade plywood has significant patches up to 1", is a solid surface, but is not sanded or smooth.

"D" grade plywood has unrepaired holes is not smooth or sanded. It is the roughest of surfaces.

Plywood is available in home centers in 4' x 8' sheets with thicknesses ranging from ¼" to 1".

Particle board is an engineered wood product made from wood chips, saw dust, or sawmill shavings and a binder. It is used for cabinets, utility shelves, furniture, and more. Most assemble it yourself furniture is constructed from particle board which may contain formaldehyde that gives off fumes, which will dissipate over time.

Cabinet construction. A kitchen cabinet has a box frame and finished cabinet door or drawer front. The oldest and simplest cabinet design has a painted plywood box frame with higher quality grade "A" plywood used for the doors. In newer construction, particle board may be used for the box section with grade "A" plywood used for the doors. The particle board box has a laminate surface adhered to the base product. This produces a hard surface that is easy to clean.

Higher quality cabinets have hardwood doors and drawer fronts made of maple, oak, cherry, or walnut wood. The box frame may have some plywood or particle board but these will be made from higher quality grade "A" plywood.

The best drawer construction will have a dove tail joint compared to simple butt or miter joint. A dove tail joint is a set of interlocking pieces which create a strong bond. Less expensive cabinet doors and drawer fronts are also available in plastics that resemble hardwood.

There are many types of cabinet hardware available in the market. Older cabinet doors are attached to the box with a simple hinge set either inside or outside the door. Higher quality hinges are spring loaded and adjustable. Adjustments are made to the hinge allowing the door to close tight against the cabinet box.

The drawer slides are the metal runners easing the in/out function of the drawer. The drawer is prevented from being pulled all the way out by the slide lock. High quality drawer slides may also have a self-closing feature which pulls the drawer closed.

Drawer pulls also come in a wide range of quality. A low cost plastic drawer pull tells a lot about the overall cabinet construction. A high quality cherry wood cabinet will have an ornate metal or ceramic drawer pull that compliments the wood.

Kitchen Countertops

Most modest homes come with a *laminate counter top*. Laminate counter tops are made by gluing a laminate surface onto a particle board base. Laminate countertops are easy to clean but can burn if a hot pot is left on them. These countertops can stain but most stains can be removed with a baking powder paste. Laminate can be cut or scratched and can separate from the base wood.

The solid surface countertop is made using high performance resin systems such as acrylic and unsaturated polyester. Solid surface products can be scratched. Scratches can be removed with sanding. This product is easy to burn, so care must be exercised in cooking. Using hot pads on solid surface countertops is advised.

This product can be cleaned and then dried using ammonia based cleaner or soapy water. Standing water for a long time can dull the finish on a solid surface countertop.

Granite has become popular as a countertop. Granite is a natural stone that comes in unique colors and shades created in nature. Because it is natural stone, granite will have imperfections like hairline cracks, color variations, and fissures. These are part of the appeal of this type of countertop.

Granite requires regular maintenance with periodic resealing. Stains on granite can be difficult to remove but not impossible. Because it is a natural stone, there will be some areas weaker than others that may crack over time.

The original milling and polishing process will hide cracks, so it is not easy to inspect a piece to see if there are any. While granite is tolerant of heat, placing hot pans on a cold surface can weaken it over time. Cracks can be repaired.

Marble is also a natural stone that is cut from a quarry. Marble has a beautiful finish and comes in several natural colors, but like granite requires similar maintenance and periodic resealing. Stains on marble countertops can be difficult to remove. Both granite and marble can last a lifetime but do wear over time.

Soapstone is also a stone that is cut from a quarry that is used for countertops. It has a high amount of talc in it which, when you touch it, gives it a slippery feeling. Soapstone varies in hardness depending on the amount of talc and quartz it contains.

The talc in soapstone makes the stone soft while the quartz in soapstone makes it hard. Soapstone is a good solution for heavy duty use but will show wear over time. It is impervious to most chemicals and liquids, but it can scratch.

Some people like soapstone's natural patina and don't mind the wear patterns that develop over time. Note: In some older New England homes, the basement has a utility sink made from soap stone.

Kitchen Flow

An efficient kitchen has easy access between the refrigerator, sink, and range. This is called the work triangle of the kitchen. Normal traffic flow should not go through the kitchen work triangle.

Work areas in the kitchen should include countertop space next to the refrigerator and range. The kitchen should have a window for direct sunlight. The ideal kitchen window is located above the sink.

Kitchen types. Older homes have large kitchens with an informal eating area. In colonial days, these were known as keeping rooms. Dining rooms in older homes were reserved for more formal dinners.

In ranch style homes the dining room is often called a dining area since it flows from the kitchen. It's not an enclosed room with four walls.

Bungalows and Cape Cod homes often have a narrow rectangular area known as a galley kitchen. Galley kitchens are compact but have all the necessary components of a full kitchen. The identifying feature of a galley kitchen is there is no eating area. It is the very efficient galley as seen in a ship.

In modern larger homes, the kitchen flows into an open area family room that has an informal dining or breakfast area. A separate dining room is reserved for more formal dinners.

Bathrooms

A full bathroom has a sink, a toilet, and bath tub and/or shower. A modest older home would have a wall hung sink which is one without a base cabinet. The toilet is simple and functional. As quality improves there is a wood based vanity cabinet similar to the kitchen cabinets. The vanity top is finished with a similar laminate or solid surface product found in the kitchen.

Older houses had ceramic tile covering the lower half of the bath's wall surface. The bath tub area has ceramic tile from the tub to the ceiling. Bathroom flooring in older bathrooms was ceramic tile. An old house may have a separate tub on legs with no ceramic finishes. If a shower was present, water came from a separate pipe that ran up from the hot and cold water supply. These showers had an oblong frame above the bathtub that held the shower curtain.

Due to the moisture coming from the shower, modern day bathrooms are designed to include floor to ceiling ceramic tile surfaces. Newer bathroom tubs, showers, and surrounding walls are made from a single preformed piece of fiberglass construction.

This eliminates any chance of water leakage. Newer bathrooms will also have an exhaust fan to remove moist air. Some bathrooms are showers only and some have a larger whirlpool tub. Whirlpool tubs may be made of fiberglass or solid surface materials such as Corian.

A more expensive home might have a steam shower or a shower with multiple side water jets. A more luxurious home may have a small sauna. Flooring finishes in today's bathrooms are similar to those found in modern day kitchens.

Porches, Garage and Outbuildings

Stoops, porches, decks, and patios. The front and rear door stoop provides access to the entry doors of the house. Since the entry doors are on grade, a stoop is not required in homes built on slab. A stoop in its simplest form is a set of stairs. By adding a roof over the stoop you create a small open porch. The porch may or may not have railings depending on local building codes.

A covered porch can be long in the front of the house, sometimes wrapping around one side and creating an open front porch, known as a veranda. Verandas are trimmed with columns to support the roof and enclosed with a railing. Unheated porches are not counted as GLA.

A rear exit may lead to a wood deck or enclosed screen porch. An enclosed porch is often called a three season porch since it can be used in all but the coldest winter months.

A Florida room is a three season porch with a base knee wall topped with jalousie windows. Jalousie windows have a mechanism for opening and closing a stack of glass slats to let air and light to the room. The windows are covered by a screen. A three season porch is not counted as GLA.

A patio is a paved area used for outdoor dining. Paving materials for patios vary from simple brick to ornate tile. *A lanai* is a popular feature in southern climates. A lanai is a screened in porch or enclosed patio built into the main living area.

Garages. The four styles of garages are the detached, attached, built in, and basement garage.

A detached garage is set away from the main house. In a detached garage the owner must walk from the garage to the house.

An attached garage is connected to the main house at ground level. An attached garage may have finished area above it that is connected to the living area on the second floor. Since it offers protection from the elements and intruders, an attached garage is more desirable than a detached garage.

A built in garage is inserted into the main living area of the house at the ground level. It exists in two story construction and is distinguished from an attached garage by being in the main living area.

Broker's Nugget
Because it *reduces the utility area* and has a stairway up to the living area, the basement garage is considered to be *less desirable* than an attached garage.

A basement garage is located below level under the main house.

Garages can be simple affairs with exposed 2x4 wall framing and open roof rafters. Some garages are finished with drywall, electric outlets, and pull down stairs.

Pull down stairs in a garage provide access to a storage area which may have a subfloor. Garages can be oversized to allow space for a workshop.

In southern climates, a smaller garage space may be created to house a golf cart. The garage floor can be a simple poured concrete or a nicer sealed finish with a drain. Fire rated drywall or plaster is installed between the garage walls /ceilings and living spaces.

Sheds, barns, or carriage house. A more global term to describe other buildings on a building lot is "out-buildings." Sheds are small structures that provide additional storage space. Care must be taken on a small shed to insure that it is considered real property. If a shed sits on concrete blocks it is personal property since it is not attached to the land. Sheds should be added to the Purchase and Sales agreement indicating they are included in the sale.

Barns are larger and are attached to the land and are real property. A barn can be considered a version of a garage and they contribute some value to the overall property. Some barns may have had the second floor converted to living area.

To be considered GLA, the finished area in a barn must be heated and/or cooled and have a finished interior, electricity, and plumbing. If it is used as an apartment, it needs a kitchen. If there is a bedroom, there must be a bathroom. However, depending on the utility and quality, barn living area is more like finished attic or basement space, adding some value but not as much as the main house.

A carriage house may be found on a large older estate. It was originally designed for a horse drawn carriage. In modern use it is more similar to a garage. The area above the garage area was often finished living area.

Pool, tennis courts, and other buildings. These items appeal to individuals and not the general public. They should only contribute to value based on their depreciated cost.

Depreciated cost is the cost new of the item less depreciation. Every product has an expected useful life. As it ages the products remaining useful life declines. An average quality tennis court may have a useful life of twenty years with a first cost of $30,000. If the tennis court is ten years old it has depreciated 50% (10 years of age ÷ 20 years of useful life). Its depreciated value is $15,000 ($30,000 cost new less 50% depreciation). It can also suffer from functional obsolescence described next for pools.

If a swimming pool is in a northern climate used only in summer, it also has functional obsolescence (a form of depreciation due to lack of usability). As a general rule the value of a swimming pool is reduced by 25% for every season it is not usable. In Florida, there is almost no value lost because the pool is usable most of the year. Even in warm climates, a heated pool is considered a plus.

In Massachusetts there is about a 75% functional loss for the same pool since it is not usable in three of the four seasons. The value of a swimming pool varies with buyer's needs. Buyers should not pay more for a swimming pool than the cost to install a new one. A swimming pool heater can add another month or so to its usable time frame.

Unless requested in the offer to purchase documents, an above ground swimming pool is considered personal property and is not included in the sale of the property.

Tennis court values are affected in the same manner as a swimming pool. Value contribution for a tennis court should never exceed the cost to build it new. The value of a tennis court diminishes if it is only usable in some seasons.

Other out-buildings may include riding stables or buildings used for extra storage or workshop. If out-buildings have a particular use to the buyer, then they add value. In most markets, buyers will not pay for specialty items of little interest to them. Every specialty item reduces the number of buyers interested in the property. Specialty items tend to create a smaller market which increases the time required to sell the property.

When selling a property with specialty items, the seller has to balance marketing time in exchange for the buyer who will pay for the specialty item. The issue will come down to "should I sell now to this buyer for a smaller price, or wait an undetermined amount of time for a buyer who will pay for the specialty items?"

14 HOUSE SYSTEMS

Water and Sewer Systems

Water Systems—Public. Many properties have access to a municipal water supply. A municipal water supply allows the water to flow into the house through water pipes located in the street. In cases of emergency, the municipality may shut off water to the house using a valve located off the property in the sidewalk.

The water pipe coming into the house is attached to a water meter for billing purposes.

Broker's Note-
Everyone should know this
To allow the property owner to turn off water to the house, a shut off valve is located next to the water meter.

The water bill sent by the municipality includes charges for both water and sewer usage, although it can only measure water usage. If the house uses a lot of water for irrigation and pools, it is paying additional charges for sewer discharge, even though this water does not go through the sewer system.

A second meter may be installed to measure lawn and pool water that does not go into the sewer system. The second water meter allows high water users to reduce the amount of the water bill that includes charges for sewer usage.

Water meters often have an electronic reading device attached to the exterior of the house and wired to the meter. This means meter readers no longer have to go inside the house to read the water meter.

The quality of the water is monitored and maintained by the municipality. In some communities there may be a neighborhood water company that maintains wells for the small community.

If you are in a metropolitan area, there may be a large reservoir that serves many cities and towns. In rural areas the town will have its own wells and provide water to the town.

When water is in short supply, a municipality may invoke a water ban restricting lawn watering. Some owners may choose to dig a private well and use the well water for irrigation, if permitted.

Water System—Private. When a public water system is not available, the property will have a private well. The well is drilled into the bedrock in the ground until it reaches the water table. There is a sealed well casing into which a submersible pump is lowered.

The submersible pump moves water through a pipe and into the house where it is connected to a small storage tank. The storage tank is kept under pressure so that when a water faucet is opened the pressurized water flows to the bowl, sink, tub or shower. When the water pressure drops in the tank, the pump is activated to recharge the tank. There may be additional filters and/or water softening devices to improve quality of the water.

Sewer systems—Public. much like public water systems some communities have public sewer systems. In a public sewer system, all waste water is drained through the house in a series of pipes to the final exit point in the house foundation. When the house is on a slab foundation, waste water drainage is through piping that protrudes though the slab into the drainage piping under the slab. The homeowner is responsible for repairs to the drains from the house to the main street line or connecting stub. From the stub or connecting point, the municipality pays for the repair.

Sewer Systems—Private. States may have laws regarding private sewer systems. It is one more aspect of building codes, and comes under the jurisdiction of the municipal health department, or similar agency.

A private sewer system, also known as a septic system, consists of a storage tank, distribution box, and a leaching field (soil absorption system). The storage tank is made of concrete, fiberglass, or plastic and is buried in the ground. It has a capacity to store 750 to 1,000 gallons or more of waste water. Sewerage solids settle to the bottom of the tank, scum accumulates at the top, and the effluent or soiled water flows into the distribution box and then into a series of small pipes. The small pipes are laid in trenches filled with small stones.

The effluent water flows through the piping and is distributed in the leaching field where it is decomposed. The leaching field develops a "bio mat" that feeds on the organic matter in the waste water. The bio-mat is the name of the black tar like substance consisting of organic material, microorganisms, and anaerobic bacteria that feed on the effluent and process it back to clean water. Anaerobic means without oxygen. Anaerobic bacteria thrive in an atmosphere without oxygen.

The septic system storage tank is pumped as needed to remove the solids and scum. Solids and scum are removed by a company that pumps the materials from the septic system storage tank into a tanker truck. Overtime, a septic system can fail due to the drain field becoming ineffective.

A septic system should last 30 years although some last much longer and some a shorter time due to local conditions. Usage of a septic system may impact its lifespan. For example, two people put much less demand on a septic system than a larger family.

Municipalities may have rules on a private sewer system when homes have a private well. The municipality will establish the rules on the required distance between the well and the sewer system. The clean water source must not be contaminated with bacteria from the waste system. Well water quality should be tested each year or as prescribed by the municipality. A water quality test should be part of the home inspection on purchase of a property with a private well.

Septic systems require a more rigorous management. Tips on managing a private system include the following.

Do not use a garbage disposal as it can overload the system.

Do not flush anything other than toilet paper in toilets.

Do not dispose of paint, oil, grease, disposable diapers, paper towels or other paper products into drains.

Repair leaks that drain into the sewer lines to avoid unnecessary water entering the septic system.

Use low flow shower fixtures.

Plant only grass over the septic tank and leaching field as roots can clog and damage the piping in the leaching field.

Do not park a heavy vehicle in the area where the septic storage tank is located.

Keep roof drains, sump pump water and other rain and surface water away from the leaching field.

Excess surface water can prevent the soil from cleansing the waste water.

Have the septic system inspected every 1-2 years and pumped every 3-5 years.

In case of emergency, have a map of the septic system location near the main waste water drain.

Heating Ventilation and Air Conditioning (HVAC)

Heating systems include Forced Warm Air (FWA), Forced Hot Water (FHW), steam systems, and electric baseboard systems. In parts of the country with moderate temperatures, a heat pump system may be used. The main fuels are oil, gas, and electricity. Geothermal heat pump systems are becoming more popular in colder climates.

After buying a new house you should have an energy audit completed. The gas or electric company may provide this service, often for free. This will provide tips on how to better insulate the house, and where you can save energy costs.

Forced Warm Air (FWA). FWA systems consist of a heating unit where gas or oil flame warms the metal heat exchanger. There is also an electric FWA system that heats the air similar to an electric baseboard unit. A fan moves cooler air through the heat exchanger where it is warmed.

In gas or oil systems, hot gases are exhausted through the chimney or through a direct power vent through the outside wall. The warm air inside the heat exchanger is blown through a series of ducts to areas needing heat. It is sometimes called the HVAC system indicating heating, ventilating, and air conditioning system.

Ductwork is a channel or conduit that allows warm or cooled air to be moved to the areas where needed. Ductwork is often made of tin or sheet metal. A section of ductwork may be six feet long with a rectangular shape of varying sizes. To conserve energy, it is often wrapped in insulation.

Modern ductwork is a flexible insulated tube 6" or more in diameter. It is often used in attic installations, where the distance to move the air is short.

Warm air enters the rooms through registers in the floor or ceiling. The ductwork ends at a vent that can be opened or closed to control the air flow and temperature in various parts of the house.

FWA systems have a cold air return duct that allows cold air to flow back to the heating unit to be heated again. The cold air return ducts should not be blocked by furniture or rugs.

Room air is made dryer by the heating process. A humidifier may be added to the system to increase moisture in the house.

How the Air Conditioning (AC) system works. Much like a refrigerator, the AC system uses Freon or similar refrigerant gas. Freon is DuPont's trade name for chlorofluorocarbon (CFC). Freon has been phased out by newer products that are safer for the environment.

The condenser is located outside the house on a concrete pad. The condenser compresses the gas into a liquid and heat is extracted from the gas.

The heat is released into the air around the condenser. A fan over the condenser motor is used to move the warm air away from the compressor.

In the HVAC system, the compressed refrigerant is pumped to the indoor cooling coil where it expands and evaporates. Evaporation cools the copper coil and the air around it. The cool air is sent through the ducts into the living spaces. The warmed refrigerant gas returns to the outside compressor completing the cycle.

In an HVAC system, both the heating and air conditioning systems are controlled by a thermostat which has a switch to select either heating or cooling. The room temperature is controlled by the thermostat.

The AC or heating unit will continue to operate until the set temperature is reached. If the house is on a slab, the heating unit is located in a utility closet in the main living area. If the house has a basement, it is located there. A large house may have a second system in the attic area which serves the second floor.

Forced Hot Water system (FHW). The forced hot water heating system (FHW) has a boiler instead of a warm air chamber. The boiler is full of water which is heated by oil or gas. The boiler has a circulating pump that moves the hot water through a series of insulated copper pipes to the baseboards or radiators in each room.

Hot water baseboards are cast iron which includes cast iron radiators, or finned copper tubing. There are pros and cons of copper tubing and fins vs. cast iron baseboard. Both will have competing 100% energy efficiency. Both use the convection process. The main difference is a sense of comfort level caused by the cast iron baseboard heating. Cast iron baseboard releases heat slower than finned copper tubing.

The process of convection is cold air being warmed by the hot heating element then rising into the room. The warm air rises up and moves through the room to the ceiling, since it is lighter than cold air.

Copper finned baseboards have a series of fins that are soldered to the copper pipe. A copper fin system is faster to heat and quicker to cool. The baseboard unit fins disburse the heat over a wide area not just the surface of the copper pipe.

The amount of air moving through the system is controlled by opening or closing the flexible vent at the top of the baseboard heating unit. To "balance the system" you adjust the slat in the first room to allow less warm air into the room. This allows more hot water to continue on to the next room.

Baseboard cast iron radiators and older upright radiators have a series of cast iron sections through which the hot water moves. The cast iron radiator type of unit may have a flow control valve to allow more or less hot water (heat) into the unit and then the room. The flow control valve diverts hot water around the baseboard to continue on to the next radiator. This allows you to "balance the system" so that the first room does not become very hot while trying to warm the last room on the circuit.

In a large house there may be multiple heating zones. Each zone is on a separate loop controlled by its own circulating pump and thermostat.

Sometimes air gets into the pipe system and may need to be released by a process known as bleeding.

Hot water boilers can provide "continuous hot water." Think of the main boiler as a pot of water. You can insert a copper coil in the pot of hot water.

This is now the hot water supply line for the house. Cold water enters at the beginning of coil and is heated by the hot water in the pot. Hot water comes out the other side of the coil.

The boiler runs as needed to reheat the main boiler water. Continuous hot water systems will run during summer months in order to heat the water. The system is designed to create a continuous flow of hot water that meets the needs of a large household.

Steam Heating System. Steam systems are similar to FHW in that there is a boiler and radiators for heat distribution. However, instead of hot water, steam is generated and moves through iron pipes to the radiators in the living area. The steam system radiator is different from the FHW radiator in that there is no continuous loop of water. The steam rises to the radiator and moves through the radiator sections to its end, warming the radiator as it goes.

At the opposite end of the steam radiator is a valve. The steam valve is a device that is open when cold and closed when hot. As the hot steam rises into the radiator, cold air is pushed out through the open steam valve. As soon as the hot steam hits the steam valve, it heats it, causing it to close.

A radiator releases heat until the steam condenses back into water. The condensed water returns to the boiler by gravity in the same steam pipes. When the steam valve opens, more steam heats the radiator until the room thermostat is satisfied. Control of how fast the radiator heats up is managed by a dial on the steam valve controlling how fast air escapes. You use the steam control value to "balance the system."

Electric baseboard. Electric baseboard is a low cost heating installation but has a higher cost of operation. Electric baseboard heat is considered inferior to other systems. It consists of a baseboard strip that looks like a hot water baseboard strip. The baseboard has an electric component with a similar arrangement of fins to distribute the heat. Electricity flows to a resistor in the unit that converts it to heat which is then radiated out to a series of fins. Convection takes the cold air at the base of the room, warms it against the fins and rises as warm air. Each strip has a temperature control switch to control temperature in each room.

Radiant floor heating. Radiant floor heating is a forced hot water system with tubing and flashing that are installed under the finished floor. The radiant heating tubes have a separate circulating pump and thermostat. Tubing and flashing are placed under any floor surface and may be installed over a sealed concrete floor. Radiant floor heating is also available in an electric version. Care must be taken to insure proper installation under ceramic tile. If a radiant floor heating system fails, the whole floor needs to be replaced.

Heat Pump System. A heat pump system extracts heat from the air or the ground and moves (or pumps) it to a specific destination. A heat pump can extract heat from the ground because the first ten feet of the earth's surface has a constant temperature of 50° to 60°.

Heat pump systems work best in moderate climates where the exterior air temperature range is narrow. A heat pump may have both a heating and cooling unit. When the house needs to be cooled, the heat pump system is identical to the AC process.

To heat the house, the pumping process is reversed so that warm air moves into the house and cold air is released outside the house. Ground source heat pumps or geothermal heat pumps are more efficient than "air to air" heat pumps.

Solar Heat. With energy costs continuing to increase and technology continuing to improve, it is worth understanding the basics of solar heating. Solar energy comes from the sun and is converted to energy with photovoltaic panels or solar thermal panels. Photovoltaic panels convert sunlight to electricity, which is used anywhere in the house.

Solar thermal panels work like the Radiant Floor Heating systems. The sun warms a fluid in the system's closed loop which circulates through the solar panel on the roof. The warm fluid is pumped to a water storage tank where it circulates through a coiled copper tube, transferring the heat to the water in the tank. The heated water provides hot water for the house. This is augmented with a traditional electric heating element for times when solar heat is not enough to warm the fluid in the loop.

Hot Water, Electric, Lighting, and Plumbing

Hot water system. A standalone hot water heater provides hot water for the house. Hot water heaters can be electric, gas, or oil fired. The hot water may also be connected to a solar panel system.

Hot water tanks come in varying sizes, between thirty and eighty gallons. Thirty gallon tanks are typical in most single family homes. Heating systems with a hot water boiler have the option for a tankless hot water feature. In this instance hot water is generated from the main boiler.

Standalone tankless hot water heaters are becoming more popular. It is a fast heat source converting cold water to hot water instantaneously. Cold water enters and hot water exits. There is no energy wasted in keeping water hot while waiting to be used.

Electrical System. Electricity comes into the house on a wire either from a pole along the street or underground. Electricity comes into an electric meter used for billing and then to the fuse or circuit breaker distribution box. The amount of electricity available to the house is 60, 100, or 200 amps. An Amp (ampere) is a measure of the electrical current strength. Today, 60 ampere service is considered marginal. 100 amps will serve a small ranch or cape. 200 amps are found in larger homes. The more electrical appliances you use, the more amps are required.

Electricity is distributed through the fuses or circuit breakers into the wires that connect to the plug outlets and wall switches which control lighting. In modern construction, there is often a light switch that allows a bedroom light to be turned on from a wall switch. In some homes built between 1965 and 1973 aluminum electrical wiring may be present, and not copper wire. The home inspector should identify the presence of aluminum wiring as there is a risk of fire caused by oxidation of the aluminum.

The electrical system must be grounded. Grounding provides protection in the event of a short circuit. A green wire connects the electrical system to a ground connector. A ground connector may be a cold water pipe or an iron rod driven into the ground near the electric meter. This is the main ground wire for the system, and should never be removed.

Lighting is an important part of a home. Older homes often have a minimum number of lighting fixtures in the entry foyer, dining room, kitchen, halls, and bathrooms. In newer construction, recessed lighting in the kitchen and family room provide additional work space lighting.

Under-counter lighting also provides good work lighting for food preparation. Bathrooms should have an exhaust fan to remove moist air from showers.

The quality of electrical fixtures can vary from a low cost affair to grand chandeliers. There should be a light on the outside of the house next to the front and back doors. An outdoor electrical outlet is handy for yard work. In more expensive homes, outdoor lighting is used to illuminate walkways and the house itself.

Plumbing. The cold water line enters the house through a meter. There is a master shut off valve at the water meter, and one for each water line for each fixture. Cold water lines run to all the cold water uses.

One cold water line is run to the hot water tank. The cold water enters the hot water tank and exits as hot water. Both lines are brought to the kitchen sink, bathroom vanities, bathroom tub or shower, and washer hookups.

A cold water line is brought to the toilets and to the exterior faucet for outside activities. All plumbing fixtures drain into the waste water pipes leading to the lowest part of the house and then to the street sewer system or the private sewer system.

Water lines can be copper or plastic depending on the state's building code. Where allowed, rigid plastic tubing is used for hot and cold water lines known as CPVC (chlorinated polyvinyl chloride). This pipe is off-white in color and is ½ to ¾ inch diameter.

PEX is a cross-linked polyethylene used for hot and cold water lines. It is more flexible than CPVC and is often used in radiant heating systems installed on the floor. It is colored red (hot) and blue (cold); it also comes in white.

In most houses build from the late 60's, plastic pipe may be used for drains and venting. PVC (polyvinyl chloride), or a black plastic pipe ABS (acrylonitrile butadiene styrene) are used. These pipes are typically a wider diameter of 2 to 4 inches.

Older drain systems use copper, cast iron, and galvanized iron. Corrosion caused by drain clearing chemicals can weaken these pipes. The home inspector will look for signs of corrosion, leaks, or blisters.

15 SKILLS TO DEVELOP

Before you skip this Chapter thinking you will never be doing any manual labor yourself, remember that you may be contracting for these services. It is helpful to understand what contractors do to be in a better position to select good quality help for a fair price. Also, you need to be aware of the environmental/health hazards present in a home that may be exacerbated by contractors.

Homeownership requires repairs and maintenance. Anything you cannot do yourself should be done by paid professionals. As a general tip on all home repairs and maintenance, always read the directions, and follow all safety precautions.

Be aware of your state's construction lien law, if there is one. Essentially this law insures that sub-contractors are paid for work done on your home. If you hire a general contractor (GC), who then employs sub-contractors(SC), you may be exposing yourself to a risk of double payments. If you pay the GC, who then fails to pay the SC, the SC can put a lien on your property forcing you to pay them for the work they did, even though you paid the GC. To protect yourself, make arrangements with the GC for you to pay the SC directly, or have all SC sign a waiver or release of lien form stating that they will only look to the GC for payment.

Check with your local building department for required building permits before beginning any alteration or renovation on your home. If for any reason you need to have any digging done on your property, check with Dig Safe System, Inc. Dig Safe System, Inc. is a free communication network, assisting excavators, contractors and property owners in complying with state law by notifying the appropriate utilities before digging.

Dangers Found In Homes

Before delving into the various aspects of repairing and maintaining your home, it is important to understand some of the health risks that may be found in a dwelling.

These descriptions may sound scary to the first time buyer, but there is nothing here that cannot be corrected. A house that is 50+ years old has been exposed to a lifetime of evolution in building products.

When first introduced, they appeared to be safe. Later they are found to have a health risk of one form or another. In most cases they can be left in place with no harm. In others the hazard should be removed. There is a cost and a procedure for removal of the hazard.

Who pays the cost is negotiated between buyer and seller. So if you have the perfect house in the perfect neighborhood, but it has one of these hazards, talk to the abatement experts and get a budget to have it removed.

Lead paint may be present in many older homes. Eating lead paint is dangerous. Children under the age of 6 are most vulnerable to lead hazards. Also dust with paint particles can be created by windows and doors swiping adjacent surfaces.

While teething, children can chew on a painted surface that contains lead. Elevated lead in their blood can cause damage to brain cells and/or organs. Lead hazards can also affect a fetus during pregnancy.

About 75% of homes build prior to 1978 may contain some lead based paint. A lead paint test should be done as part of a pre-purchase home inspection.

Never scrape or sand painted surfaces, or disassemble painted wood components without first testing for lead. Although home test kits are available for your use, testing by a certified or licensed lead test technician is the safest method. Most tests are conducted with an x-ray fluorescence instrument, which gives a specific reading. An abatement, renovation, or painting contractor should be certified and insured.

EPA, state, and local guidelines should be followed to assure that the components tested have not exceeded the prescribed limits. The EPA has specific guidelines for testing and disturbing lead paint, which include specific protective clothing, respiration devices, work barriers, cleaning of work areas and disposal methods. State and local rules may exist.

Lead solder was also used in assembling copper piping in the house water distribution system. In some cases, lead can leach into the drinking water.

In 1986, Congress banned the use of lead solder containing greater than 0.2% lead, and restricted the lead content of faucets, pipes and other plumbing materials to 8.0%.

For older homes, a lead in water test should be considered during the pre-purchase inspection. The test will show if the EPA limit of 15 parts per billion(ppb) is exceeded. If it is, corrective steps can be implemented.

Higher than normal lead levels are not a deal breaker, but the risks and costs of abatement should enter the equation.

Asbestos is a known carcinogen sometimes found in materials in older homes. The American Cancer Society has found evidence in humans and laboratory animals that asbestos can increase the risks of some types of cancers. Asbestos becomes a hazard to us when it is disturbed causing fibers to become airborne, or friable.

Inhaled fibers can stick to throat mucus, trachea (windpipe) or bronchi, the network of air ways in the lungs, can penetrate the outer lining of the lung, and cannot always be cleared by coughing or swallowing. Lung cancer is known as mesothelioma.

Asbestos was used as insulation around pipes and air ducts. It can also be found in flooring, roofing, exterior siding, older furnaces and boilers. It may be in the thin cement board applied to walls and ceilings near the boilers and furnaces.

Positive identification can be made by sending a sample to a qualified laboratory for analysis. Samples could be taken by your home inspector or a qualified technician. Removal should always be done by a certified and insured asbestos abatement contractor.

Urea-Formaldehyde Foam Insulation (UFFI) was an insulation product applied to un-insulated homes during the 1970s and early 1980s. UFFI was injected as foam into exterior wall cavities and in some roof and floor cavities. In some cases formaldehyde gas leached from the product.

It was considered an indoor air quality hazard and was banned in the United States in 1982 by the Consumer Product Safety Commission. However, it was found the product cured and became benign over time. The ban was overturned by the U.S. Court.

Formaldehyde can also be found in building materials such as plywood, particle board, and carpeting and sensed as a new house smell. Small amounts of formaldehyde gas are considered harmless, but can be an irritant to some people with sensitivity.

Radon gas is a product of decaying uranium and can be found anywhere in the world. Next to tobacco smoke, high concentrations of radon gas in homes is considered a leading cause of lung cancer by the Surgeon General. A test for radon gas should be considered during the home inspection.

Radon is measured in picocuries per liter (pc/l) of air. The recommended level for remediation is 4.0 pc/l or higher.

Radon is easy and cost effective to correct. Installing a PVC pipe into one or more locations in the basement floor connected to a fan in the attic vents the gas to the exterior. The fan system sucks the radon out of the soil under the basement floor before it escapes into the indoor air.

Mold is a fungus similar to a mushroom or yeast. Spores are released into the air as part of the mold reproduction process. Spores grow in humid environments. High levels of certain mold species can be toxic to humans.

Blackened spots observed on wood or drywall is suspected to be mold. Air conditioning systems are vulnerable when not maintained or have dirty filters. Spores clinging to the condensation on the cooling coils and fed by dust and dirt allow larger quantities of mold to be released into the indoor air.

Testing for mold should be done by a qualified specialist during the home inspection. Mold levels exceeding EPA standards will require mitigation by a qualified service provider, and generally involves washing suspect surfaces with special agents.

How to minimize mold in your home:

A musty smell or eye and throat irritation are signs of a mold problem. Water stains on drywall ceilings, or floors should be investigated.

Repair all water leaks and allow exposed areas to dry. Mold can grow in less than a day.

Vent humid air from bathrooms, kitchens and laundry areas, to the outdoors. Keep dryer exhaust systems clear.

A de-humidifier with an automatic pump and discharge to a plumbing fixture installed in the basement or lowest living area can remove excess moisture from the indoor air. Humidity should be maintained below 60%. Air conditioning can de-humidify the air in the living spaces.

Exterior drainage and landscaping should slope away from foundations.

A leak-detection system could be installed to set off an alarm when water intrusion is sensed.

Mold should be removed without delay. Scrub mold off hard surfaces with detergent and water, and dry the area. See the EPA's web site for additional information.

Chinese drywall is a fairly new concern for homes. It may have been installed in homes built from 2001-2009, mostly in the southeast and especially in Florida and Louisiana.

A large amount of drywall was imported from China to the U.S. to meet unusual demand caused by two factors. First is the unprecedented growth in residential construction in the boom period through 2006. Second are the hurricanes in 2004-2005 which caused a tremendous amount of damage, requiring above average repairs and reconstruction.

The main issue with this drywall is a higher concentration of sulfur and strontium which release a caustic gas. The caustic gas attacks copper and metal elements near the drywall. This will be seen as blackened copper elements. Copper wires will normally have a bright copper color. When exposed to a caustic gas, the copper turns black, and begins to oxidize or erode the metal.

It will cause problems with HVAC systems eroding the copper cooling coils, eventually piercing them and releasing the refrigerant used in the cooling system. It can also affect personal property such as precious metals and mirrors.

Summary of home dangers: During the process of buying a home, be particularly aware of lead paint, asbestos, radon gas, mold, and discolored metal. You should consider adding these test services to the home inspection menu, or if the inspector suspects any of these hazards.

If you're a do-it-yourselfer, follow proper safety procedures. When hiring contractors, be sure they are qualified or certified in the specialty, follow procedures, and are properly insured.

Painting: Interior & Exterior

Learning to paint is not difficult, and it is a skill that will eventually be needed when you own a home.

If you go to a hardware store, there are many staffers who can give you tips on a specific project. There is a lot of information on the Internet, although it can be confusing and contradictory.

To begin you need to determine if you will use latex or oil based paint. The key factor is what is on the wall now, and the best source is the current owner. If the existing paint is oil based, you will need to get some expert advice on how to prepare the wall to paint over it with a latex paint.

Most modern painting is done with latex or acrylic paint. Unless you want to become a professional painter, stick with latex paints.

Ninety percent of a good paint job is in the preparation of the surface. Interior walls or ceilings need to be filled (spackling compound of some sort), sanded smooth, and vacuumed clean to eliminate dust.

If there are good sized holes, they should be patched and built up to the flat surface. Wood trim holes should be filled with wood putty or filler. Walls are then washed. Tri-sodium phosphate (TSP) is good product to wash walls making them as clean as possible. Be sure to wear gloves and eye protection.

It is not a good idea to paint over existing wallpaper. Existing wallpaper can be removed with a steamer, scraping to remove the paper, and glue to get down to a clean flat surface that can be painted.

If it is new drywall, you may need to apply a primer first. You may also need a primer if there was a lot of patching, or if the color change is dramatic in shade, e.g. dark blue to ivory. In most cases a primer is needed if covering an oil based surface with a latex paint.

A gloss paint finish is hard and shiny, often used on woodwork. The gloss finish is durable and easy to clean. A gloss finish is also used on main walls in areas of heavy traffic or moisture, such as a play room, kitchen, or bath.

A satin or semi-gloss finish is 50% flat finish and 50% gloss finish. The satin finish has some luster, but not the shiny effect of gloss.

A flat finish has no luster or reflection and is found in the main rooms such as living room, dining room, family room, and bedrooms. Ceilings are finished with a white flat ceiling paint. Decorators add a small amount of the wall color to tint the ceiling paint.

You will need a selection of paint brushes, rollers, and roller extensions. Other painting supplies include paint tape, drop cloths, paint roller pans, liners, and a step ladder. Remove as much hardware as possible to prevent paint splatter. It is quicker to tape over hardware, but the finished job always shows some splatter, reducing the crisp look.

A typical room will have three paint applications, the wood trim doors and windows in a gloss finish, the walls in a flat finish, and the ceiling in a tinted white.

Start with the wood trim. Use paint tape to cover wall sections and window glass. Use drop cloth to protect the floor. Next do the walls after protecting the woodwork and ceiling with tape. Use a brush to paint the edges next to the paint tape. Be careful not to get paint on protected surfaces.

Once the edging is done, use the roller to fill in the wall. Then paint the ceiling after protecting the walls with paint tape. Do the ceiling edges first with a brush, then do the main part of the ceiling with a roller. Use the roller with roller extension for the ceiling. When dry, replace all hardware.

Be sure to save any leftover paint for touchups. Label each can with color as well as where it was used and when.

Painting—Exterior. Exterior painting can be a big job, but there are many small jobs within the skill set of most homeowners. You may need to paint a porch, garage or out-building. If you have a small one story ranch, and feel comfortable on a short ladder, you may do it yourself.

Anything over one story that needs extension ladders should be left to the pros. You may need to paint a concrete patio, deck, or metal railings on a stoop. Resealing a driveway is in this category since it is like painting the driveway.

When looking at the existing paint you may see signs of poor preparation or moisture from the last paint job. Paint can peel, blister, wrinkle, chalk, mildew, sag, or fail to dry.

Almost all of this is caused by poor preparation of the surface, excess moisture or poor quality paint. You will find plenty of help on how to prepare the surface from your local hardware or paint supply store. Techniques and process will vary depending on where you live. For do it yourselfers, use latex paints. Oil based paints are good, but require a lot of cleanup.

Plumbing Fundamentals

Many homeowners will not try a plumbing job since it is complex and often requires special tools. However, most anyone can learn to change a washer or plunge out a stopped up toilet. Every homeowner should know where the main water shut off valve is in the house. In case of a broken water line or failed hot water tank, the first thing to do is shut the water off at its source.

There are a few places where water can break through the water lines causing a flood. If the water heater fails or if the washing machine hot or cold water lines burst, you will get a flood.

Good maintenance practice is to replace the water heater before its normal warranty period ends. The hoses that connect the water lines to the washing machine may be braided stainless steel, or reinforced rubber to minimize the chance of their bursting.

Neither lasts forever and a good maintenance practice is to replace every 3-5 years. Most new homes have shut off values for the washer hoses. Get in the habit of turning off the water supply when not using the washer.

The kitchen sink has a few items that a homeowner can address. Most garbage disposal units have a reset button on the bottom of the motor. If the garbage disposal is overloaded the motors circuit breaker trips and shuts off power. After clearing the grinder area, the power can be turned back on by pushing the reset button.

Never put your hand into the grinder area to remove something. You can pull out a fork knife or spoon by its end. You may use some tongs to grab the end. If it's slippery, put some tape, sticky side out to grasp the utensil.

If something small like a bottle cap has fallen in, use a stick (top of a broom handle works). Put tape, sticky side out, on the bottom and press onto the item. Gently pull up to remove the lost item.

Under the kitchen sink is the drain line. Some plastic drains have wing nut collars that allow you to disconnect the trap section of the drain. The trap is the U-shaped pipe in the drain line.

The trap prevents sewer gas from filtering up through the drain. Because of its shape, it is also a place where drain clogging may occur. If the drain is clogged, you may be able to remove the trap to clear the drain.

Alternatively, if you have older copper connected drain lines you may be able to clear the drain by using a cleaning product designed to dissolve the clog.

If you have an older steam heating system, you may need to periodically check the boilers water level to add water. Some water escapes the system in the form of steam. Over time the water in the boiler is depleted.

There is a water shut off valve that allows you to add water to the boiler. There will be a glass tube on the side of the boiler that shows the water level. There will be an indicator, either on the glass tube or on the boiler that shows where the water level should be.

Turn on the water supply while watching the water level in the glass tube, until it reaches the desired level. Some modern systems have an automatic fill device that does this for you. If you do not have a maintenance service contract on the boiler, you will need to drain the boiler about twice a year to remove old rusty water. Your home inspector should teach you about maintenance items you need to do for the boiler.

Those living in a northern climate should be aware of the potential for pipes freezing and bursting. If you will be away for an extended period, don't set the temperature so low that pipes might freeze. Consider that the heating system may fail, or you may lose power. It's a good idea to have someone drop by daily to check on the house. You can also use a temperature monitoring device that can call you if the temperature drops below a preset level.

Electric Fundamentals

This is not intended to be a course on electricity, but a brief overview. Electricity flows to your house on a wire (the hot wire). Its natural tendency is to reach the ground where it dissipates. Lightning is a good example of electricity in its natural state. When you see a flash of lightning, the positive electric charges are seeking the earth to be grounded.

So an electric circuit is made up of a hot wire and a ground wire. They are kept apart in a normal state. If you put a light bulb between the hot wire and the ground wire the electricity flows into the light bulb, trying to reach the ground. The light bulb uses the electricity to create light from the heated filament in the vacuum of the bulb.

If there were a fault in the light fixture that allowed the hot wire to connect with the ground wire, then there would be nothing to stop the flow of electricity. That is the function of the circuit breaker.

As with plumbing, many homeowners should not take on any major electrical jobs. However, everyone should know where the electric sub panel is with the circuit breakers or fuses.

Circuit breakers should be labeled for the section of the house being protected. When a circuit is tripped, the breaker moves to the center position. After fixing the cause of the tripped circuit, you reset it by turning it off, then on by moving the breaker switch.

When a fuse is overloaded it "blows." This means the connecting metal has melted and the flow of electricity stops. You replace the fuse with the same amperage that was there. Do not increase the circuit capacity by putting a larger amp fuse in a smaller circuit. This is dangerous and could cause a fire.

A circuit breaker or fuse is a protection between the electric source and the area of the house drawing the electric service. The main reason a circuit draws more amps than it should is because it has been grounded by mistake.

This may be due to a faulty appliance or light fixture, or someone working on the line may connect the hot wire to the ground wire. Circuit breakers or fuses have limits (number of amps). The usual range is 15, 20, 30 or 50 amps. If the circuit under protection begins to draw more amps than the breaker allows, it trips the circuit, stopping the flow of electricity.

You can overload a circuit by putting several appliances on at one time. Do not override the capacity a circuit was designed for: this could lead to a fire. You sometimes hear of a fire being caused by faulty wiring. This can occur in old houses where the wiring is frayed, or perhaps repaired by an unskilled homeowner.

Most modern construction will use a Ground Fault Circuit Interrupt (GFCI) outlet in areas near water. They are used in bathrooms, kitchen sink areas, and also for outdoor outlets. Older homes will not have these safety devices, in most cases.

The GFCI outlet is designed to trip (**C**ircuit **I**nterrupt) if the appliance plugged into it is grounded (**G**round **F**ault). It is sensitive and will trip in an instant with as little as .005 amps of change.

Typical scenario is you drop a hair dryer into the sink full of water. The GFCI outlet has a small button that will pop out if tripped. If tripped, unplug the appliance, and reset the trip switch.

If you have no power in an outlet that is protected by GFCI, it may have been tripped from a thunder storm or excess moisture. Before you check the main circuit breaker for the room, see if the GFCI has been tripped (button popped out, or indicator light).

Sometimes there are two or more outlets protected by a single GFCI outlet. In this case the outlet is not a GFCI outlet but has a statement on it that it is GFCI protected. Look at other outlets near the one not working to find the master GFCI outlet. Reset this one.

Within the past several years, codes require that new home construction have AFCI circuit breakers in the electric panel (Arc Fault Circuit Interrupter). This device is an upgrade of the older circuit breaker switch.

It is designed to minimize the risk of fires caused by arcing in circuitry. An arc fault occurs when electricity jumps from the hot wire to the ground wire creating a spark. You observe this sometimes when you pull a plug out from the wall plug. You see a small spark. If wires are frayed its possible for the electricity to jump the distance from the hot to the ground wire. If this happens the hot arc created could start a fire.

Refinishing Wood Flooring

This skill is not difficult, but requires some physical strength. When considering an older house, look for worn and stained hardwood floors, or you may see worn carpeting which covers an old hardwood floor. Hardwood floors are often made of ¾ inch thick oak boards about 3" wide.

Underneath the worn or stained surface is a wonderful finish that goes through the entire board. Your job is to remove the old stained surface revealing the next new layer. You do this by sanding off the old finish, and applying a new sealer. When done it will look like a new installation.

The first step is to rent floor sanding equipment from your local tool rental company. This is a large main floor sander and a smaller circular sander for the edges. The larger floor sander is a rotating drum to which a piece of sandpaper has been attached.

You remove the old finish in three passes of coarse, medium and fine sandpaper. The smaller circular edger is used close to the baseboard in the same three passes. You will need a small palm sander for the corners.

When sanding wear eye, ear, and dust mask for protection and old sturdy boots or shoes. Wear long pants and a long sleeve shirt. Sanding may be hot work but it is important to avoid injury from any flying debris.

Before beginning, clear the room of all furniture. Sanding machines have a dust collector bag that needs to be emptied. Attach a coarse paper to the main sander and the same grade course paper to the edger. The sander is moved parallel with the hardwood flooring in the same direction the hardwood boards run, not crosswise against the grain.

Start in the center of the room, moving the sander in the direction of the boards to the wall. Lower the sander to the floor in a slow motion and let it pull you along in a constant motion to the wall. As you reach the wall, raise the sander from the floor. Do not leave the rotating drum on the floor without movement. It will dig a hole.

Now move backward, lowering the drum again. Repeat in overlaps until your first pass on the main floor is finished. Change the worn sandpaper as needed. Empty the dust bag as needed.

Now use the edger and sand along the baseboard, using a similar technique of contact and movement. Once the edging is done, use a small palm sander to do the corners and hard to reach places. Vacuum up the fine dust. Repeat the sanding process with the medium and fine sandpaper. This is adequate for most floor finishing jobs in an older house.

For perfection you can also rent a floor buffing machine used with a fine sand paper or sand screen. Use the buffer across the grain to help highlight imperfections and blend in the edges.

A final step is using the orbital sander to blend in any light scratches or floor imperfections. In old houses it is possible to have a deep gouge in the floor. Fill these with a matching wood filler. Do not sand the area around it to match the depth of the indentation.

Finishing the floor needs thought. Do you want to stain the floor to a different color? Most hardwood is beautiful in its natural state, however you can stain it to any shade you like, much like refinishing a piece of furniture.

After staining the finish, apply a polyurethane, high gloss (think basketball court), semi-gloss, or satin finish. It's a matter of taste, but satin is often used in living areas.

Polyurethane is available as a water or oil base. Water based is easier to work with, faster drying and easy to clean up (with water). Oil based has higher Volatile Organic Compounds (VOC), is smellier, needs turpentine or paint solvent for cleanup, and takes longer to dry. Most water based products do a fine job and are easier for the homeowner to use.

Read the directions on the polyurethane product. You may need to lightly sand the floor or use steel wool between applications. Use a slow pour of the product into a paint pan to eliminate air bubbles which can transfer to the floor.

Many light applications are better than one thick application. After the final polyurethane coat, give the room a few days to harden the finish. This is a good time to put small sliding casters or felt on the feet and legs of furniture to ease sliding and minimize scratching the newly refinished floor.

Wall Papering

If you wish to make a bolder statement in a room, a nice decorative wall paper is a good solution. Wallpaper is designed to last 15 years compared to paint which lasts 3-5 years.

Wallpapering is a good solution for an older home with wall surfaces that are irregular due to age and many years of patching. There are many options including bamboo grass finishes that can add a dramatic new look, and cover up an old wall at the same time.

Wallpapering is a skill that most homeowners will not need to develop, however if you are interested you can find all you need at your local building supply store. You will also find "how to" videos on the Internet.

Other Skills

You may also develop skills in installing carpeting, ceramic tile, wood flooring, and laminate flooring. You may have or are willing to learn carpentry skills to finish a basement or attic room, kitchen and bath cabinet installation.

You may learn or have masonry skills to repair or install stoops, walkways, or patios. If you are interested in learning any particular skill, I have found the Internet is a good starting point to get a wide view of opinions on how to do most any task.

Oftentimes there will by a short how-to video on the process. Next purchase a how-to book on the subject. If it's a small project and the task is not complex, you can do it yourself.

For more complex tasks, you should work with a professional on the first project to learn the skills necessary to do a professional job. This way you can develop the skill for the next time you have a similar project.

Don't rush into unfamiliar areas. Poor workmanship may impact the property value, and any savings you earned by doing it yourself may be offset in a loss in property value.

Trade or Vocational Schools: If you have a trade or vocational school near you, they often have classes for the general public. You can learn a lot about carpentry, plumbing and/or electricity. If you are already a home owner and have a project in mind, you may be able to get some of the students to do some of the work at a reasonable rate under the tutelage of the teacher.

Exterior Maintenance

Exterior maintenance includes the care of the yard and the house exterior. Yard care varies from region to region of the country. Most yard maintenance includes lawn mowing, bush trimming, tree pruning, mulching, and weeding of flower and shrubbery beds. Northern climates also require snow and ice removal.

Leaf raking, gutter cleaning, exterior window cleaning, lawn watering, fertilizing, and aeration of the yard are all part of exterior maintenance. Exterior maintenance may also include the care of an in ground sprinkler system or swimming pool.

Exterior maintenance is not complicated. However, to maximize the value of your home, you need to be aware of the periodic care necessary to maintain the grounds and exterior systems.

Financial Skills in Home Maintenance

The ongoing maintenance of your home will require a system for managing periodic expenses. Expenses under a fixed amount of $1,000, for example, may be purchased from a vendor or service provider based on your own experience and trust factor with whomever you choose.

For maintenance or repairs costing over $1,000, comparison shop by requesting bids from at least three providers. Before asking for bids, prepare a detailed description of the work you want completed. This helps ensure the providers involved are bidding on the same work.

Without bidding guidelines, three roofing bids may vary by several thousand dollars. For example, one bid may include the removal of the existing roof, one may include a high quality architectural shingle, and one bid may include a low cost basic shingle.

Bids for products and services such as a new roof or a new heating system will include a range of quality and price. The middle range bid will most often give you adequate quality for a fair price.

Take into consideration the overall quality of your neighborhood. Potential buyers don't expect and won't pay for top quality finishes in an average neighborhood. Balance your selections of service providers to match your neighborhood standards.

Financial calculator. When managing costs a financial calculator, or even better, a computer worksheet program such as Excel is helpful. If you have no experience with a worksheet program consider taking a class to learn how to use this tool. Adult education courses are available at trade schools, community colleges, or community education centers. See the addendum for a short tutorial in how to use a financial calculator (HP 12c) and an Excel worksheet program. Consider this a starting point in your use of these tools. The manual and course work will round out your skills.

Prepare a budget. A budget will enlighten you on where you're spending your money. The basis for your budget is what you spent last year. Look at your checkbook from last year and classify each check into an expense category.

The main expense categories are shelter, utilities, transportation, food, clothing, and entertainment. Other major expense categories include insurance, retirement, education, and savings. Beneath each major category, sub-expense categories might include items such as auto and home insurance, fuel, and home repairs. See the addendum for a simple budgeting tool you can create in Excel.

As a homeowner, from time to time you will need to purchase a big ticket item such as a television, furniture, or carpeting. These are considered capital expenditures. A capital expense is anything with a lifespan over one year.

There are two types of expense budgets. The first is an annual *operating budget* which shows the planned costs for one year. Second is the *capital budget* which anticipates the purchase of big ticket items. A savings line in an operating budget is used to accumulate a sum of money to purchase big ticket items.

As consumers, we have been encouraged to use credit cards. Using a credit card is expensive. You not only pay for the product or service you're purchasing, but you also pay a finance change. A better discipline is to anticipate your future needs and save towards those goals. This is not always possible, but it is a good habit to develop over time.

A budget allows you to prepare in advance for future expenditures. For example, you know you want to purchase a new entertainment center which will cost $5,000.

To achieve that goal, you save each year until you have accumulated the $5,000 you need. This is the point at which you purchase your entertainment center. This is known as a sinking fund. See the addendum for more information on how to calculate sinking funds.

16 CONCLUSION

This life planning "how to" book took you through every aspect of homeownership from the first glimmer of an idea that you might want to buy a house to owning your retirement home with no mortgage. You now know how to save for that first down payment. You now know your credit score and how to keep it high.

You also know a good deal more about real estate including the underlying land, deeds, mortgages and limitations imposed on land use by government powers. You are well versed in the various types of houses and condominiums. While not yet a home builder you know how a house is constructed, the important components and finishes that go into a house and how they contribute to value.

You are not yet a real estate appraiser, but you know a lot about how value is created from the location of the property, the neighborhood and the community. You know about the Gross Living Area (GLA) of a house, how it is calculated and what GLA is not. You know how to find factual information about houses from many sources including assessor's offices, county or municipal registry of deeds/court houses.

You have a good understanding of what it takes to maintain a home, and how that contributes to value. You know about the major systems including electric, plumbing, water and sewer, heating and cooling that make a house livable.

You are not yet a real estate lawyer but you know how to read and understand the important contracts used in home purchasing including offers to purchase, purchase and sales agreements, mortgages, and closing documents including the HUD-1 form. You also know how to add protective language to the offer and the purchase and sales contracts to protect your rights and interests.

Though not yet a bank loan officer or mortgage broker, you know how to shop for a loan, the differences between an interest rate and the annual percentage rate (APR). You know the differences between a fixed rate and a variable rate loan and when the variable rate may be useful to you. You know how escrow accounts work and what charges to expect in closing costs.

You still have a ways to go to be a real estate broker, but you are now skilled in finding properties listed for sale, how to negotiate an asking price to a contract price, and how to manage all of the steps involved with completing the sale. This includes the loan application, home inspection, preparing to move, and the final inspection. You know how to prepare your house for sale, and how to search the market for comparable properties to help you understand its market value.

A few more courses may be necessary before you are a home inspector, but more importantly you know the importance of the home inspection and how to find a qualified expert in your area.

You may not want to be a tax accountant or Certified Public Accountant (CPA), but you know how mortgage interest and property taxes affect your taxable income and the rules on capital gains tax.

The Certified Financial Planner skills needed to establish and manage budgets, as well as to plan for your financial long term goals are also now available to you.

Life insurance can provide peace of mind to insure that your plans for your family can still be completed, even if an accident or illness cuts your life short. You now know how to manage your life insurance needs over a lifetime to provide protection for the least cost.

Having reached this point in the book, you are ready to buy that house and to start taking advantage of all the tangible and sometimes more importantly, the intangible values of home ownership, so without further ado:

LET'S BUY A HOUSE

ADDENDUM

Conventions Used In the Book

Excel is used as the worksheet program in discussing calculations, but most any worksheet program will do. The Hewlett Packard HP-12c is the financial calculator for discussing the calculations; however, most all financial calculators will have similar capability.

Results are occasionally displayed in whole dollars only for ease of reading; however calculations include cents. Percentages are displayed with 1-4 decimal places; however, the calculations often are not rounded, so there may be slight differences if you try to replicate the calculations with different rounding.

Search engines and web sites: Data from the Internet can be helpful, and there are many ways to find information. There are also many different web sites that offer competing services.

The Internet is in constant change, and what may be a helpful site now can be replaced by another tomorrow. The book refers to sites that are popular as of this writing. See the addendum for Using the Internet to Find Data. It will show you how to generically search the Internet for new sites that may offer better services. I have also created a web site to augment the book at www.letsbuyahouse.info. Periodically it will be updated to reflect changes in the pertinent web sites referred to in the book.

One final caution in using the internet is to be watchful for scams and rogue sites. Most users today are very careful of what sites they trust and how to deal with unsolicited or junk e-mail. Never divulge your contact information except to trusted sources.

The 2003-2011 Real Estate Market

The worst recession since the 1929 depression occurred from December 2007 to June 2010. For the first time in history, property values declined significantly. Some observers took a dim view of owning a single family home and lost confidence in the premise that real estate will always appreciate in value.

In my opinion this event was artificially created, and the declining market values were simply a correction for past mistakes. Not everyone lost value in their home during this period. Let's understand the fundamental forces that were in play. It is in fact a complex set of events, and there are several other books that deal with it in great detail.

Banks are able to make loans from deposits on hand. People make deposits into savings accounts or certificates of deposit. The bank pays a rate of interest to the depositor of 3.0%. The bank then lends the money to borrowers for a mortgage at 6.0%. The difference provided income to the bank to cover its expenses, and to provide profits for the bank and its shareholders.

Banks were limited in the amount they could lend, based on deposits. They were adverse to losses, so they required a 20% down payment, and the borrower had to have a good credit rating and a good employment history. The bank wanted to avoid a foreclosure.

Now enter third-party investors such as Fannie Mae and Freddie Mac. These are quasi-governmental agencies whose main purpose is to encourage first-time home buyers. Banks sell loans to these agencies.

With a Fannie Mae or Freddie Mac backed loan, a borrower can get a mortgage with a 3% down payment. The mortgage becomes a security that can be sold to Fannie Mae/Freddie Mac.

The term used for mortgage loans sold to third parties like Fannie Mae or Freddie Mac is "Collateralized Mortgage Backed Security (CMBS)." The loan is sold to Fannie Mae/Freddie Mac, and the bank gets the face value of the loan back into their deposit base. The bank continues to service the loan, essentially sending the monthly mortgage statement, and handling the escrow payments. The bank in turn pays the mortgage payments to Fannie Mae/Freddie Mac.

The ability to sell mortgages to third parties means the bank can make many more loans, since the principal keeps getting returned to the bank. The investors in Fannie Mae/Freddie Mac get the income generated by the mortgage loans they purchase. Lenders assemble many loans known as a portfolio and sell the portfolio in bulk. A typical portfolio may be $10,000,000 for 50 mortgages.

Like any investment, they purchase a portion of a mortgage portfolio and in return get the income from the loan payments.

The Collateralized Mortgage Backed Security (CMBS) was successful in the Fannie Mae/Freddie Mac model, and it became attractive to Wall Street investment banks. However, Wall Street took it a step further. Instead of just selling the mortgage payments in total to the investor, they "Sliced it and diced it."

By using more complex formulas, they were able to layer the loans so that different investors could take part in the investment pool with different rates of return based on the risk level. To protect against high losses, an insurance factor was added.

The CMBS model worked fine when traditional banking practices were in play with due diligence on potential borrowers. Then greed stepped in as well as supply and demand forces in the market for CMBS products. There came a point when investors wanted more of the CMBS product, but as mortgage brokers lamented, "We have made a loan to everyone that qualifies."

This results in a relaxation of qualifications. There were "No Doc" loans, where the borrower did not have to show any documentation regarding their income. Loan to Value Ratios reached 100% and more, essentially a purchase with no down payment.

The last piece then fell into place with the large supply of unqualified buyers entering the market, driving up prices. This artificially created excess demand fueled the construction industry to build more housing.

It takes a long time to build a house, so the supply of houses could not keep up with demand for houses. As a result of the shortage, buyers bid higher and higher for properties. This drove up housing values.

With values increasing, speculators or "Flippers" entered the market. An investor buys a unit that is to be constructed in a condominium or sub-division. The investor had no intention of living in the property.

It was not unusual for a speculator to buy a unit for $150,000 and 12 months later sell it for $180,000. Considering a small down payment, of say $5,000, they convert $5,000 into $30,000 in one year. They can do this for 5 units at a time with $25,000 starting capital. The speculators added to the increasing artificial demand.

At the top of the market in 2006, interest rates started to increase to curb increasing inflation. Higher interest rates slowed the demand for housing.

Many buyers had selected adjustable rate loans, assuming their property value would increase and they would be able to refinance at the same or lower rate in 2-3 years.

As variable rates increased, borrowers found they could not make the mortgage payment and started to put their property on the market. New buyers were slowing their purchases due to increasing mortgage rates. This reversed the supply and demand trend with more houses on the market with fewer buyers.

As the market slowed, it also hurt the speculators. When it came time to close on the loan, there was no buyer. The speculator was forced to take ownership, not just for one, but for several properties.

Now with more property on the market and fewer buyers, values started to decline. From 2006 to 2009, values declined in most markets. In 2010, values started to level off with some increases. Values are dependent on the community.

The decline in housing values during this period resulted from the increases in value caused by artificially created excess housing demand. This particular scenario is not likely to happen again, much like the Great Depression of 1929 has never been repeated.

However, as consumers we should be watchful of the next unprecedented run up in housing values. When housing values increase rapidly there may be more at work than simple economic growth.

Trust Deed

When you purchase real estate, a deed is recorded transferring ownership from the seller to you, the buyer. This deed, whether it is a quit claim or warranty or other type, puts ownership in your name.

If you get a mortgage, the loan is recorded next, documenting the mortgage lien. This essentially puts a lien on the property preventing you from selling it until the loan is repaid. There are two parties to the transaction: you and the lender. An important part of this process is that you hold title to the property directly, with the mortgage as a lien against the property.

The mortgage contains language that gives the lender the right to take the property and sell it to satisfy the outstanding debt if you default on the loan terms. Each state has a process which the lender must follow to exercise this right.

A trust deed is different from a mortgage in important ways, especially around the process by which the lender can take back the property if you default on the loan terms.

In a trust deed there are three parties. The trustor is the borrower, the trustee holds the title in trust, and the beneficiary of the trust is the lender. Transactions involving trust deeds are structured so that the lender gives the borrower (trustor) the money to buy the property, the seller executes a grant deed giving the property to the trustor (for a moment you have title), and the borrower/trustor immediately executes a trust deed giving the property to the trustee to be held in trust for the lender/beneficiary. In this transaction, title is held by the trustee, not you.

If the borrower defaults on the loan, the trustee has the power to foreclose on the property on behalf of the beneficiary. In most states, a deed of trust (but not a mortgage) can contain a special "power of sale" clause that permits the trustee to exercise these powers. Here is the standard conveyance clause from a Freddie Mac "uniform instrument": *"Borrower irrevocably grants and conveys to Trustee, in trust, with power of sale, the following described property..."*

An attorney explained that in California, where trust deeds are used, the lender has two choices if they must foreclose: judicial and non-judicial. A non-judicial foreclosure is the least complicated and most often used but does require a power of sale clause authorizing the lender to sell the property in case of default.

It follows the prescribed rules on notification and auction for the state of California. When complete, any funds not recovered are a loss to the lender. This is known as the deficiency.

A deficiency is created when the amount recovered in the foreclosure auction is not enough to repay the loan balance and fees incurred in the foreclosure process. The amount recovered is often not enough to repay the loan balance plus fees built up in the foreclosure process.

A judicial foreclosure involves a court case whereby the lender can look to other assets owned by the borrower to satisfy the debt, or the deficiency. It is more complex and takes longer. If there is no power of sale clause, it may be required.

Additionally, the borrower may have one year after the foreclosure auction to reclaim the property. They would have to pay the lender back the amount owed, plus costs and fees incurred, and interest on the obligation. This is the right of redemption.

Assuming the lender was the high bidder at the auction with the outstanding loan balance plus fees, they cannot sell the property for a year. If it was purchased by another bidder, and the bid was enough to repay the loan and fees, then the redemption period is 3 months.

Hopefully you will never need to know the details of these features. If you pay the loan on time as agreed to, you will never have to worry about this process.

Rent vs. Buy Calculations

When you purchase a home with a mortgage there are three major forces at work:

1. Deductions from your income taxes.
2. A mortgage balance decreases over time.
3. Real estate values increase over time.

Buy Option. Suppose a property is purchased for $200,000 with 3.5% ($7,000) down payment (gifted from relative), with a $193,000 mortgage. Mortgage terms are 30 year fixed rate at 4.5%. The monthly payment for principal and interest is $978. Calculations:

Mortgage Calculation	Amounts	Annually
Price	$200,000	
Down payment 3.5% gifted	$7,000	
Mortgage	$193,000	
Term	30	
Interest Rate	4.50%	
monthly payment (Excel PMT function)	$977.90	$11,734.83

In Excel the mortgage payment function is [=PMT(Rate/12,term*12,PV)]. The mortgage amount of $193,000 is the present value (PV). To calculate a monthly payment the annual interest rate of 4.5% (.045) is divided by twelve. The annual term of thirty years is converted to months by multiplying by twelve. The result is a negative number indicating a cash outflow or payment. The payment can be shown as a positive number by adding a minus sign in front of the PMT function as =-PMT.

The Internal Revenue Service allows deductions for owner-occupied mortgage interest expense for mortgages up to $1,000,000, as well as for property taxes. This also includes second homes as well as the interest on equity loans up to $100,000.

In the early years of a loan, the interest expense is close to 100% of the payment. Assume annual taxes on the property are $2,000. Federal taxes are assumed for this example to be in the 25% marginal tax bracket, and the state income tax is assumed to be 5%. These two deductions are $4,120 shown in these calculations:

Calculations:

Tax Deduction	Monthly	Annually
Interest Expense - declines slightly over time	$978	$11,735
Base Property Taxes increases slightly over time	$167	$2,000
Total Deductible		$13,735
Federal Marginal Tax Rate	25%	
State Marginal Tax Rate	5%	
Total Tax Rate for savings		30%
Total Tax Savings	$343	$4,120

Because this is not an 80% loan-to-value ratio, Private Mortgage Insurance (PMI) is estimated at $65 per one hundred thousand of loan value per month ($193,000 ÷ $100,000 = 1.93) or $125 per month (1.93 × $65.00).

The net ownership expense is $927 ($925 rounded) per month. This includes the monthly mortgage payment of $978, plus the PMI of $125, plus property tax of $167, less tax deduction of $343.

Calculations:

Item	Monthly	Annually
Principle and Interest	$978	$11,735
PMI - insurance $65 per $100,000 mortgage	$125	$1,505
Taxes	$167	$2,000
Less Deduction (See calculation)	($343)	($4,120)
Total	$927	$11,120
Rounded	$925	$11,100

After five years of ownership, I do a comparison of own vs. rent as if the property is sold. Usually two things have happened. The amount owed on the mortgage has declined and the value of the property has increased. PMI is no longer needed because LTV is now 80% or better. The outstanding mortgage is calculated on a financial calculator or in Excel using the present value function (PV). Here are the steps for the HP-12c to estimate how much of a remaining mortgage is owed after five years. This is done in two steps on the financial calculator. If you are unfamiliar with the HP-12c read the section later in this addendum on The Basics of Using a Financial Calculator.

Calculate the original monthly payment. The interest rate is 4.5% for a term of 30 years with a $193,000 loan. This calculates to $977.90 monthly.

Calculate Mortgage Payment

	n	i	PV	PMT	FV
Variables	30 years	4.5%	$193,000	????	not used
Key	30 [g] [n]	4.5 [g] [i]	193000	PMT	
Answer				-977.90	

Don't clear the registers for the next step.

After this calculation all of the registers have the correct values. You only have to change the number of years left on the mortgage.

Calculate Remaining Mortgage Balance

	n	i	PV	PMT	FV
Variables	25 years	4.5%	193000	-977.90	not used
Key	**25 [g] [n]**		**PV**		
Answer			175935		

The second step calculates the remaining mortgage after five years. Change the term from 30 years (360 months) to 25 years (300 months). This is the remaining term of the loan after paying for five years, solve for the Present Value (PV). The outstanding mortgage balance after five years is $175,935.

The property has increased in value at an estimated 2.25% annually. This is an estimate, but a well-founded one (it is the average CPI for the last five years). For this analysis I use a very conservative growth estimate, considering the recent recession. In other parts of this book I use a more typical rate of 4.0%. The value in five years is $223,540. This is the beginning value of $200,000, increased 2.25% annually compounded. To calculate the compounded total of 11.77% you can multiply 1.0225×1.0225 five times or you can use the financial calculators exponent function. Enter 1.0255, then key 5 and Y^X. Calculations:

Equity Increase in Property Value	Rates	Annually
Purchase Price		$200,000
Estimated Annual Increase	2.25%	
Increase Compounded 5 years	11.77%	$23,540
Projected Sales Price		$223,540

A sales commission of 5% ($11,177) is taken for the real estate broker's selling commission. The outstanding mortgage is paid ($175,935). The net proceeds are $36,428. This is a $29,428 increase over the $7,000 down payment. Calculations:

Projected Sales Price		$223,540
Less Sales Commission	5%	$11,177
Less Outstanding Mortgage Balance		$175,935
Equals Proceeds		$36,428
Original Down payment		$7,000
Increase in equity in 5 years		$29,428

Rent Option. Alternatively you could rent an apartment for $925 a month. This is the same as our net expense from the ownership calculations. Rent will typically increase at the rate of inflation, estimated at 2.25% or about $1,030 monthly at the end of five years. Calculations:

Equity Increase in Rent Expense	Rates	Monthly
Starting Rent		$925
Inflation	2.25%	
Term	5	
Increase / rent after 5 years	11.77%	$1,034
Rounded		$1,030

Comparing the Two Models. I calculate the equivalent ownership costs at the end of five years. The tax deduction has changed, caused by declining deductible interest and increased taxes estimated at the rate of inflation. The new interest expense can be estimated by taking the loan rate of 4.5% times the outstanding balance ($175,935) or $7,917 ($175,935 × .045) at the end of five years. Property taxes have increased to $2,235 ($2,000 × 1.1177. This is the 11.77% compounded rate of inflation from above. Income tax savings are now $3,046. Calculations:

Tax Deduction		Annually
Outstanding Balance		$175,935
PMI Insurance - No longer needed		$0
Interest Expense - in Five Years	4.50%	$7,917
Base Property Tax increased at 2.25% inflation	$2,000	$2,235
Total Deductible		$10,152
Federal Marginal Tax Rate	25%	
State Marginal Tax Rate	5%	
Total Tax Rate for Savings		30%
Total Tax Savings		$3,046

LET'S BUY A HOUSE

We calculated the Loan to Value (LTV) ratio in five years with the estimated market value and the outstanding loan balance. It is about 79% ($175,935 ÷ $223,540). The loan is now less than 80% of the value so PMI can be eliminated. Calculations:

PMI Test	Values
Value in 5 Years	$223,540
Balance owed on Mortgage	$175,935
LTV	79%

Lastly I calculate housing costs to be the loan payment of $978 ($11,735 annually) plus property taxes less deductions. The new ownership cost of housing is $910. The deductions have gone down but the PMI has been eliminated. Calculations:

Item	Monthly	Annually
Principle and Interest	$978	$11,735
Taxes		$2,235
Less Deduction (See calculation)		($3,046)
Total	$910	$10,924
Rounded	$910	$10,900

At the end of five years net equity has built up to $29,428 in ownership and nothing in the rental model.

Projected Sales Price		$223,540
Less Sales Commission	5%	$11,177
Less Outstanding Mortgage Balance		$175,935
Equals Proceeds		$36,428
Original Down payment		$7,000
Increase in equity in 5 years		$29,428

At the end of five years rent is $1,030 and ownership costs are $910.

There are a few other items to consider. These include property maintenance, repairs, and replacement of major items that are not factored in as an expense in the ownership model. Consider cutting the lawn, pruning the bushes, and shoveling snow as part of the sweat equity to gain the $29,428 increase in value. You must replace items that break like an appliance. This is also true on major items such as the roof or heating system. However, the property improvements in condition are a factor in the property's market value. Over time most improvement investments will be recouped partially in the sales price.

The Valuation Process

In your search for a home you will learn what makes one house more valuable than another. The more houses you look at, the more skilled you become at estimating the value of the house. Most buyers will accept opinions from a wide range of market participants, but in the end they rely on their own judgment. I know few people who have bought a house based on what the seller thought it was worth, or the real estate broker.

Smart buyers don't want to overpay for a property. They do want to be competitive in bidding for a house they want. In the end the buyer is competing against other buyers, not the seller.

If you know the market value of a house, you can be a competitive bidder without overpaying.

Market Value. This is a very important foundation block of the appraisal process. Market value is defined in every appraisal report. There is more than one definition of market value, and there is more than one type of value. I include the standard definition to help set the foundation.

Market Value (Appraisal Foundation). The most probable price which a property should bring in a competitive and open market under all conditions requisite to a fair sale, the buyer and seller each acting prudently and knowledgeably, and assuming the price is not affected by undue stimulus. Implicit in this definition is the consummation of a sale as of a specified date and the passing of title from seller to buyer under conditions whereby:

- *buyer and seller are typically motivated;*
- *both parties are well informed or well advised, and acting in what they consider their best interest;*
- *a reasonable time is allowed for exposure in the open market;*
- *payment is made in terms of cash in U.S. dollars or in terms of financial arrangements comparable thereto; and*
- *the price represents the normal consideration for the property sold unaffected by special or creative financing or sales concessions granted by anyone associated with the sale.*

This is the definition of *market value* from the *Dictionary of Real Estate Appraisal,* 5th ed. (Chicago: Appraisal Institute, 2010), p. 123, definition #3.

The key point here is that the value is the *most probable price*. It's not the highest or the lowest. It's not the value to the seller or the buyer. It's not the value a daughter would pay to live next to her mother. It's not the value a mechanic would pay because there is an over-sized garage where he can run his business. It is the value that the majority of the market participants would pay.

The next key point is that it is a current value. It's not what the owner paid three years ago. It's not what it will be worth in three years when something changes. It is what the market will pay now (a reasonable time).

A Quick Overview of Other Foundation Steps

The property must be legally identified. This is not an issue for most existing homes. If you are buying new construction, be sure you have a good legal definition of the land. Environmental issues are mostly around buried oil tanks. Be sure the site does not have any. Are there any easements or encroachments on the property? Is the property in a flood zone?

You should have a good sales history of the property starting with the current listing price. If you are in a state that reports price transfers, you can get the sales history from the property field card, available in the local assessor's office.

Develop a summary description of the area and neighborhood. This will be the foundation of location factors when you compare sales and listings in other neighborhoods. What makes this neighborhood special? Is it the town it's in, the school district, its proximity to highways or commuter rail station? Is it the ambiance of the subdivision, the reputation of quality built homes, or access to desirable amenities such as parks, trails, mountains, lakes etc.?

What makes the site valuable? Is it level, wooded, large for the area, well landscaped? Does it have views? Is it waterfront property? Is it buffered by conservation land?

If it's a city location, is it on a bus line, or other public transportation? Does it have parking? Is it close to desirable amenities such as ballparks, museums, schools, theatres, (live and or movie), music symphony hall, etc.?

The improvement is a critical part of the value. You should be able to identify its style (ranch, split, multi-level, cape, colonial, etc.). You need to know its Gross Living Area (GLA) above grade. Count finished basement or finished attic areas separately.

Know the room count including total rooms, bedrooms and bathrooms. A standard Ranch will show rooms as 6/3/2 indicating 6 rooms, 3 bedrooms and two baths. A Classic Colonial will have 8/4/2.5 indicating 8 rooms, 4 bedrooms and 2 ½ baths.

Quality: Read the section on houses to get a solid understanding of components that go into a house. For simplicity, consider most houses as average quality. Your rating moves up with higher quality of finishes. Items that are better than average are *good* quality, then *very good* and finally *excellent* quality. Consider:

Framing: 2 x 4, or 2 x 6 framing studs, insulation

Heat: FHW, FWA, steam, electric baseboard, fuel: gas, oil, electric

Cooling: Central Air conditioning, wall AC units, none

Water and Sewer: public, private, adequate for size of house.
Kitchens: cabinets, countertops, appliances, lighting, flooring
Baths: flooring, wainscot, whirlpool tub, steam shower, sauna, vanity
Flooring: hardwood, carpet
Ceilings: height, tray ceiling, cathedral
Millwork: hardwoods, painted, none
Central staircase: functional, elaborate, hardwoods
Fireplace: none, simple, elaborate floor to ceiling
Lighting: simple, recessed, chandeliers
Exterior siding: brick, wood clapboard or shingle, vinyl, composite
Roof: asphalt or wood shingle, architectural, clay tile, metal, slate
Garage: attached, detached, built in, basement, finished, over sized
Other: patio, deck, porch, outbuildings
Landscaping: simple, professional, well maintained, sprinkler system

Condition: Properties come in a wide range of ages. Here is a simple rule to estimate effective age. Take the subject's actual age and divide by 2. A thirty-year-old house has a starting effective age of 15 years. Now look at how it has been maintained. If it still has the original kitchen but has updates to carpeting, roofing, electrical and or heating, consider it average. If the kitchen has been updated as well, move its effective age down a little to 10 years. If the house is worn and shows deferred maintenance, move the effective age up to 20 years. For houses over 60 years, set its effective age at 30 years, and then move up or down based on updates and condition.

Functional issues: Did you notice any functional issues? Boxcar bedrooms, bedrooms with no access to a bath, older kitchen with a pantry, older baths with tub on legs, above average ceiling height of 10+ feet. Electrical service 60 amps or less. Non-functioning septic system. Is there aluminum wiring?

Utilities: What is the heating type (FWA, FHW, steam, electric baseboard)? How old is it? What is the fuel source: oil, gas electric? Does it have central air conditioning? Is there Public water, and Public sewer?

Hazardous materials: Is there any asbestos, Chinese drywall, lead paint, mold, radon gas, termites etc.?

Garage: How many spaces? What is the garage type: attached, detached, built in, basement garage? How is the interior finished: open studs, finished drywall, electric service, lighting, or workshop area?

Porch Deck & Patio: Is there a porch? Is it enclosed or open? Are there decks or patios?

Fireplaces: Is there a fireplace? How many? What type: traditional masonry or gas fire log?

Selecting Your Comparables Sales

Appraisers use the general term "comparable" to indicate the property being compared to the subject. The comparable could be a sale or a current listing. Try not to use listings, unless they support a lower value.

Here is big concept for you to understand. It is the *principle of substitution.* It simply means that one item can easily be substituted for another. Why would you pay $150 for product "A" when you could buy product "B" for $125? This of course assumes that A and B are fairly equal. The same is true in real estate. Why would you pay $180,000 for a 3 bedroom ranch if there is a similar one on the market for $160,000? This is where listings can be helpful. When list prices are very high for the market, they are not helpful. Any seller can list his or her property for any price. It does not mean that it is a competitive market price. However, if there is a reasonably priced house listed for sale, it can support a lower value.

This is the most important first step in valuing your subject property. You need three good recent closed sales that will focus in on the value of your subject property. Ideally the identical house on the right sold yesterday. The one across the street sold last week, again identical, and the one just to your left sold two weeks ago, again identical. The sales prices were $199,000, $200,000 and $201,000. Estimating that yours is worth about $200,000 is not hard.

In the real world, sales data is much more imperfect and far flung in both distance and time. However you can still select three good sales that will close in on a value. Your first sale should be one right in the neighborhood. Even if it is an older sale, or one that is a slightly different style, get the best sale from the neighborhood. Next get the most recent sale of a very similar property, even if it's across town or even in another town. Now get a sale that is almost identical to the subject in style, size, quality, age, condition, and features.

From these three you can adjust in to a value indicator reflecting the neighborhood, the market and the house.

Other guidelines: Don't go more than one style up or down. If you are valuing a ranch you can use a spilt level or a cape but not a gambrel or colonial. If you are valuing a cape, you can use a split, or a gambrel but not a colonial.

Don't use sales that are very different in size, not more than 30%. For a 1,200 square foot ranch you can use sales from 850 to 1,600 square feet. Larger or smaller become less comparable.

Don't use sales that have very different lot sizes. A house on a 5-acre lot is not a good comparable for one on a 1-acre lot.

Don't use sales with very different quality. The high end brick colonial with cherry kitchen, hardwood floors, and 9' ceilings is not a good comparable for a standard finished colonial.

Bracket your sales: If your final value indicator is $200,000, then the original sales range before adjustments should be above and below $200,000 and after adjustments the values should converge. Avoid the situation where all three sales are smaller, older and of inferior quality that sold between $150,000 and $175,000, and then adjusted up to $200,000.

Organizing Your Data

This is a simple grid that you can use to organize your subject and three sales. The Excel version is available on www.letsbuyahouse.info:

Sales Comparable Grid							
Subject		Comparable 1		Comparable 2		Comparable 3	
Street:							
City, State:							
Element of Comparison	Description	Item/ Desc.	Adjustment	Item/ Desc.	Adjustment	Item/ Desc.	Adjustment
List Price							
Sales Price							
Price/SF							
Days on Market							
As Of Date							
Rooms/Bedrooms AG	/ /	/ /		/ /		/ /	
GLA							
Location							
View							
Design (Style)							
Lot Size							
Quality / Appeal							
Effective Age/Cond.							
Heat/CAC							
Deck, Patio, Porch							
Garage							
Fireplace							
Finished Basement							
Finished Attic							
Net Adj Total							
Adj Sales Price							

Adjusting the Comparable Sales

The Adjustment Process: Appraisers use the terms superior or inferior when rating a sale. You can *use better or worse.* The sales are used to estimate the value of the subject. If the sale is *better* than the subject, you *subtract* a value from its sales price reflecting how much better the market thought that feature was worth. If the sale is *worse* than the subject, you *add* a value. This is important, and sometimes it's easy to get the adjustment going in the wrong direction, so here is a quick summary:

Element of Comparison	Subject	Comparable 1	
Quality	Average	Better	Minus (-)
Condition	Average	Worse	Plus (+)

For the subject and each sale fill, in the first five blocks. If it's a sale, enter the sales price. If it is a listing, enter the list price and estimate a discount. This might be 5-10%. Calculate an estimated sales price based on the list price less the discount. The listing price is discounted since most listings sell for less than the list price. Move down the grid to the Gross Living Area (GLA) and enter that for the subject and three sales. You will note that for the comparable sales each column is split in two. The left side (shaded box) is for the actual data; the right side will be for your adjustment.

Now back to the top and calculate the price per square foot. This is the sales price divided by the GLA. If you know the days on market from MLS listings, enter that next. It's not critical but can be useful in looking at listings. If they have been on the market for a long time, they may be over-priced.

Enter today's date for the subject in the *As of date field*. Your valuation is based on the time you did the analysis. For the sales and listings, enter the date that the property sold or when it was listed, if you have it. This data is helpful in seeing if values are increasing or decreasing.

Room Count: This is entered as 6/3/1 indicating 6 rooms, 3 bedrooms and 1 bath. The usual convention is to adjust for Gross Living Area on the next line, and not to adjust by room count. The exception is for baths. If there is a difference in number of baths then it is adjusted here. As a starting point use $1,000 for an additional ½ bath and $3,000 for a full bath. It will vary based on markets, quality and condition.

Gross Living Area: Houses will have different sizes. Start with the average price per square foot of the three sales you are using. For each of the comparable sales, divide the sales price by the sales GLA. For example if a 2,000 square foot house sold for $200,000 its price per square foot is $100.00 ($200,000 / 2,000). Suppose the average of the three sales is $100.00. This $100 value per square foot is for the total property and includes many items that occur only once. Remember that GLA is the measure of the above grade living area. When you use the GLA to calculate the value per square foot, the result is an indicator of value for the whole property. The value per square foot includes the land, kitchen and baths, fireplaces, garage, decks, electrical, water and sewer connections. Also, for slight differences in size it should include the main heating/cooling systems. The next 100 square feet of area will be less than the average sales price per square foot of the market comparables. Start with 25% of the average or $25.00 ($100.00 per square foot × 25%). A difference of 300 square feet would be a $7,500 adjustment ($25.00 × 300 square feet). You can adjust the rate for your market and particular house. A newer house of high quality will have a higher percentage of the average price per square foot, and an older house of lower quality will have less of a percentage.

Location: Enter *Average* for the subject. For each sale use your judgment to say the comparable is better, equal, or worse.

View: Enter *Average* for the subject. For each sale use your judgment to say the comparable is better, equal, or worse.

Design (Style): Enter the subject's and sale houses styles. It is likely to be a ranch, split level, multi-level, cape, or colonial. Use terms standard for your market. In selecting the comparables, try as much as possible to select the same design styles. It is more complicated when you are trying to compare a ranch to a cape to a colonial. If you must use a very different design and it is clearly better or worse than the subject, make the adjustment here.

Lot Size: Enter the subject's lot size either in square feet or acres. Enter the lot size for each sale. If there is not much difference in lot size, consider them of equal value. If one of the sales is much larger or smaller, make an adjustment. When using square feet, estimate a value per square foot difference, say $1.00. If the subject is 10,000 square feet and the sale is 15,000 square feet the adjustment is -$5,000 (10,000 - 15,000 × $1.00). Always round this to the nearest $1,000. If you are working in acres, set the value of an extra acre at a reasonable number, say $5,000. If the subject has 4 acres and the sale has 2 acres the adjustment is +$10,000 (4-2 × $5,000). Round to the nearest $1,000. The example values per unit of $1.00 per square foot or $5,000 per acre are just a starting point. You will use your knowledge of the market to refine this.

Quality/Appeal: **Don't confuse quality with condition.** A house may have carpeted floors and the sale has hardwood floors, but they are worn. They are still a *better quality* finish, but in *worse condition.* Only consider the quality of the finish here. You will adjust for condition separately.

Estimate the subject's quality as average. For each comparable sale use your judgment to say the comparable is better, equal, or worse. This is subjective and you have to weigh everything that you know about the subject and how it compares to the sale. If they are fairly similar, then they are equal. The sale is better or worse by its finishes in the kitchen, baths, flooring, ceiling height, millwork, staircase, ceiling styles, floor-to-ceiling stone fireplace, lighting, exterior finish, roof finish, and landscaping.

Effective Age/Condition: Estimate the effective age of the subject and comps. Select as a starting point an estimate of 1% of the sales price for each year of difference in the effective age. If the subject's effective age is 15 years, and the sale's effective age is 20 years then the difference is 5 years or 5% of the sales price. Multiply the percent times the sales price and round to the nearest $1,000. Example: Sale 1 sells for $200,000 and was in worse condition by 5 years or 5%. The adjustment is +$10,000 (20 years effective age of the sale - 15 years effective age of the subject = 5 years or 5% × $200,000 sales price).

Heat/CAC: This will be a lump sum adjustment. If there is a market-perceived difference in the type of heating or cooling, make it here. For small starter homes the market might pay $2,000 less for a house with electric heat compared to a FWA system. It might pay $3,000 more for a house with air conditioning compared to one without. If you are in the south where air conditioning is almost mandatory then the value will be higher. In the northern climates, it is needed less and many homes do not have it, so the market will not pay as much.

Deck/Patio/Porch: These are small adjustments reflecting the small contributing values of these items. Round to the nearest $1,000. You can leave out very small adjustments.

Garage: For a small older property, you might look at $2,000 per garage bay. If the sale has a two-car garage and the subject has none, the adjustment would be -$4,000. If you are comparing a basement garage to a detached garage, it needs a little more thought.

To build a new two-car attached garage will cost about $15,000. To make a basement garage, the builder simply modifies one of the basement foundation walls to allow an opening for the garage doors. You actually lose a good portion of the basement to the garage. An attached garage allows direct entry to the house. It is easy to unload the shopping. With a basement garage you have to walk up a flight of stairs to unload shopping. You can start with a value for a basement garage bay of about $1,000.

Fireplace: This will vary with the type of fireplace. A simple brick fireplace starts around $3,000, if it is a gas fire log, about $1,000. A floor-to-ceiling stone fireplace in a family room with a cathedral ceiling might be $10,000. Again, these are just starting points. You will refine them based on your market.

Finished Basement: Things to consider. What is the quality of the finish, its age and condition? Is the area heated and/or cooled? Is there a walk-out to grade level? Is it a split level with some daylight windows? Is there a bath? Sometimes there will be a fireplace in the lower level. This is counted in the fireplace adjustment, so don't double count it here. Using the GLA adjustment guide above I said that the overall value per square foot was $100, and the value of more or less GLA was 25% of that or $25.00. Based on that, the value per square foot of finished basement space is less than that. Start with 15%. If the basement finished area is 400 square feet, then the value is $6,000 (400 × $15)

Finished Attic: This is similar to the finished basement space. It adds some value, but less than the overall value per square foot, and less than the GLA adjustment. Start with $15, and refine for the market.

Other Items: The grid has three extra lines for you to add any particular item that may be available in your market. This might be for a pool, outbuilding, tennis courts, or anything else.

Net Adjusted Total: Total all of the individual adjustments both pluses and minuses for a net adjustment.

Adjusted Sales Price: Add the *Net Adjusted Total* to the sales price for each sale. This is now the indicated value of the subject based on this sale.

Refinements

When you have completed the analysis for the three comps, you now look again at your adjustments to see if they can be refined. Look at the lowest value indicator and the highest value indicator. Now look at the individual adjustments for those comps. Does anything stand out as an adjustment that might be pushing this sale high or low. It might be the location or view adjustment. These are subjective and you initially made an estimate of what you thought the market would pay for the view or location. If you change that adjustment higher or lower it might bring the sales indicators closer.

Now look at the quality and condition adjustments. Can they be refined?

If the GLA or Lot Size adjustment rate is changed to a higher or lower rate, will it tighten up the range of indicators?

Now look at the adjustments for individual features. Perhaps the market is paying more for the garage, fireplace, or finished attic or basement space.

Reconciliation

The three comparable sales are individually an indicator of value for the subject. Each sale has its strengths and weaknesses. From these three adjusted value indicators you will form your opinion of the market value of your subject property. The first step is to see the range of values:

Range	Value
Low	
Average	
High	
Range	
Value	

Enter the low and high values. Calculate the average and round to the closest $1,000. Calculate the range of values as the High indicator minus the low indicator.

The final value that you reconcile to will be within this range and fairly close to the midpoint. Revisit the sales to see which ones had the fewest adjustments, and are more similar to the subject. You can weight these more heavily. In the end it is your opinion, and certainly it will be different from the seller's opinion, the broker's opinion, the assessor's opinion and the appraiser's opinion. However, these opinions should not be wildly different.

A Completed Example:

Sales Comparable Grid							
Subject		Comparable 1		Comparable 2		Comparable 3	
Street: 100 Elm Stret		203 Elm Street		27 Cherry Street		56 Maple Street	
City, State: Anytown, FL		Anytown, FL		Anytown, FL		Anytown, FL	
Element of Comparison	Description	Item/Desc.	Adjustment	Item/Desc.	Adjustment	Item/Desc.	Adjustment
List Price	$152,000	$145,000		$152,000		$160,000	
Sales Price		$140,000		$149,000		$155,000	
Price/SF	NA	$127		$124		$119	
Days on Market	45	$20		$30		$50	
As Of Date	04/01/12	02/01/12		01/01/12		03/01/12	
Rooms/Bedrooms AG	6 /3 /1	6/3 /1		6/3 /1.5	-$1,000	6/3 /1	
GLA	1,200	1,100	+$3,000	1,200	$0	1,300	-$3,000
Location	Average	equal		equal		equal	
View	Average	equal		equal		equal	
Design (Style)	Ranch	Ranch		Ranch		Ranch	
Lot Size	10,000	9,000	+$1,000	10,000	$0	11,000	-$1,000
Quality / Appeal	Average	Average		Average		Average	
Effective Age/Cond.	15	19	+$6,000	15	$0	11	-$6,000
Heat/CAC	FWA/No	FWA.No		FWA.No		FWA.No	
Deck, Patio, Porch	deck	deck		deck		deck	
Garage	1 Car Att	1 Car Att		1 Car Att		none	+$2,000
Fireplace	1	1		1		1	
Finished Basement	none	none		none		none	
Finished Attic	none	none		none		none	
Net Adj Total			+$10,000		-$1,000		-$8,000
Adj Sales Price			$150,000		$148,000		$147,000

In this example the subject is a small ranch listed for sale for $152,000 and has been on the market for 45 days. It has 6 rooms 3 bedrooms and 1 bath on a 10,000 square foot lot. Its effective age is estimated to be 15 years. It has a deck, 1-car attached garage and one fireplace. Location and view is average. There is no finished basement or attic space.

After researching the market there are three similar recent sales in the subject's immediate neighborhood. Sale #2 had a superior ½ bath and was adjusted down $1,000. The price per square foot ranged from $119 to $127 with an average of $124. The adjustment for differences in GLA was set at $30. Sale #1 is 100 square feet smaller. The adjustment is $3,000 (100 × $30). Sale #2 has the same GLA, so no adjustment. Sale #3 is 100 square feet larger (better). It is adjusted down -$3,000 (-100 × $30).

Difference in lot size is adjusted at the rate of $1.00 per square foot of land size differences.

Differences in effective age are based on 1% for each year. Sale #1 is 4 years or 4% older (worse). The rounded adjustment up is $6,000 ($140,000 × .04 = $5,600 rounded to $6,000). Sale #2 is equal, so no adjustment. Sale # 3 is adjusted down -$6,000 ($155,000 × .04 = $6,200 rounded to $6,000.), since its effective age is 4 years better than the subject.

Sale #3 is adjusted up $2,000 for lack of a garage.

Reconciliation

Range	Value
Low	$147,000
Average	$148,333
High	$150,000
Range	$3,000
Value	$148,000

The average value indicator is $148,333. Sale #2 had the fewest adjustments with an indicated value of $148,000. I conclude the estimated market value is $148,000.

How Do You Use This Knowledge?

The subject is listed for $152,000. Your data says it will not sell for less than $147,000, or more than $150,000. Now you can use other market knowledge to help you to determine your offer price.

A buyer's or Seller's Market: In a buyer's market the buyer has an advantage because there are too many properties on the market for the number of buyers.

This is based on the number of month's supply of inventory. If ranches similar to this one sell about 20 units a month and there are 80 units on the market, then the month's supply of inventory is 4 months (80 units of supply ÷ 20 units of demand). This is how the markets are divided:

Under 3 month's supply is a seller's market (a shortage of supply)
3-6 month's supply is neutral (a balanced market)
Over 6 month's supply is a buyer's market (an oversupply)

Don't forget that your data came from the current market, so the indicated values reflect the oversupply or shortage.

If it is a buyer's market, you might go with a low offer of $145,000 hoping to get it for the $147,000.

If it is a seller's market you might offer $148,000 to stay competitive, and hope to get it for $149,000.

If it is a balanced market you might offer $147,000 hoping to get it for $148,000.

Even in a buyer's market there is no advantage in making a very low offer of say $135,000. The sellers know that they can get at least $147,000 for it so any low offer will be rejected.

To stay competitive you need to be close to the value range.

Homeowner's Property Insurance

This section provides an overview of the coverage provided in a standard Homeowner's Insurance Policy (HOI). It also offers suggestions for selecting the right coverage for your needs. When you purchase a home with a mortgage, the lender will need to protect their investment from damage through an insurance policy.

The lender will require you to pay for the insurance, typically for at least the replacement cost of the house. This may be less than the loan since the property value includes both land and building, and the insurance is just for the building.

The lender will need to be named as a "loss payee." This protects its interest in the property. If the property is damaged, the insurance company will issue the check to you and the loss payee. The bank is only added to the check as a loss payee when the damage is to the property. It is not added for a loss to other items that are covered by the policy.

Like car insurance, HOI is underwritten by an insurance company. You may purchase the policy directly from an insurance company, or you may purchase a policy through an independent insurance agent.

If you feel comfortable in selecting the insurance company and coverage you need, you will not need the services of an independent agent. Otherwise, an independent agent can help you to select the policy best suited for your needs.

An insurance policy is a contract. In a dispute, the contract will prevail. Contracts can be difficult to interpret and often times there are gray areas. An insurance agent can help interpret the contract in your favor when there is a gray area.

Look for a referral from friends or relatives or other professionals in the real estate business. It's helpful to understand the terms insurance agents will use as you consider the coverage you will need.

Deductibles. The deductible is the amount deducted from the total payment made by the insurance company in the case of a loss. For example, if you have a $10,000 loss and a $2,000 deductible, the insurance company will pay $8,000.

Replacement Cost. Depending on the section of the insurance policy in which it occurs, replacement cost has two important meanings. In Coverage A, the dwelling or house, replacement cost refers to how much it will cost to rebuild the house itself.

Replacement cost in Coverage C. This is for your belongings and refers to the additional insurance coverage necessary to replace a loss with a new item. If you do not have replacement cost insurance for coverage C, then the insurance company will only reimburse you for the depreciated value of the damaged items. Before purchasing HOI, be sure you understand how replacement cost is applied under Coverage Section A and Coverage C.

The Homeowners Insurance Policy (HOI): The standard home owner's policy covers the following areas:

A. The dwelling or house
B. Other structures
C. Your belongings
D. Additional living expenses
E. Liability insurance
F. Medical payments

Coverage A, the dwelling or house: This is the insurance coverage needed to rebuild the house if it is destroyed. When you first buy the house you will have 100% replacement cost coverage. However, 10-20 years later it is possible that the cost to replace the house exceeds its insured value.

If at least 80% of the replacement cost is insured, then the policy will cover the total loss. Less than 80% coverage will result in the insurance payment being prorated. For example, if the cost to rebuild the house today is $200,000 and the HOI insurance limit is $125,000 for the dwelling (62.5% coverage), then the policy will pay for 62.5% of the loss.

If you have a kitchen fire and it costs $30,000 to replace the kitchen, the policy with 62.5% prorated coverage will pay $18,750 (62.5% of $30,000). It is important to understand the amount of coverage provided since you will have to pay any difference between the insurance payment and the actual cost to rebuild.

For Coverage A, the HOI covers *everything except what is excluded.* This may seem odd but it is important. On the first page of your insurance policy it will state that you are covered for everything that might damage the house except for those events that are excluded from coverage.

Most policies will exclude coverage for floods, war, nuclear accidents or attacks. Depending on the state, coverage may be excluded or limited for tornadoes, earthquakes, and other unusual weather events.

When buying HOI, read through the exclusions carefully to see what is not covered. Consider the specialty coverage if you live in an area that experiences extreme weather. In a separate HOI policy you may add specialty coverage for exclusions such as flood, earthquake, hurricane, tornadoes, and others.

Specialty coverage such as acts of war or nuclear accident is also available through Lloyd's of London. If you are purchasing a home near a nuclear power plant, you may have coverage through the Price-Anderson Act which provides coverage in the event of a nuclear accident.

It is important to know the cost of rebuilding the house if it were destroyed. Replacement cost estimate for Coverage A (the house) is usually calculated on a cost per square foot basis. The cost per square foot might begin at $150 for a slab ranch, $175 for an average house and $200 or more for a more expensive home.

If the house has a mortgage, the mortgage lender will insist on coverage for the full replacement cost of the building. As owner, you will also be interested in the amount necessary to replace the house if it is destroyed. Your insurance agent can help determine the amount of coverage necessary to replace the house.

If you buy hurricane or flood insurance, you can also get additional protection for unusual cost increases in the event of a major disaster. If a large area is hit with a disaster, costs can increase dramatically due to a shortage of labor and supplies.

Estimating the amount of your coverage for dwelling insurance is not as simple as insuring the house for the purchase price. When you purchased the property, the sales price included the value of the land. The value of the land is not included in a HOI. Depending on its location, a significant part of the value of the property may be in the land.

Over time the house may have depreciated somewhat in value. For example, if you pay $300,000 for a house and the land value is $125,000, the depreciated value of the house is $175,000 ($300,000 total price - $125,000 land value = $175,000 value of the depreciated house). A 1,250 square foot house with a $160 per square foot cost to rebuild should have $200,000 in Coverage A replacement cost (1,250 square feet × $160).

Using the example above, if you're insured for $300,000 you will be paying for insurance you do not need. If you're insured for $175,000 you will be under insured.

Replacement Cost vs. Reproduction Cost: Replacement cost coverage is adequate for the average home. If the house must be rebuilt, replacement costs cover the use of current modern materials and finishes. For example, a 90-year-old colonial will be rebuilt as a modern new colonial.

Replacement costs may not be adequate for an antique or Victorian house which may have elaborate millwork, stained glass windows, elaborate parquet wood floors with intricate designs, marble fireplaces, and other features from a bygone era. In these homes, the HOI should provide *reproduction cost* coverage. Reproduction cost insurance allows the house to be rebuilt to its original standard of design and finish.

You may also be able to purchase "Ordinance or Law" coverage. This covers the costs needed to bring an older house into compliance with current building codes. For example, if a fire partially destroys the house, and the municipal office in charge of building codes states that you must bring all of your plumbing and electric service up to the current code, then this coverage will cover those costs.

Coverage B other structures: Other structures coverage includes items such as a detached garage, shed, pool, or fence. The standard HOI coverage for other structures starts at 10% of the amount specified for the dwelling in coverage A. If the coverage A dwelling amount was $200,000, then the coverage B amount for other structures is $20,000.

Be certain the 10% amount allocated for other structures is adequate. Other structures coverage may be raised but not lowered. Coverage B also covers everything except what is excluded. Be sure to read carefully through the list of exclusions in the coverage B section of the policy under consideration.

Coverage C—Your Belongings: Coverage C insures the contents of the home. The contents will include furniture, electronics, clothing, dishes, gas grills, and all other personal property. In coverage C the terminology is different. Coverage C introduces the term *"named perils."* Some typical perils are:

Fire or lightning, windstorm or hail, explosion, riots or civil disturbance, aircraft, vehicle, smoke, vandalism or malicious mischief, loss from theft, glass breakage, volcanic eruption, falling objects, collapse due to weight of ice, snow or sleet, freezing to plumbing, heating/air conditioning or household appliances, accidental discharge or overflow of water from plumbing or a heating/air-conditioning system, sudden and accidental discharge of an artificially generated electrical current, sudden and accidental tearing apart, cracking, burning or bulging of a heating/air-conditioning system, a fire-prevention sprinkler system or an appliance for heating water

Here is a list of a few perils commonly EXCLUDED from homeowners policies
(Check your policy for specific exclusions):

1. Damage caused by flood
2. Damage caused by earthquake
3. Damage caused by war or nuclear accident
4. Damage caused by earth movement

Coverage C is for specific items called *"named perils."* Only named perils are covered by insurance. In the case of a loss, the homeowner must show that the loss was to one or more of the named perils. Coverage C is usually 50% of coverage A. In our example this would be $100,000, or 50% of $200,000.

To prove the loss, you must first show that you owned the items damaged by a named perils. To avoid problems I recommend taking photographs of the entire contents of the home. In the case of a loss, it will be your responsibility to prove that you owned that $2,000 high definition flat screen TV.

Be sure coverage C specifies *replacement cost* of the loss. Unless replacement cost is spelled out in the policy the items will be covered at their depreciated value. For example, if a five-year-old TV cost $2,000 new, its depreciated value may be $500. The replacement TV today may cost $2,500. Without replacement cost coverage you will be allowed $500 not $2,500. If the deductible is $1,000, you will get nothing.

A HOI policy will have a long list of coverage limits on items that are easily stolen such as cash, jewelry, fine art, and electronics. For example, the coverage limit for stolen cash might be $200.

Valuable personal property should be covered in a separate insurance schedule called a "rider." In a rider, you declare the value of each item up front and pay an additional premium for insurance coverage. In some cases you may need to have the item appraised by an appropriate expert to establish its value.

There will be a deductible for losses under coverage C. If someone steals your TV worth $2,500 and you have a $1,000 deductible, you get $1,500. However scheduled items covered on a rider normally do not have to pay the deductible. If your $5,000 diamond necklace is stolen and it is a scheduled item on a rider, you get $5,000.

Coverage D is for additional expenses for loss of use. If you have a loss to your home and you cannot live in it, this section covers your stay in a motel or other temporary housing.

The standard HOI policy provides a 20% limit for loss of use. In our example this would be $40,000 (20% of $200,000). Typically there is no time limit as to how long you have a loss of use. If it takes six months to rebuild, you are covered up to $40,000 (20% of coverage A). $40,000 is the maximum that would be paid under Coverage D and would include your increased living expenses. If the time to rebuild is extensive, the insurance provider may place a trailer on the property.

Coverage D also provides insurance for other expenses that result from a loss. For example, if you have a kitchen fire, you may still be able sleep in the house but cannot prepare meals; the insurer will pay for the increased cost of outside meals. If the cost for breakfast for a family of four is $10 at home, and the restaurant cost is $20.00, the company will pay the difference in cost.

Coverage E liability: Liability insurance covers you personally for incidents that occur on your property or anywhere else in the world. For example, if someone slips and falls on your property you are covered by your liability insurance. If you accidently injure someone at another location, you're protected. Your HOI liability insurance will also cover property damage caused by you off site. Standard liability insurance typically gives you $100,000 of coverage. Insurance agents will often recommend $500,000 in coverage.

They may also discuss an umbrella policy which will provide additional insurance for both auto and homeowner's policies.

Coverage F Medical Payments: The standard HOI policy provides $1,000 in coverage to reimburse for medical expenses caused by you. When purchasing HOI, for a small additional premium, you may increase your medical coverage to $5,000.

Considering the deductible: Higher deductibles mean lower premiums. The decision concerning the amount of your deductible should be based on determining the risk of loss.

What is the probability that your house will burn down compared to the cost of having a low deductible? The answer to this question can be calculated by using a break even analysis. For example, the annual premium is $200 with a $1,000 deductible, or $100 with a $2,000 deductible. If you choose the $2,000 deductible policy you will save $100 annually on your premium. If you have no claims in ten years you will break even. An informed decision on an HOI involves evaluating the risk of a loss over the next ten years. You may choose the lower cost premium and hope there are no claims for the next ten years.

The Condominium Homeowner's Policy

When purchasing a condominium there will be two insurance policies in effect. The master condominium association carries a policy that insures the common areas of the development. The second is your HOI policy that provides insurance coverage for your specific unit.

The master condominium association insurance covers all the areas held in common by the owners. Common areas include the roads, landscaping, swimming pools, tennis courts, and clubhouse. The master association insurance also covers the main portion of your unit's building. The master policy will cover the exterior of the building, the building foundation, the roof, the hallways, and the utility lines coming into your unit.

It is important to understand the insurance coverage provided by the master association versus the coverage you should carry for your unit. When purchasing their policy, the master association has an option to provide either "studs out" coverage or "all inclusive coverage."

Studs out is also known as "bare walls," and all inclusive is also known as "Single Entity." A "studs out" policy provides coverage from the perimeter unpainted drywall (the finished studs) to the full exterior of the building. This means that if the building were destroyed the master association policy would pay to rebuild the building up to the interior unfinished drywall of your unit.

If the master association carries a "studs out" policy, your HOI policy must cover the cost of repairing all the interior finishes to your unit. Interior finishes include the interior walls, doors, kitchen cabinets, plumbing, electrical fixtures, appliances, flooring, and interior painting.

If the master association carries a policy with "all inclusive coverage," then their policy covers all of the interior finishes to your unit. Be sure to read all the material sent by the master association to be sure their insurance policy does not change. To lower cost, a master association may start out with "all inclusive coverage" and at a later date change it to a "studs out" policy.

The Master Association Policy Deductible. To lower the cost of insurance, a master association may choose an Insurance policy with a high deductible.

A well-managed master association will have the amount of the insurance deductible held in their "reserve for replacement" account.

If there is a loss, the master association's deductible is available for rebuilding. If the master association does not have enough cash to pay the insurance deductible, a special assessment may be levied against each unit owner and/or rebuilding may be delayed.

Loss Assessment. If the condominium's master insurance does not cover all of the losses from a disaster, the association may assess the unit owners for the uncovered loss. You can purchase Loss Assessment coverage in your policy.

If there is an uncovered loss, and your association assesses you a one-time special assessment to pay it, then Loss Assessment coverage can help pay your portion of the special assessment. The standard coverage for loss assessment is $1,000, but higher limits may be available.

Specialty Coverage. Condominium owners may add specialty coverage for exclusions such as flood, earthquake, hurricane, tornadoes and other acts not covered in a standard HOI policy. If your condominium is in a flood zone, the master association policy will carry flood insurance to cover the common areas of the development.

However, you also need to protect the contents of your unit from flood damage. Through a separate insurance provider, you may purchase coverage for flood, earthquake, hurricane, or tornadoes.

Coverage C–Condominium Contents Value. The concept of "named perils" also exists when purchasing HOI on the contents of your condominium unit. In coverage C, only the listed items such as TV, stereo, computer or those you prove you owned are covered by your insurance. I recommend photographing the contents of each room.

The pictures are used to make a list of the items that would need to be replaced. Save the list and photos and give a copy to your agent. This will help determine the appropriate amount of your coverage. It will also serve as proof of ownership in the event of a loss. For more information, see Coverage C in the Home Owner's Insurance section.

Coverage D, E and F for condominiums is the same as in the single family dwelling.

Plan vs. Actual Budget Worksheet

Here is a way to set up a plan vs. actual worksheet on your own computer to track your budget. The Excel models are available on www.letsbuyahouse.info. If you only have a few income and expense items, you can collect the data monthly from your checking account and credit cards. However as you get older and life becomes more complicated, you can get help with accounting systems like Quicken or QuickBooks. There is some learning needed to master these more sophisticated accounting systems.

Courses are often available at your community adult education center, local high school, trade school or community college, and others. You can research on line for [Personal Financial Systems]. You can also visit your local office supply store to read the features and benefits of the various offerings without being inundated with web ads.

Accounting systems are not expensive, and many will have the budget process as well as income and expense tracking. Some will link to your checking account so you can download your transactions. Then you only have to classify the type of expense for each entry.

The following example shows a spreadsheet from an Excel model. This is an abbreviated format of the budget showing just the first quarter of reporting. It does not show all twelve months. Note that it is not necessary to repeat the Column "A" labels. I use the hide function to hide columns. For example, if you just want to show the actual columns, you hide columns "B" through "O" If you just want to see the variance columns you hide "A" through "AC" To see them again you highlight the columns and unhide them. You use the merge cell function to allow the titles PLAN, ACTUAL, and VARIANCE to be centered over their respective columns.

	PLAN				ACTUAL				VARIANCE			
	A	B	C	D	N	O	P	Q	R	AD	AE	AF	AP
1		PLAN					ACTUAL				VARIANCE			
2 Income	Jan	Feb	Mar	Total	Jan	Feb	Mar	Total	Jan	Feb	Mar	Total
3 -Net pay	$10			$10	$9			$9	$1	$0	$0	$1
4 -Other				$0				$0	$0	$0	$0	$0
5 Total income	$10	$0	$0	$10	$9	$0	$0	$9	$1	$0	$0	$1
6												
7 Expenses	Jan	Feb	Mar	Total	Jan	Feb	Mar	Total	Jan	Feb	Mar	Total
8 Shelter				$0				$0	$0	$0	$0	$0
9 Utilities				$0				$0	$0	$0	$0	$0
10 Transportation				$0				$0	$0	$0	$0	$0
11 - Car Loan				$0				$0	$0	$0	$0	$0
12 - Auto insurance				$0				$0	$0	$0	$0	$0
13 -Gas				$0				$0	$0	$0	$0	$0
14 -Repairs				$0				$0	$0	$0	$0	$0
15 Food				$0				$0	$0	$0	$0	$0
16 Clothing				$0				$0	$0	$0	$0	$0
17 Entertainment				$0				$0	$0	$0	$0	$0
18 Insurance				$0				$0	$0	$0	$0	$0
19 - Life				$0				$0	$0	$0	$0	$0
20 -Property				$0				$0	$0	$0	$0	$0
21 Retirement				$0				$0	$0	$0	$0	$0
22 Education				$0				$0	$0	$0	$0	$0
23 Savings				$0				$0	$0	$0	$0	$0
24 Total Expenses	$0	$0	$0	$0	$0	$0	$0	$0	$0	$0	$0	$0
25 Difference	$10	$0	$0	$10	$9	$0	$0	$9	$1	$0	$0	$1

In an Excel worksheet, enter all of the income categories in column "A." Leave a row for Total Income. Leave a blank row between income and expenses. Enter the "Expenses" title in column "A," row 7, then all the expense items you want to track. Leave a row for Total Expenses (A24) and the Difference (A25) then label twelve columns for the months January through December. This is row 2 for income and (in the example row 7) for the expenses. Your row may vary depending on the number of income sources you are tracking. Note the $10 entered in cell B3 and how it calculates to N3, B5, B25, N5 and N25.

	A	B	C	D	E	F	G	H	I	J	K	L	M	N
1							**PLAN**							
2	**Income**	Jan	Feb	Mar	Apr	May	Jun	Jul	Aug	Sep	Oct	Nov	Dec	Total
3	-Net pay	$10												$10
4	-Other													$0
5	Total income	$10	$0	$0	$0	$0	$0	$0	$0	$0	$0	$0	$0	$10
6														
7	**Expenses**	Jan	Feb	Mar	Apr	May	Jun	Jul	Aug	Sep	Oct	Nov	Dec	Total
8	Shelter													$0
9	Utilities													$0
10	Transportation													$0
11	- Car Loan													$0
12	- Auto insurance													$0
13	-Gas													$0
14	-Repairs													$0
15	Food													$0
16	Clothing													$0
17	Entertainment													$0
18	Insurance													$0
19	- Life													$0
20	-Property													$0
21	Retirement													$0
22	Education													$0
23	Savings													$0
24	Total Expenses	$0	$0	$0	$0	$0	$0	$0	$0	$0	$0	$0	$0	$0
25	Difference	$10	$0	$0	$0	$0	$0	$0	$0	$0	$0	$0	$0	$10

Make a total column (N) to the right of December, and have that cell sum Jan-Dec, then copy the calculation formula down the column, so it calculates the total for each row. This is your total budget for that item for the year. In the Total income row #5, sum all the income for each column (B3 through B4). Copy this cell from Jan to Feb-Dec.

This now calculates your total income by month. In the Total Expenses row, #24 in the example, sum all of the expense lines by month (B8:B23), then copy this cell to Feb-Dec. These are your total expenses by month. Now calculate the difference (row 25) (Total Income(B5) – Total Expenses(B24)). Copy this cell to Feb-Dec. Note that the Difference row shows the $10 in cell B25 and N25.

Next copy all of the PLAN cells to the right and label it ACTUAL. This is where you will enter your actual expenses each month. (Leave Column O blank as a separator).

In Excel you highlight the cells you want to copy. In the example this would be B1:N25. Highlight, then copy, then click on the cell where you want to copy the cells. In the example this is P1. Now paste into P1. Re-label the cells from PLAN to ACTUAL. Note in the example below that the cell columns start with "A" then jump to "P." This is because I hid columns "B" through "Q," the PLAN columns. Note The $9 entered in cell B4 and how it calculates to AB3, P5 and AB5.

	A	P	Q	R	S	T	U	V	W	X	Y	Z	AA	AB
1							**ACTUAL**							
2	**Income**	Jan	Feb	Mar	Apr	May	Jun	Jul	Aug	Sep	Oct	Nov	Dec	Total
3	-Net pay	$9												$9
4	-Other													$0
5	Total income	$9	$0	$0	$0	$0	$0	$0	$0	$0	$0	$0	$0	$9
6														
7	**Expenses**	Jan	Feb	Mar	Apr	May	Jun	Jul	Aug	Sep	Oct	Nov	Dec	Total
8	Shelter													$0
9	Utilities													$0
10	Transportation													$0
11	- Car Loan													$0
12	- Auto insurance													$0
13	-Gas													$0
14	-Repairs													$0
15	Food													$0
16	Clothing													$0
17	Entertainment													$0
18	Insurance													$0
19	- Life													$0
20	-Property													$0
21	Retirement													$0
22	Education													$0
23	Savings													$0
24	Total Expenses	$0	$0	$0	$0	$0	$0	$0	$0	$0	$0	$0	$0	$0
25	Difference	$9	$0	$0	$0	$0	$0	$0	$0	$0	$0	$0	$0	$9

Note that the Difference row shows the $9 in cell P25 and AB25. You are finished with the actual section.

Finally, copy one more time and label it PLAN vs. ACTUAL - Variance. This is the variance between what you planned to do, and what you actually did. Leave column AC as a separator.

	A	AD	AE	AF	AG	AH	AI	AJ	AK	AL	AM	AN	AO	AP
1						PLAN VS. ACTUAL- Variance								
2	**Income**	Jan	Feb	Mar	Apr	May	Jun	Jul	Aug	Sep	Oct	Nov	Dec	Total
3	-Net pay	-$1	$0	$0	$0	$0	$0	$0	$0	$0	$0	$0	$0	-$1
4	-Other	$0	$0	$0	$0	$0	$0	$0	$0	$0	$0	$0	$0	$0
5	Total income	-$1	$0	$0	$0	$0	$0	$0	$0	$0	$0	$0	$0	-$1
6														
7	**Expenses**	Jan	Feb	Mar	Apr	May	Jun	Jul	Aug	Sep	Oct	Nov	Dec	Total
8	Shelter	$0	$0	$0	$0	$0	$0	$0	$0	$0	$0	$0	$0	$0
9	Utilities	$0	$0	$0	$0	$0	$0	$0	$0	$0	$0	$0	$0	$0
10	Transportation	$0	$0	$0	$0	$0	$0	$0	$0	$0	$0	$0	$0	$0
11	- Car Loan	$0	$0	$0	$0	$0	$0	$0	$0	$0	$0	$0	$0	$0
12	- Auto insurance	$0	$0	$0	$0	$0	$0	$0	$0	$0	$0	$0	$0	$0
13	-Gas	$0	$0	$0	$0	$0	$0	$0	$0	$0	$0	$0	$0	$0
14	-Repairs	$0	$0	$0	$0	$0	$0	$0	$0	$0	$0	$0	$0	$0
15	Food	$0	$0	$0	$0	$0	$0	$0	$0	$0	$0	$0	$0	$0
16	Clothing	$0	$0	$0	$0	$0	$0	$0	$0	$0	$0	$0	$0	$0
17	Entertainment	$0	$0	$0	$0	$0	$0	$0	$0	$0	$0	$0	$0	$0
18	Insurance	$0	$0	$0	$0	$0	$0	$0	$0	$0	$0	$0	$0	$0
19	- Life	$0	$0	$0	$0	$0	$0	$0	$0	$0	$0	$0	$0	$0
20	-Property	$0	$0	$0	$0	$0	$0	$0	$0	$0	$0	$0	$0	$0
21	Retirement	$0	$0	$0	$0	$0	$0	$0	$0	$0	$0	$0	$0	$0
22	Education	$0	$0	$0	$0	$0	$0	$0	$0	$0	$0	$0	$0	$0
23	Savings	$0	$0	$0	$0	$0	$0	$0	$0	$0	$0	$0	$0	$0
24	Total Expenses	$0	$0	$0	$0	$0	$0	$0	$0	$0	$0	$0	$0	$0
25	Difference	-$1	$0	$0	$0	$0	$0	$0	$0	$0	$0	$0	$0	-$1

In the cell AD3, enter a calculation to subtract the plan amount (Q3) from the actual amount (C3). (=Q3-C3). This calculation will show a negative number when you are under plan and a positive number when over plan.

If at the end of the year your total income variance is -$1,500 (a negative number), you are under plan by $1,500. If your planned income was $36,500, and your actual income was $35,000, you're $1,500 under plan.

Now copy this cell to all of the other columns. Then copy this row to all the other rows. This now calculates the difference between what you planned to spend and what you actually spent: any negative numbers indicate you are under plan. Note the calculated variance of -$1 in cell AD3 and how it calculates to AP3, AD5 and AP5. The $9.00 actual - $10.00 plan is a -$1.00 variance. In this test it is $1.00 under plan.

It is good to be over plan on income, and under plan on expenses. You now have a powerful tool to see how you are spending your money and areas where you can improve.

Using the budget. Save this master template for future use (Master Budget worksheet), and then create a worksheet for this year's budget (Budget current year). Using that worksheet, enter your budgeted amount for each category.

Once the budget is set, you can hide these columns so that what you see when you open the worksheet is the ACTUAL and VARIANCE portions.

While the budget is by month, be aware that the number of weeks in each month varies. The year has fifty two (52) weeks. When I divide it up into four quarters there are thirteen weeks in each quarter, and this is divided up into cycles of 4, 4, and 5.

If you get paid weekly, you see this as a bonus paycheck once a quarter. If you get paid every two weeks, you get twenty six paychecks; if you get paid bi-monthly you get twenty four paychecks.

Just be aware of this anomaly. It will cause some months to show more income than others. If desired, you can smooth out your income line and show a uniform amount each month, essentially your annual pay divided by twelve. If paid weekly, you can budget based on three 4-week cycles and save the extra pay check.

As you use a worksheet, you may find a need to add a row for a new expense that was not in place at the beginning of the year or you may want to change a category into subcategories.

Example: You choose to break food expense down to subcategories of food at home, and outside dining. Just insert a row where you want it, copy the row above it down to the new row, re-label it, put in the PLAN data for the rest of the year, enter zero amounts into any plan or actual cells that are not used.

For example, if you add a row to track dining out food in April, then put zeroes in the plan and actual cells for January, February, and March. When done, it should reflect the new item. If this will be an ongoing change, then also correct the master budget, so it will be there for next year.

The Basics of Using a Financial Calculator

This will introduce you to the Hewlett-Packard 12c financial calculator. They are available in office supply stores. You will see two versions, the basic and the platinum model. Either works fine. The platinum is faster for a higher cost.

If you don't want to learn reverse polish notation (RPN), you will like the platinum 12c better since it has an option to complete traditional calculations. For this discussion I will refer to the basic 12c calculator. The main exterior difference is the basic 12c uses gold as the color of functions, while the platinum model uses red as the function color. The original 12c calculator:

The calculator is turned on with the bottom left [ON] key. Note that each key has a main value on the top of the key in white, such as [n], [i], [PV], [PMT], and [FV] on the top left row. These are the financial registers. Also note that there are functions above the key in gold.

The functions above the financial registers (top left five keys) are [AMORT], [INT], [NPV], [RND], and [IRR]. Also note the functions printed below the main key in blue.

The functions below the financial registers are [12×], [12÷], [CF0], [CFj], and [Nj]. Each key can do three things. Next to the [ON] key is a gold key labeled [f] for function. Next to the [f] (function) key is a blue key labeled [g], which selects the blue function on a key.

We will simply refer to these keys as [f] and [g] keys. If the calculation calls for monthly payments when the term is 30 years, enter 30 [g] [n]. This multiplies 30 times 12 and stores it in the[n] register.

To use the n key just press [n]. To use the [AMORT] function press [f] then [n.] You can read this as do [AMORT] function (AMORT is amortization). To multiply a number by 12 press [g] then [n].

The 12c is capable of a lot more functions that will not be discussed here. On occasion you will use the [f] and [g] function keys.

Calculator basics. The calculator has many registers where it stores information. Periodically you need to clear the registers so that no leftover value will affect the calculation. On the second row above the gold key note the bracket that is labeled ┌-------CLEAR------┐ just over the [XY] key.

These are the clear register functions labeled [Σ] [PRGM] [FIN] [REG] [PREFIX]. You are mainly interested in the CLEAR financial registers [FIN] and CLEAR all registers [REG].

To clear the financial registers press [f] then [FIN]. To clear all registers including the financial registers key [f] [REG]. Use the [CLX] key to clear the display. If you accidently enter 300 when you meant 30 press [CLX] to clear it and enter 30. If you already stored the value by pressing [ENTER], simply key again and press enter again.

The calculator can display 0-9 decimals. Press [f] key and a number to set the decimal places. To show two decimal places press [f] 2.

Look at the display areas under the numbers. It should be blank. If you press the [f] key a small f is displayed. This confirms that the function key has been pressed. If you press the [g] key a small [g] is displayed.

A financial calculator has the ability to calculate payments either at the beginning of the month or the end of the month. Under the 7 key it shows BEG, this sets the calculator to beginning of the month payments. Press [g] and the number 7. The display shows BEGIN.

If you see BEGIN in the display you have accidently turned on this feature. You will not use it for this work so it should always be blank. To switch to end of month calculations press [g] [8]. This key is labeled END and will clear the display. It sets the calculations to payments being received at the end of the month, which is where it needs to be for the mortgage calculations.

You may accidently turn on a date function. If you see [D.MY] displayed, key [g] [5] to clear. It does not affect these calculations, but may distract you if you see it on and don't know what it is.

You can use the financial calculator for simple calculations, but you need to learn one more idiosyncrasy of the 12c. It uses logic taken from mathematics known as *reverse polish notation*.

If curious you can look up its history on the Internet. Regular algebraic calculations are computed as 3×4 = 12. In reverse polish notation the calculations are 3 enter 4 ×. If you have the platinum version you can turn on the algebraic form of calculations with [f] [ALG] (above the [ENTER] and [EEX] keys).

To use common calculator commands of division [÷], multiplication [×], subtraction [-] , and addition [+], use the form of 3 [enter] 4 +. These keys are on the right side of the calculator

To divide two numbers: 12 [ENTER] 3 ÷ answer of 4 is displayed.

To multiply two numbers: 12 [ENTER] 12 × answer of 144 is displayed.

To subtract two numbers: 12 [ENTER] 3 – answer of 9 is displayed.
To add two numbers: 3 [ENTER] 4 + answer of 7 is displayed.

Let's do some simple exercises:
Turn on the calculator. Clear all registers [f] [REG].

Function	Key Strokes	Result
set decimals to 0	[f] 0	0
Addition	3 [ENTER] 4 +	7
Subtraction	126 [ENTER] 100-	26
Multiplication	10 [ENTER] 100 ×	1000
set decimals to 2	[f] 2	1000.00
Clear all registers	[f] REG	
Turn on European date format	[g] 4	D.MY in display
Turn off European date format	[g] 5	blank display
set decimals to 4	[f] 4	0.0000

Doing Financial Calculations. Calculating the mortgage payment is used frequently when buying a home. There are many online calculators available on the Internet but often they are linked to a site that collects information about you first. Learning how to compute payments yourself is handy. Also, once you learn the basics of calculating the mortgage payment, it is easy to compute variations such as the outstanding mortgage balance after a certain number of years.

A mortgage loan is for a certain amount or its present value [PV] at a fixed interest rate [i] for a period of time [n]. You want to know what the monthly payment will be [PMT]. These are the financial keys. PV stands for present value. This is the present value of the loan on the first day it is made.

From the lender's point of view, they give you the amount of the loan and you give them the monthly payments for [n] years. Let's calculate the payment for a $100,000 loan at 5% interest rate for 30 years. Note that the interest rate is entered as a whole number. Technically 5% is .05. The HP 12c uses the convention of the interest rate as a whole number. A fractional rate of 6.5% is entered as 6.5.

Function	Key Strokes	Result
Clear all registers	[f] REG	
set decimals to 2	[f] 2	0.00
Enter years	30 [n]	30.00
Enter interest rate	5 [i]	5.00
Enter loan amount	100000 [PV]	100000.00
solve for annual payment	[PMT]	-6504.14
Change the sign	[CHS]	6504.14

One final convention is how the answer is displayed. In the example, the mortgage payment is a negative number -6504.14. This is in keeping with financial analysis conventions and the direction of cash flows. When you receive a cash flow it is positive number. When you make a payment it is a negative number.

View the examples from the borrower's point of view. When the loan is made the borrower receives $100,000 (a positive number). You then make payments back to the lender (a negative number).

Change sign: One more useful key is the change sign [CHS]. This will change minus to plus and plus to minus.

In the last step solve for payment: [PMT], note the calculator flashes [running], indicating it is computing the answer.

The display shows -6,505.14. You would have to pay $6,505.14 each year for thirty years to repay the $100,000 loan. This would be correct if the loan called for annual payments. Mortgages usually call for monthly payments. You cannot just divide the annual payment by twelve to get the monthly payment. This would be close but not exact. The HP 12c helps in this process by using the [12×] and [12÷] keys. This is the monthly calculation:

Mortgage Calculation - with monthly payments		
Function	Key Strokes	Result
Clear all registers	[f] REG	
set decimals to 2	[f] 2	0.00
Enter years × 12	30 [g] [n]	360.00
Enter interest rate ÷ 12	5 [g] [i]	0.42
Enter loan amount	100000 [PV]	100000.00
solve for annual payment	[PMT]	-536.82
Change the sign	[CHS]	536.82

Note the only difference is the [g] key is pressed in front of the [n] and [i] keys and the display shows your entry × 12 or ÷ 12.

Using a Worksheet Program like EXCEL

This will introduce you to the Excel worksheet program. It is part of Microsoft Office which is available in office supply stores.

When you first start Excel you see a blank worksheet. This is a sample of the rows and columns:

	A	B	C	D
1				
2				
3				
4				
5				

Worksheet programs are simply an automated version of an accountant's worksheet.

At the heart of it is the ability to add a column of numbers or a row of numbers. The box where a row and a column intersect is called a cell. In the example above the intersection of column A and row one is called cell A1. The cell to its right is cell B1. The cell below A1 is A2. I can perform arithmetic on values in various cells.

	B	C	D	E
2	2	4	6	12
3	4	8	12	24
4	6	12	18	36
5	8	16	24	48
6	20	40	60	120

Above I entered the numbers 2, 4, 6 in cells B2, C2 and D2. In cell E2 I put in a formula to add up the values in cells B2 through D2. I added up all of the rows 2 through 6. I entered values in cells B2 through D5. Then I put a formula in cell B6 through D6 to add up the column of numbers. Here is the worksheet with the values and formulas displayed:

	B	C	D	E
2	2	4	6	=SUM(B2:D2)
3	4	8	12	=SUM(B3:D3)
4	6	12	18	=SUM(B4:D4)
5	8	16	24	=SUM(B5:D5)
6	=SUM(B2:B5)	=SUM(C2:C5)	=SUM(D2:D5)	=SUM(B6:D6)

We used the SUM formula to add up the rows and columns. In cell E2 you see the formula =SUM(B2:D2). The first = sign is an instruction to Excel that the next thing it sees will be a formula. SUM is an Excel formula that adds or SUMS a range of cells.

A cell range is a group of cells that are included in the calculation. In the formula in cell E2 the range of cells is (B2:D2). This is read as cell B2 through D2. The total formula is read as "sum the values in the range of cells B2 through D2 and put the results here in cell E2." I use the data in the cells to show basic calculations.

	B	C	D	E
2	2	4	6	=SUM(B2:D2)
3	4	8	12	=SUM(B3:D3)
4	6	12	18	=SUM(B4:D4)
5	8	16	24	=SUM(B5:D5)
6	=SUM(B2:B5)	=SUM(C2:C5)	=SUM(D2:D5)	=SUM(B6:D6)
7				
8		result	formula	
9	Subtraction	4	=D2-B2	
10	Multiplication	48	=D3*B3	
11	Division	3	=D5/B5	
12	Exponentiation	16	=B2^C2	
13	Addition	32	=D5+B5	

To subtract two numbers the formula is =D2-B2. I put the formula in cell D9. The value in cell D2 is 6. The value in cell B2 is 2. The result in cell C9 is 4 (6-2). Multiplication uses the asterisk [*]. The formula is =D3*B3. The value in D3 is 12, the value in B3 is 4, the result is 48 (cell C10) (4 times 12).

Division uses the [/] symbol. The formula is =D5/B5. The value in D5 is 24, the value in B5 is 8, the result is 3 (cell C11) (24 / 8).

Exponentiation uses the [^] symbol. The formula is =B2^C2. The value in B2 is 2, the value in C2 is 4, the result is 16 in cell C12 (2 raised to the 4th power).

Addition uses the [+] symbol. The formula is =D5+B5. The value in D5 is 24, the value in B5 is 8, the result is 32 in cell C13 (24 + 8).

Like the financial calculator, Excel calculates payments either at the beginning of the month or the end of the month. This is selected in the formula. If you select the 0 option, then it is calculated as if payments were received at the end of the period. This is the default option. For our purposes you can ignore this option and always default to end of month payments

Doing Financial Calculations with Excel. A mortgage loan is for a certain amount [PV] at a fixed interest rate [i] for a period of time [n]. You want to know what the monthly payment will be [PMT]. These are the same financial terms explained for the HP-12c.

PV stands for present value. This is the present value of the loan on the first day it is made. From the lender's point of view, the bank or broker gives you the amount of the loan and you give them the monthly payments for [n] years or [n] number of periods (nper). Let's calculate the payment for a

$100,000 loan at 5% interest rate for 30 years. Note that the interest rate is entered as a decimal. This is different from the HP-12c where you entered a whole number for the interest rate. Technically 5% is .05.

The Excel formula is =PMT(rate,nper,PV,[FV],[type]). For our purposes we do not use [FV] or [type]. FV is the future value, and in mortgage calculations the future value is always zero since the mortgage is paid off at the end of the loan period. Type is the option to select beginning of period payments (type =1) or end of period payments (type =0). We can skip the type since payments are at the end of period.

This leaves us with =PMT(rate,nper,PV). You can enter the values directly in the formula or refer to a cell that has the value. To enter directly it is [=PMT(.05,30,100000)]. To use cell references it is:

	B	C
2	Rate (i)	5%
3	Term (n)or nper	30
4	PV	100000
5	PMT Formula	($6,505.14)
6	Result	($6,504.14)

In cell C2 you enter the interest rate of .05 or 5%. In cell C3 you enter the term of thirty years. In cell C4 you enter the present value of the mortgage of $100,000. In cell C5 you enter the formula, but instead of entering values, you enter the cell numbers. In this case, rate is in cell C2, term, or number of periods or nper is in cell C3, and the present value of the mortgage of $100,000 is in cell C4. The result will be displayed in cell C5.

You can now easily convert the formula from annual payments to monthly payments. You divide the interest rate by twelve and multiply the term by twelve:

	B	C
2	Rate (i)	0.05
3	Term (n)or nper	30
4	PV	100000
5	PMT Formula	=PMT(C2/12,C3*12,C4)
6	Result	-536.82

Change sign: On the HP-12c you used the change sign (CHS) key to convert a negative number to a positive number. In Excel you can put a minus sign [-] in front of the PMT formula. This tells Excel to subtract the result. This ends up as a positive number since two negatives make a positive.

	B	C
2	Rate (i)	0.05
3	Term (n)or nper	30
4	PV	100000
5	PMT Formula	=-PMT(C2/12,C3*12,C4)
6	Result	536.82

How to Calculate a Sinking Fund

The sinking fund. When I talked about the capital budget I said you needed to put aside money to save for a planned big ticket purchase such as a large high definition TV. In financing this is known as a sinking fund. It answers the question: "How much do I need to save each month to reach a particular total amount?"

There are three variables in this question. The first is how much will you need in the future, or the Future Value (FV). For example, if you determine in 5 years you need $50,000 for the down payment, then $50,000 is the future value you are saving towards. Next is the term. How many years will you need to save in order to reach your goal of $50,000? If you want to buy your house in five years, then your TERM ([n] for number of years) is five. Last is the interest rate of the savings account, say 4%. This is the interest rate [i].

If you solve this on a financial calculator, you want to know the payment you need to make each month in order to have your *Sinking Fund* grow to $50,000 in five years at 4% annual interest. After clearing the calculator you enter 50000, FV, 5 g n, 4 g i , and then press the PMT key. The answer is -754.16.

Calculate Sinking Fund to reach a Future Value				
	n	i	PV	PMT	FV
Variables	5 years	4%	not used	????	$50,000
Key	5 [g] [n]	4 [g] [i]		**PMT**	50000
Answer				-754.16	

You need to save $754.16 monthly to grow to $50,000 in five years at a 4% annual interest rate.

In Excel you use the PMT function.

	A	B	C
1		Annual	Monthly
2	Future Value (FV)	$50,000	$50,000
3	Term (nper)	5	60
4	RATE	4%	0.333%
5			
6	PMT	($9,231.36)	($754.16)

Note that the answer is a negative number. This reflects a payment by you, or an out-flow of cash. At the end you withdraw $50,000 or in-flow of cash back to you (a positive cash flow). You can refine this to a monthly calculation by multiplying the years by twelve, now 60 months, and dividing the interest rate by twelve.

The formula in cell B6 is PMT (rate,nper,,FV,type). This skips the FV field since it is not used. There are 2 commas after nper. This skips over the entry for a Present Value (PV). You would only use this if you were starting with some money. If you had $10,000 to start your down payment fund:

A	B	C
	Annual	Monthly
1 Present Value (PV)	($10,000)	($10,000)
2 Future Value (FV)	$50,000	$50,000
3 Term (nper)	5	60
4 RATE	4%	0%
5		
6 PMT	($6,985.08)	($569.99)

Now you only have to put in $6,985.08 or $569.99 monthly. Note that the present value (PV) is a negative number, again reflecting an outflow movement of money to the savings account.

The type of payment reflects whether you make the deposit at the beginning of the period (1) or the end of the period (0). It defaults to end of period, indicating the payment is made at the end of the year, or end of the month. This is the typical process.

Calculating a sinking fund is an important financial skill in budgeting. The day your first child is born, you can sit down with your financial calculator to determine how much you have to set aside each year to save for college education, starting in 18 years.

You can calculate how much you need to put into your retirement fund to create your nest egg.

Term Life Insurance Calculator

While not related to buying a house, *mortgage term life insurance* should be consider when getting a mortgage.

Mortgage life insurance is not Private Mortgage Insurance (PMI), which protects the lender in case you default on the mortgage. Mortgage life insurance is designed to pay off your mortgage in the event of your death.

The *Mortgage Term Life Insurance* product is structured as a decreasing term life insurance policy. The benefit amount decreases as the mortgage balance decreases. In contrast, there is *level premium term life insurance.* Level life insurance has a fixed benefit amount until it expires.

Many types of life insurance policies are available in the market. For this discussion I are using a level premium term life insurance policy. Level premium life insurance is offered as an alternative to the typical term mortgage life insurance that may be offered to you when you apply for a loan.

The main difference is that the mortgage life insurance death benefit declines with the outstanding mortgage balance while the level premium term life insurance has a fixed death benefit amount until it expires.

If you want to explore other life insurance options, talk to a life insurance agent and/or a Certified Financial Planner ™, (CFP®).

If you are inclined to have insurance, then a level premium term policy is better than mortgage life insurance for several reasons. The cost of term life insurance is lowest when you are young and in good health. If over your lifetime you purchase more than one home or refinance your home, you will need to get a new mortgage life insurance policy each time. As you age the cost of your mortgage life insurance will increase.

In the event of your death, there are other things that need your consideration. For example, you may decide to pay for your children's college education and build a retirement income reserve.

There may be debts that have to be paid such as cars, vacation homes, equity lines taken out for special purposes, medical expense and the cost of a funeral. The financial protection needed to protect loved ones varies over a lifetime.

You also decide whether both partners involved in the purchase of a home will be insured. In a traditional husband-wife partnership with children, consideration is given to the need to cover losses if either dies pre-maturely.

If both work, then the loss of either income will affect the ability of the surviving spouse to maintain the family lifestyle. If one partner is at home raising the children, then the loss of that partner will require replacement services such as a nanny, day care and/or chauffer services.

A simple way to determine your insurance needs is to make a list of the items you want to protect and project how long you will need the protection. The following will not be interesting to everyone, but it is a simplified approach to determining your term life insurance needs. If you are not comfortable doing this on your own, you should consider the services of a Certified Financial Planner ™ (CFP®).

You learned about sinking funds earlier, and essentially that is what you are setting up when you start saving for retirement or a college fund, or anything else. This example will set up two funds, one for retirement and one for college. Interest earned on non-sheltered investments are taxable. But, to make it simple I assume the 8% earnings rate is after taxes. Because this is a long term investment plan, I use a rate that is expected from a balanced portfolio of stocks that carry some risk, but with a long holding period, is considered reasonable.

Factors	Retirement	College
Present Value	$500,000	$100,000
Rate	3%	3%
Term	35	20
Future Value	$1,406,931	$180,611
Rounded	$1,400,000	$180,000
Rate	8%	8%
Term	35	20

The first step for the retirement fund is to estimate the future value of today's purchasing power. If you determine you will need an additional $500,000 in today's dollars and that inflation over the next thirty-five years will average 3% annually, then to maintain today's lifestyle your future fund should be about $1,400,000 in thirty-five years. This is the future value (FV) function.

Assuming that your monthly investment yields 8% annually on average over the next thirty-five years, then the monthly payment into your sinking fund should be $610 or $7,324 annually (the payment function[PMT]).

Calculate Sinking Fund for Retirement					
	n	i	PV	PMT	FV
Variables	35 years	8%	not used	????	$1,400,000
Key	35 [g] [n]	8 [g] [i]		**PMT**	1400000
Answer				-610.32	

Next look at what you need for a college fund. An additional $180,000 in twenty years, is $306 monthly or $3,667 annually.

Calculate Sinking Fund for College Tuition

	n	i	PV	PMT	FV
Variables	20 years	8%	not used	????	$180,000
Key	20 [g] [n]	8 [g] [i]		PMT	180000
Answer				-305.59	

If you are buying a house with a $300,000 mortgage and a 30 year fixed mortgage interest rate of 5%, then your monthly mortgage payment is $1,610.

Mortgage	$300,000
Rate	5%
Term	30
payment	$1,610
Annual	$19,326

The mortgage principal will decrease over the thirty years exemplified here:

Time		5	10	15	20	25	30	35
Item/Age	30	35	40	45	50	55	60	65
Mortgage balance	$300,000	$214,660	$148,163	$96,348	$55,974	$24,514	$0	

At the end of five years, you have a remaining mortgage balance of $214,660 and it decreases until paid off in thirty years.

If you upgrade your house during this period, the total mortgage balance will increase and may require additional coverage.

Now calculate the total amount of insurance protection you will need until age 65:

Time		5	10	15	20	25	30	35
Item/Age	30	35	40	45	50	55	60	65
Mortgage balance	$300,000	$214,660	$148,163	$96,348	$55,974	$24,514	$0	
Retirement Fund	$1,400,000	$1,355,156	$1,288,345	$1,188,806	$1,040,510	$819,571	$490,405	$0
College Fund	$180,000	$157,546	$124,093	$74,253	$0			
Total	$1,880,000	$1,727,362	$1,560,601	$1,359,408	$1,096,483	$844,084	$490,405	$0
Coverage Needed	$1,880,000	$1,880,000	$1,727,362	$1,560,601	$1,359,408	$1,096,483	$844,084	$490,405

This indicates that $1,880,000 in insurance is needed at age 30 and will decline to zero at age 65. I can now structure several term life insurance policies to cover this declining need for insurance protection.

Term Age	30	35	40	45	50	55	60	65
Term to Age 65	$500,000	$500,000	$500,000	$500,000	$500,000	$500,000	$500,000	$500,000
Term to Age 60	$300,000	$300,000	$300,000	$300,000	$300,000	$300,000	$300,000	
Term to Age 55	$300,000	$300,000	$300,000	$300,000	$300,000	$300,000		
Term to Age 50	$300,000	$300,000	$300,000	$300,000	$300,000			
Term to age 45	$200,000	$200,000	$200,000	$200,000				
Term to age 40	$200,000	$200,000	$200,000					
Term to Age 35	$100,000	$100,000						
Total Coverage		$1,900,000	$1,800,000	$1,600,000	$1,400,000	$1,100,000	$800,000	$500,000
Difference		$20,000	$72,638	$39,399	$40,592	$3,517	-$44,084	$9,595

If you purchase seven insurance policies with varying coverage amounts for different terms, you will achieve the coverage and minimize the cost. Term life insurance costs decline for shorter periods at younger ages. So the cost per $1,000 of coverage for the policy for five years (term to age 35) will be the least expensive, and the policy for $500,000 to age 65 will be the most expensive. In total, this will be less expensive than purchasing a single policy for $1,900,000 coverage to age sixty five.

This structured coverage gives the protection you need until you retire. At that point your mortgage will be gone, retirement income will be established, your college responsibilities completed, and your eventual demise will not affect the lifestyle of your partner.

One last point that is outside the area of real estate but is something to consider in life planning, is the need to have additional money available to fund long term care.

There are many options available to handle long term care needs, however, as my CFP® succinctly put it: "no money, no options." Once you get older, there is a possibility you may need some form of extended care services including assisted living or skilled nursing home facilities. Having either long term care insurance or additional savings available is a hedge against that need.

The Good Faith Estimate

The Good Faith Estimate (GFE) is a summary of what the lender expects the charges to be for processing the loan. It is divided into costs that

**won't change
might change up to 10%
could change more than 10%**

As the borrower, you will receive the Good Faith Estimate when you apply for the loan, which is 1-3 months before you close.

It is designed to allow you to comparison shop 3-4 loans from different lenders.

The form is self-explanatory, but this is a quick overview

Top section	Information on the lender for this loan.
Important Dates	Loans are time sensitive. This summarizes how long this loan will be good for. It must be long enough for you to do your closing.
Summary of Loan	These should all be checked NO (in most cases).
Escrow account	This tells you how much the lender will need monthly for taxes, home insurance and PMI if any.
Summary of settlement charges	This is the amount you will pay to complete the loan closing. "A" are loan costs, "B" are closing costs.
"A" Loan Costs	This is the additional amount you pay for the interest rate quoted based on your credit rating, type of loan, term and purpose.
"B" Closing Costs	These are all the other costs to complete the loan.
What can change	Self-explanatory.
The Tradeoff table	The lender can offer you the same basic loan trading off interest rate, points paid, and closing costs. If you want to roll some of your closing costs into the loan, you can see the effect here.
The Shopping Cart	You can summarize up to four loans from different lenders to compare rates and terms.

OMB Approval No. 2502-0265

Good Faith Estimate (GFE)

Name of Originator		Borrower	
Originator Address		Property Address	
Originator Phone Number			
Originator Email		Date of GFE	

Purpose

This GFE gives you an estimate of your settlement charges and loan terms if you are approved for this loan. For more information, see HUD's *Special Information Booklet* on settlement charges, your *Truth-in-Lending Disclosures*, and other consumer information at www.hud.gov/respa. If you decide you would like to proceed with this loan, contact us.

Shopping for your loan

Only you can shop for the best loan for you. Compare this GFE with other loan offers, so you can find the best loan. Use the shopping chart on page 3 to compare all the offers you receive.

Important dates

1. The interest rate for this GFE is available through [_____]. After this time, the interest rate, some of your loan Origination Charges, and the monthly payment shown below can change until you lock your interest rate.

2. This estimate for all other settlement charges is available through [_____].

3. After you lock your interest rate, you must go to settlement within [__] days (your rate lock period) to receive the locked interest rate.

4. You must lock the interest rate at least [__] days before settlement.

Summary of your loan

Your initial loan amount is	$
Your loan term is	years
Your initial interest rate is	%
Your initial monthly amount owed for principal, interest, and any mortgage insurance is	$ per month
Can your interest rate rise?	☐ No ☐ Yes, it can rise to a maximum of %. The first change will be in
Even if you make payments on time, can your loan balance rise?	☐ No ☐ Yes, it can rise to a maximum of $
Even if you make payments on time, can your monthly amount owed for principal, interest, and any mortgage insurance rise?	☐ No ☐ Yes, the first increase can be in and the monthly amount owed can rise to $. The maximum it can ever rise to is $
Does your loan have a prepayment penalty?	☐ No ☐ Yes, your maximum prepayment penalty is $
Does your loan have a balloon payment?	☐ No ☐ Yes, you have a balloon payment of $ due in years.

Escrow account information

Some lenders require an escrow account to hold funds for paying property taxes or other property-related charges in addition to your monthly amount owed of $ [_____].

Do we require you to have an escrow account for your loan?

☐ No, you do not have an escrow account. You must pay these charges directly when due.

☐ Yes, you have an escrow account. It may or may not cover all of these charges. Ask us.

Summary of your settlement charges

A	Your Adjusted Origination Charges *(See page 2.)*	$
B	Your Charges for All Other Settlement Services *(See page 2.)*	$
A + B	**Total Estimated Settlement Charges**	$

Good Faith Estimate (HUD-GFE) 1

Understanding
your estimated
settlement charges

Your Adjusted Origination Charges

1. Our origination charge
This charge is for getting this loan for you.

2. Your credit or charge (points) for the specific interest rate chosen

☐ The credit or charge for the interest rate of [　　　] % is included in "Our origination charge." (See item 1 above.)

☐ You receive a credit of $[　　　] for this interest rate of [　　　] %. This credit **reduces** your settlement charges.

☐ You pay a charge of $[　　　] for this interest rate of [　　　] %. This charge (points) **increases** your total settlement charges.

The tradeoff table on page 3 shows that you can change your total settlement charges by choosing a different interest rate for this loan.

A Your Adjusted Origination Charges | $

Your Charges for All Other Settlement Services

Some of these charges can change at settlement. See the top of page 3 for more information.

3. Required services that we select
These charges are for services we require to complete your settlement. We will choose the providers of these services.
Service　　　　　　Charge

4. Title services and lender's title insurance
This charge includes the services of a title or settlement agent, for example, and title insurance to protect the lender, if required.

5. Owner's title insurance
You may purchase an owner's title insurance policy to protect your interest in the property.

6. Required services that you can shop for
These charges are for other services that are required to complete your settlement. We can identify providers of these services or you can shop for them yourself. Our estimates for providing these services are below.
Service　　　　　　Charge

7. Government recording charges
These charges are for state and local fees to record your loan and title documents.

8. Transfer taxes
These charges are for state and local fees on mortgages and home sales.

9. Initial deposit for your escrow account
This charge is held in an escrow account to pay future recurring charges on your property and includes ☐ all property taxes, ☐ all insurance, and ☐ other [　　　]

10. Daily interest charges
This charge is for the daily interest on your loan from the day of your settlement until the first day of the next month or the first day of your normal mortgage payment cycle. This amount is $[　　　] per day for [　　] days (if your settlement is [　　　]).

11. Homeowner's insurance
This charge is for the insurance you must buy for the property to protect from a loss, such as fire.
Policy　　　　　　Charge

B Your Charges for All Other Settlement Services | $

A + B Total Estimated Settlement Charges | $

Good Faith Estimate (HUD-GFE) 2

Instructions

Understanding which charges can change at settlement

This GFE estimates your settlement charges. At your settlement, you will receive a HUD-1, a form that lists your actual costs. Compare the charges on the HUD-1 with the charges on this GFE. Charges can change if you select your own provider and do not use the companies we identify. (See below for details.)

These charges cannot increase at settlement:	The total of these charges can increase up to 10% at settlement:	These charges can change at settlement:
• Our origination charge • Your credit or charge (points) for the specific interest rate chosen (after you lock in your interest rate) • Your adjusted origination charges (after you lock in your interest rate) • Transfer taxes	• Required services that we select • Title services and lender's title insurance (if we select them or you use companies we identify) • Owner's title insurance (if you use companies we identify) • Required services that you can shop for (if you use companies we identify) • Government recording charges	• Required services that you can shop for (if you do not use companies we identify) • Title services and lender's title insurance (if you do not use companies we identify) • Owner's title insurance (if you do not use companies we identify) • Initial deposit for your escrow account • Daily interest charges • Homeowner's insurance

Using the tradeoff table

In this GFE, we offered you this loan with a particular interest rate and estimated settlement charges. However:
- If you want to choose this same loan with **lower settlement charges**, then you will have a **higher interest rate.**
- If you want to choose this same loan with a **lower interest rate**, then you will have **higher settlement charges.**

If you would like to choose an available option, you must ask us for a new GFE.

Loan originators have the option to complete this table. Please ask for additional information if the table is not completed.

	The loan in this GFE	The same loan with lower settlement charges	The same loan with a lower interest rate
Your initial loan amount	$	$	$
Your initial interest rate¹	%	%	%
Your initial monthly amount owed	$	$	$
Change in the monthly amount owed from this GFE	No change	You will pay $ **more** every month	You will pay $ **less** every month
Change in the amount you will pay at settlement with this interest rate	No change	Your settlement charges will be **reduced** by $	Your settlement charges will **increase** by $
How much your total estimated settlement charges will be	$	$	$

¹ For an adjustable rate loan, the comparisons above are for the initial interest rate before adjustments are made.

Using the shopping chart

Use this chart to compare GFEs from different loan originators. Fill in the information by using a different column for each GFE you receive. By comparing loan offers, you can shop for the best loan.

	This loan	Loan 2	Loan 3	Loan 4
Loan originator name				
Initial loan amount				
Loan term				
Initial interest rate				
Initial monthly amount owed				
Rate lock period				
Can interest rate rise?				
Can loan balance rise?				
Can monthly amount owed rise?				
Prepayment penalty?				
Balloon payment?				
Total Estimated Settlement Charges				

If your loan is sold in the future

Some lenders may sell your loan after settlement. Any fees lenders receive in the future cannot change the loan you receive or the charges you paid at settlement.

Good Faith Estimate (HUD-GFE) 3

HUD-1 Settlement Statement

This form is provided at the loan closing. You get a copy of it 2 days before the closing. The HUD-1 settlement statement can be daunting, but it is important to have an understanding of the information it provides. Your attorney will review the HUD-1 statement and should explain all of the costs associated with the loan.

The HUD-1 statement is another excellent reason to have your attorney involved. Your attorney will get a copy of the HUD-1 a few days (48 hours) before the closing. He or she should review the HUD-1 statement to ensure no mistakes were made and the loan terms are the same as you agreed to in your loan application. There should be no surprise charges listed in the HUD-1 statement.

> Make sure you save the HUD-1 statement and review it when you prepare your taxes for the year in which you bought or sold the house. There may be items on the HUD-1 statement that are tax deductible. For example, on line 106 on page 1 in the borrower's column there is an adjustment for city or town taxes. Line 510 is a similar adjustment in the seller's column if the seller had to pay property taxes as an adjustment. From the HUD-1 statement, you or your tax accountant will get tax deduction information such as points paid.

Let's walk through the HUD-1 form and break it down into its component parts. See below for an example of the HUD-1 settlement statement.

The HUD-1 form is an accounting of all the expenses involved in the transaction for both buyer and seller. The buyer will be getting a loan from the lender and the lender will spend money to process the loan. Page 1 of the three-page HUD-1 settlement sheet summarizes all monies due from the borrower on the left side of the page. All the monies due to the seller are on the right. In our example, the buyer owes $150,000 in the left column, and the seller is due $150,000 in the right column. Page 2 details the settlement charges. Page 3 shows the comparison of the lender's Good Faith Estimate (GFE) of what the closing costs would be and the final costs shown on the HUD-1 statement.

A lot can happen in the two to three months between application and closing. The HUD-1 settlement statement is a reconciliation between what the lender told you up front in the GFE and what they are telling you at the closing. In most cases the variances are small. Now, let's take a look at the HUD-1 form starting on the top of page 3 which is the comparison of the charges estimated on the GFE and the final costs at closing.

Comparison of Good Faith Estimate (GFE) and HUD-1 Charges		Good Faith Estimate	HUD-1
Charges That Cannot Increase	HUD-1 Line Number		
Our origination charge	# 801		
Your credit or charge (points) for the specific interest rate chosen	# 802		
Your adjusted origination charges	# 803		
Transfer taxes	# 1203		

Charges That In Total Cannot Increase More Than 10%		Good Faith Estimate	HUD-1
Government recording charges	# 1201		
	#		
	#		
	#		
	#		
	#		
	#		
Total Increase between GFE and HUD-1 Charges	$ or %		

Charges That Can Change		Good Faith Estimate	HUD-1
Initial deposit for your escrow account	# 1001		
Daily interest charges $ /day	# 901		
Homeowner's insurance	# 903		
	#		
	#		
	#		

HUD-1 page 3

Comparison of Good Faith Estimate (GFE) and HUD-1 charges: At the top of page 3 you see the estimated costs and actual costs, or plan vs. actual. It is divided into the charges *that cannot change* including the lender's loan origination charge, points you are paying to reduce the interest rate, and the transfer taxes to record the deed. Next are the charges that *cannot change more that 10%* such as the cost of the real estate appraisal, the credit report, tax service fee to research outstanding property tax, and flood certificate or Private Mortgage Insurance (PMI). You may see the term Mortgage Insurance Premium (MIP), which is the term that HUD uses when the insurance is provided by them. Check the bottom line of the top section to determine any increase between the GFE and the HUD-1 charges. There should be no surprises.

The last section lists charges that *can change more than 10%*. These include your first deposit to the escrow account, daily interest charges (from the date of closing to your first mortgage payment), and your homeowner's insurance.

The first deposit for your escrow account: The GFE may not have this total at the time it was made, so in some instances the amount on the HUD-1 varies from the GFE. Variances might include the cost of three months of homeowner's insurance and three months taxes. Lender requirements vary from state to state. The lender may ask you to bring a paid invoice from your insurance agent indicating the first year's homeowners insurance has been paid.

Daily interest charges: This is an adjustment in the amount of interest charges that accrue from the day of the loan closing to the due date of the first mortgage payment. For example, the closing is scheduled for June 15th and the first mortgage payment will be due August 1st. The interest amount on the mortgage loan is $16.44 per day ($120,000 × 5% ÷ 365 days). If there were 45 days from closing to first payment, then the interest charge is $739.80 ($16.44 × 45 days).

Loan Terms

Your initial loan amount is	$
Your loan term is	Years
Your initial interest rate is	%
Your initial monthly amount owed for principal, interest, and any mortgage insurance is	$ includes ☐ Principal ☐ Interest ☐ Mortgage Insurance
Can your interest rate rise?	☐ No ☐ Yes, it can rise to a maximum of %. The first change will be on and can change again every after . Every change date, your interest rate can increase or decrease by %. Over the life of the loan, your interest rate is guaranteed to never be **lower** than % or **higher** than %.
Even if you make payments on time, can your loan balance rise?	☐ No ☐ Yes, it can rise to a maximum of $.
Even if you make payments on time, can your monthly amount owed for principal, interest, and mortgage insurance rise?	☐ No ☐ Yes, the first increase can be on and the monthly amount owed can rise to $. The maximum amount it can ever rise to is $.
Does your loan have a prepayment penalty?	☐ No ☐ Yes, your maximum prepayment penalty is $.
Does your loan have a balloon payment?	☐ No ☐ Yes, you have a balloon payment of $ due in years on .
Total monthly amount owed including escrow account payments.	☐ You do not have a monthly escrow payment for items, such as property taxes and homeowner's insurance. You must pay these items directly yourself. ☐ You have an additional monthly escrow payment of $ that results in a total initial monthly amount owed of $. This includes principal, interest, any mortgage insurance and any items checked below: ☐ Property taxes ☐ Homeowner's insurance ☐ Flood insurance ☐ ☐ ☐

Note: If you have any questions about the Settlement Charges and Loan Terms listed on this form, please contact your lender.

HUD-1 Page 3 Loan Terms

The terms of the loan are covered in the bottom 2/3rds of Page 3 of the HUD-1 form. Using our example, the section begins with the mortgage loan amount ($120,000) and the term (30 years). Next, the Loan Terms section states the interest rate of the loan (5%). The payment amount is stated ($644.19 per month) along with the items included in the payment. Boxes to be checked include those for Principal, Interest, and Mortgage Insurance (PMI). Both Principal and Interest should be checked. If you have PMI, then Mortgage Insurance will be checked as well. This is summarized from the example below:

HUD-1 Summary	Amount
Principle	$144
Interest	$500
PMI	$0
Total loan payment	$644

The rest of the form is a series of questions regarding the loan and the answers. Questions in this section include the following.

Can the interest rate rise? No. A variable rate can, but not a fixed rate.

Even if you make payments on time, can the loan balance rise? Not if you have a fixed rate mortgage.

Even if you make payments on time can the principal, interest and mortgage insurance rise? No, if you have a fixed rate mortgage.

Does the loan have a pre-payment penalty? This should be No. If yes, consider shopping for another loan. You want to maintain flexibility with your financing. If rates drop in the future, it may be worthwhile to refinance. If you have to pay a penalty to get out of this loan, it may prevent you from refinancing.

Does the loan have a balloon payment? This should be No. If yes, consider not going forward with the loan. Everyone reading this book should be using a 30 year fixed rate mortgage, at least initially. A balloon payment indicates that the loan will have to be paid off earlier than the thirty years, which may not be possible.

Total owed each month including escrow account payments. Here is where the escrow amounts for property taxes, property insurance, and flood insurance are added. This is summarized from the example as:

Plus Escrow amounts for:	Amount
Property taxes	$184
Home Insurance	$50
Flood Insurance	$0
Total Monthly escrow payments	$234

You can now total the loan payment with the escrow payments to see the total payment due. Remember that the escrow account will pay for the property tax and home insurance bills when they come due.

Monthly loan expenses	Amount
Total Loan Payment	$644
Total escrow payment	$234
Total Monthly payment	$878

This completes page 3 of the HUD-1 form. Now look at page 2 starting with settlement charges.

HUD-1 Page 2 – Settlement Charges

The HUD-1 form uses a number of expense classes: On the right side is a column for the Borrower and on the left side is a column for the seller.

L. Settlement Charges		Paid From Borrower's Funds at Settlement	Paid From Seller's Funds at Settlement
700. Total Real Estate Broker Fees			
Division of commission (line 700) as follows:			
701. $ to			
702. $ to			
703. Commission paid at settlement			
704. Listing Agent Earnest Money Retention			
705.			

(700) *Total Real Estate Broker Fees:* In most cases the seller engaged the listing broker who gets paid from the seller's funds. However, if the borrower engaged a buyer's broker and agreed to pay a 2% commission, it will be charged here to the borrower.

800. Items Payable In Connection with Loan			
801. Our origination charge	(from GFE #1)		
802. Your credit or charge (points) for the specific interest rate chosen	(from GFE #2)		
803. Your adjusted origination charges	(from GFE A)		
804. Appraisal fee to	(from GFE #3)		
805. Credit report to	(from GFE #3)		
806. Tax service to	(from GFE #3)		
807. Flood certification	(from GFE #3)		
808.			
809.			
810.			
811.			
812.			
813.			

(800) *Items Payable in Connection with Loan:* These are the lender's charges for processing the loan application. They may include the loan origination fee, points agreed upon, the real estate appraisal, the credit reports, tax service fee to research outstanding property taxes, flood certificates, and the plot survey.

900. Items Required by Lender to Be Paid In Advance			
901. Daily interest charges from to @ $ /day	(from GFE #10)		
902. Mortgage insurance premium for months to	(from GFE #3)		
903. Homeowner's insurance for years to	(from GFE #11)		
904.			
905.			

(900) *Items Required by the Lender to Be Paid in Advance:* Prepaid items are listed here. They include the interest on the loan from date of closing to the first payment, the Mortgage Insurance Premium (MIP) or Private Mortgage Insurance (PMI) if required, and buyer's homeowner's insurance.

It is easy to confuse the (900) section with the next section that covers the reserves deposited. The (900) section lists all of the costs associated with the loan up to the date of the first mortgage payment. The (1000) section lists the upfront escrow amount necessary to pay the municipal real estate tax bill due from the date of the first and ongoing mortgage payments.

1000. Reserves Deposited with Lender				
1001. Initial deposit for your escrow account		(from GFE # 9)		
1002. Homeowner's insurance	months @ $	/mo.		
1003. Mortgage insurance	months @ $	/mo.		
1004. Property taxes	months @ $	/mo.		
1005.	months @ $	/mo.		
1006.	months @ $	/mo.		
1007.	months @ $	/mo.		
1008. Aggregate Adjustment		-		

(1000) *Reserves Deposited with Lender:* The escrow account can be envisioned as a checking account which pays the property taxes and home insurance bills. To open the checking account, a deposit must be made to make sure there is enough to pay the expected bills. When the first tax bill comes in, you send it to the lender. The lender pays the bill from the escrow account. You make a deposit to the escrow account each month (in your monthly payment) to keep the balance high enough to pay future bills.

In this section of the form it tells you how much you need for the first escrow deposit. It then lists the amount of homeowner's insurance, mortgage insurance (PMI), and property taxes. This section details the number of months in advance taxes are to be collected and the tax rate per month. Escrow reserves are for 3-6 months sometimes a year. When they come due, funds from the escrow account are used to pay the property taxes, homeowner's insurance, and PMI. For example, if the community's property tax bill is paid each quarter, the lender must have enough money in the escrow account to pay the quarterly bill when it comes due.

1100. Title Charges				
1101. Title services and lender's title insurance		(from GFE #4)		
1102. Settlement or closing fee to				
1103. Owner's title insurance		(from GFE #5)		
1104. Lender's title insurance				
1105. Lender's title policy limit				
1106. Owner's title policy limit				
1107. Agent's portion of the total title insurance premium	to			
1108. Underwriter's portion of the total title insurance premium	to			
1109.				
1110.				
1111.				
1112.				
1113.				
1114.				

(1100) *Title Charges:* This section covers Title Insurance. The lender requires title insurance for the amount of the mortgage. The home buyer can purchase a policy to cover his or her portion of ownership, which I recommend. Title insurance is a small fee to pay to insure against potential problems that may occur involving clear ownership. The lender or bank's attorney completes the title search and would be the best person to arrange for the title insurance.

1200. Government Recording and Transfer Charges				
1201. Government recording charges			(from GFE #7)	
1202. Deed	Mortgage	Releases		
1203. Transfer taxes			(from GFE #8)	
1204. City/County tax/stamps	Deed	Mortgage		
1205. State tax/stamps	Deed	Mortgage		
1206.				
1207.				
1208.				

(1200) *Government Recording and Transfer Charges:* When a deed is recorded, there may be a charge for recording the new deed on the property as well as for releasing the mortgage of the seller. When recording the sale, three things happen in immediate succession. They are:

The seller's mortgage is paid off and recorded as a mortgage release.
The deed is recorded, transferring ownership from the seller to the buyer.
The mortgage is recorded, creating the lender's lien on the property.

Recording the deed process is handled differently in states that use trust deeds. See the definition of a trust deed above. In some instances there may be other transfer taxes that must be paid to the city, county and/or state. Each state has a payment guideline, but transfer taxes are often divided between the buyer and seller.

1300. Additional Settlement Charges		
1301. Required services that you can shop for	(from GFE #6)	
1302.		
1303.		
1304.		
1305.		
1306.		
1307.		

(1300) *Additional Settlement Charges:* An area for any other charges associated with the closing.

1400. Total Settlement Charges (enter on lines 103, Section J and 502, Section K)

(1400) *Total Settlement Charges:* The first box is the total to be paid by the borrower. The second box is the total to be paid by the seller. These two amounts are transferred to page 1 of the HUD-1 form.

This completes the detailed expenses on page 2 of the HUD-1 form. Now let's look at page 1, which is the summary of pages two and three.

HUD-1 Page 1

The top section of page 1 provides the particulars on the transaction. The left side of the page summarizes *the amount due from the borrower's transaction,* and the right side is *a summary of the seller's transaction.* In brief, you the borrower owe the sales price of the house, plus the settlement charges outlined on page 2 (borrower's column total), less any items paid in advance, less your deposit and loan from the bank, less any adjustments from the seller for unpaid items. This totals the amount the borrower must bring to the closing in cash or certified check.

B. Type of Loan		
1. ☐ FHA 2. ☐ RHS 3. ☐ Conv. Unins. 4. ☐ VA 5. ☐ Conv. Ins.	6. File Number: 7. Loan Number:	8. Mortgage Insurance Case Number:

C. **Note:** This form is furnished to give you a statement of actual settlement costs. Amounts paid to and by the settlement agent are shown. Items marked "(p.o.c.)" were paid outside the closing; they are shown here for informational purposes and are not included in the totals.

D. Name & Address of Borrower:	E. Name & Address of Seller:	F. Name & Address of Lender:
G. Property Location:	H. Settlement Agent: Your Name or Company Here	I. Settlement Date:
	Place of Settlement:	

HUD-1 Page 1---

Left column, Summary of Borrower's Transaction

100. Gross Amount Due from Borrower		
101. Contract sales price		
102. Personal property		
103. Settlement charges to borrower (line 1400)		0.00
104.		
105.		
Adjustment for items paid by seller in advance		
106. City/town taxes	to	/yr.
107. County taxes	to	/yr.
108. Assessments	to	/yr.
109.		
110.		
111.		
112.		
120. Gross Amount Due from Borrower		0.00
200. Amounts Paid by or in Behalf of Borrower		
201. Deposit or earnest money		
202. Principal amount of new loan(s)		
203. Existing loan(s) taken subject to		
204.		
205.		
206.		
207.		
208.		
209.		
Adjustments for items unpaid by seller		
210. City/town taxes	to	/yr.
211. County taxes	to	/yr.
212. Assessments	to	/yr.
213.		
214.		
215.		
216.		
217.		
218.		
219.		
220. Total Paid by/for Borrower		0.00
300. Cash at Settlement from/to Borrower		
301. Gross amount due from borrower (line 120)		0.00
302. Less amounts paid by/for borrower (line 220)		0.00
303. Cash ☐ From ☐ To Borrower		0.00

100. Gross Amount Due from Borrower	
101. Contract sales price	
102. Personal property	
103. Settlement charges to borrower (line 1400)	0.00
104.	
105.	

The accounting starts with the sales price of the house, plus any payments agreed to for personal property. Next the borrower's settlement charges from line 1400 on page 2 is listed.

Adjustment for items paid by seller in advance			
106. City/town taxes	to	/yr.	
107. County taxes	to	/yr.	
108. Assessments	to	/yr.	
109.			
110.			
111.			
112.			
120. Gross Amount Due from Borrower			0.00

If the seller has prepaid any taxes or assessments, they are added here. Line 120 shows the total amount the borrower needs for the sale.

200. Amounts Paid by or in Behalf of Borrower	
201. Deposit or earnest money	
202. Principal amount of new loan(s)	
203. Existing loan(s) taken subject to	
204.	
205.	
206.	
207.	
208.	
209.	

The 200 section shows all payments made. First is the deposit, next is the new loan. In rare cases the buyer may be assuming an existing mortgage, which would be shown next.

Adjustments for items unpaid by seller			
210. City/town taxes	to	/yr.	
211. County taxes	to	/yr.	
212. Assessments	to	/yr.	
213.			
214.			
215.			
216.			
217.			
218.			
219.			
220. Total Paid by/for Borrower			0.00

Next are any items that were not paid by the seller, which should have been paid. If the closing is on June 15, and the seller has paid the first quarter's taxes through March 30, then the seller owes the taxes from March 30 to June 15. This amount would be shown here.

300. Cash at Settlement from/to Borrower	
301. Gross amount due from borrower (line 120)	0.00
302. Less amounts paid by/for borrower (line 220)	0.00
303. Cash ☐ From ☐ To Borrower	0.00

The final total owed by the borrower is calculated as the Gross Amount due from the borrower (line 120) less all the amounts paid by the borrower (line 220). This is mostly the deposit and the loan. Line 303 shows the amount of cash due from the borrower at the closing.

> In a rare instance there might be cash going to the borrower. In the case of a loan with planned improvements, or an AS COMPLETED value, the amount of the loan would include the planned improvements. In that case the borrower would get cash back at the closing for the planned repairs.

Next I show the right column for the Sellers accounting.

HUD-1 Page 1---

Right Column, Summary of Seller's Transaction

400. Gross Amount Due to Seller	
401. Contract sales price	
402. Personal property	
403.	
404.	
405.	
Adjustments for items paid by seller in advance	
406. City/town taxes to /yr.	
407. County taxes to /yr.	
408. Assessments to /yr.	
409.	
410.	
411.	
412.	
420. Gross Amount Due to Seller	0.00
500. Reductions In Amount Due to Seller	
501. Excess deposit (see instructions)	
502. Settlement charges to seller (line 1400)	0.00
503. Existing loan(s) taken subject to	
504. Payoff of first mortgage loan	
505. Payoff of second mortgage loan	
506.	
507.	
508.	
509.	
Adjustments for items unpaid by seller	
510. City/town taxes to /yr.	
511. County taxes to /yr.	
512. Assessments to /yr.	
513.	
514.	
515.	
516.	
517.	
518.	
519.	
520. Total Reduction Amount Due Seller	0.00
600. Cash at Settlement to/from Seller	
601. Gross amount due to seller (line 420)	0.00
602. Less reductions in amount due seller (line 520)	0.00
603. Cash ☐ From ☐ To Seller	**0.00**

400. Gross Amount Due to Seller	
401. Contract sales price	
402. Personal property	
403.	
404.	
405.	

The accounting starts with the sales price of the house, plus any payments agreed to for personal property.

Adjustments for items paid by seller in advance			
406. City/town taxes	to	/yr.	
407. County taxes	to	/yr.	
408. Assessments	to	/yr.	
409.			
410.			
411.			
412.			
420. Gross Amount Due to Seller			0.00

Next are any items that were paid by the seller beyond the closing date. If the closing is on June 15, and the seller has paid the first AND SECOND quarter's taxes through June 30, then the seller has overpaid the taxes from June 15 to June 30. These same amounts will be shown on the buyers side in column 1 lines 106, 107 and 108. Essentially it adds the amounts to what the seller will get, and adds it to the amount the borrower owes.

500. Reductions In Amount Due to Seller	
501. Excess deposit (see instructions)	
502. Settlement charges to seller (line 1400)	0.00
503. Existing loan(s) taken subject to	
504. Payoff of first mortgage loan	
505. Payoff of second mortgage loan	
506.	
507.	
508.	
509.	

Next it deducts items that the seller has to pay. Mostly this will be the settlement charges to the seller from Page 2 line 1400. All existing loans will have to be paid shown on line 504 and 505.

Adjustments for items unpaid by seller			
510. City/town taxes	to	/yr.	
511. County taxes	to	/yr.	
512. Assessments	to	/yr.	
513.			
514.			
515.			
516.			
517.			
518.			
519.			
520. Total Reduction Amount Due Seller			0.00

Next are any items that were not paid by the seller, which should have been paid. These same amounts will be shown on the buyers side in column 1 lines 210, 211 and 212. Essentially it deducts the amounts from what the seller will get, and deducts it from the amount the borrower owes.

600. Cash at Settlement to/from Seller	
601. Gross amount due to seller (line 420)	0.00
602. Less reductions in amount due seller (line 520)	0.00
603. Cash ☐ From ☐ To Seller	0.00

The final total owed to the seller is calculated as the Gross Amount due to the seller borrower (line 601) less all the amounts paid by the seller (line 520).

Line 603 shows the amount of cash due to the seller at the closing.

In a rare instance there might be cash owed by the seller if there were insufficient proceeds from the sale to cover all of the sellers expense.

HUD-1 Settlement Statement Page 1 of 3

A. **Settlement Statement (HUD-1)**

OMB Approval No. 2502-0265

B. Type of Loan		
1. ☐ FHA 2. ☐ RHS 3. ☐ Conv. Unins. 4. ☐ VA 5. ☐ Conv. Ins.	6. File Number:	7. Loan Number:
		8. Mortgage Insurance Case Number:

C. Note: This form is furnished to give you a statement of actual settlement costs. Amounts paid to and by the settlement agent are shown. Items marked "(p.o.c.)" were paid outside the closing; they are shown here for informational purposes and are not included in the totals.

D. Name & Address of Borrower:	E. Name & Address of Seller:	F. Name & Address of Lender:
G. Property Location:	H. Settlement Agent: Your Name or Company Here Place of Settlement:	I. Settlement Date:

100. Gross Amount Due from Borrower		**400. Gross Amount Due to Seller**	
101. Contract sales price		401. Contract sales price	
102. Personal property		402. Personal property	
103. Settlement charges to borrower (line 1400)	0.00	403.	
104.		404.	
105.		405.	
Adjustment for items paid by seller in advance		**Adjustments for items paid by seller in advance**	
106. City/town taxes to /yr.		406. City/town taxes to /yr.	
107. County taxes to /yr.		407. County taxes to /yr.	
108. Assessments to /yr.		408. Assessments to /yr.	
109.		409.	
110.		410.	
111.		411.	
112.		412.	
120. Gross Amount Due from Borrower	0.00	**420. Gross Amount Due to Seller**	0.00
200. Amounts Paid by or in Behalf of Borrower		**500. Reductions in Amount Due to Seller**	
201. Deposit or earnest money		501. Excess deposit (see instructions)	
202. Principal amount of new loan(s)		502. Settlement charges to seller (line 1400)	0.00
203. Existing loan(s) taken subject to		503. Existing loan(s) taken subject to	
204.		504. Payoff of first mortgage loan	
205.		505. Payoff of second mortgage loan	
206.		506.	
207.		507.	
208.		508.	
209.		509.	
Adjustments for items unpaid by seller		**Adjustments for items unpaid by seller**	
210. City/town taxes to /yr.		510. City/town taxes to /yr.	
211. County taxes to /yr.		511. County taxes to /yr.	
212. Assessments to /yr.		512. Assessments to /yr.	
213.		513.	
214.		514.	
215.		515.	
216.		516.	
217.		517.	
218.		518.	
219.		519.	
220. Total Paid by/for Borrower	0.00	**520. Total Reduction Amount Due Seller**	0.00
300. Cash at Settlement from/to Borrower		**600. Cash at Settlement to/from Seller**	
301. Gross amount due from borrower (line 120)	0.00	601. Gross amount due to seller (line 420)	0.00
302. Less amounts paid by/for borrower (line 220)	0.00	602. Less reductions in amount due seller (line 520)	0.00
303. Cash ☐ From ☐ To Borrower	0.00	**603. Cash ☐ From ☐ To Seller**	0.00

The Public Reporting Burden for this collection of information is estimated at 35 minutes per response for collecting, reviewing, and reporting the data. This agency may not collect this information, and you are not required to complete this form, unless it displays a currently valid OMB control number. No confidentiality is assured; this disclosure is mandatory. This is designed to provide the parties to a RESPA covered transaction with information during the settlement process.

HUD-1 Settlement Statement page 2 of 3

L. Settlement Charges			
700. Total Real Estate Broker Fees		Paid From Borrower's Funds at Settlement	Paid From Seller's Funds at Settlement
Division of commission (line 700) as follows:			
701. $ to			
702. $ to			
703. Commission paid at settlement			
704. Listing Agent Earnest Money Retention			
705.			
800. Items Payable in Connection with Loan			
801. Our origination charge	(from GFE #1)		
802. Your credit or charge (points) for the specific interest rate chosen	(from GFE #2)		
803. Your adjusted origination charges	(from GFE A)		
804. Appraisal fee to	(from GFE #3)		
805. Credit report to	(from GFE #3)		
806. Tax service to	(from GFE #3)		
807. Flood certification	(from GFE #3)		
808.			
809.			
810.			
811.			
812.			
813.			
900. Items Required by Lender to Be Paid in Advance			
901. Daily interest charges from to @ $ /day	(from GFE #10)		
902. Mortgage insurance premium for months to	(from GFE #3)		
903. Homeowner's insurance for years to	(from GFE #11)		
904.			
905.			
1000. Reserves Deposited with Lender			
1001. Initial deposit for your escrow account	(from GFE # 9)		
1002. Homeowner's insurance months @ $ /mo.			
1003. Mortgage insurance months @ $ /mo.			
1004. Property taxes months @ $ /mo.			
1005. months @ $ /mo.			
1006. months @ $ /mo.			
1007. months @ $ /mo.			
1008. Aggregate Adjustment —			
1100. Title Charges			
1101. Title services and lender's title insurance	(from GFE #4)		
1102. Settlement or closing fee to			
1103. Owner's title insurance	(from GFE #5)		
1104. Lender's title insurance			
1105. Lender's title policy limit			
1106. Owner's title policy limit			
1107. Agent's portion of the total title insurance premium to			
1108. Underwriter's portion of the total title insurance premium to			
1109.			
1110.			
1111.			
1112.			
1113.			
1114.			
1200. Government Recording and Transfer Charges			
1201. Government recording charges	(from GFE #7)		
1202. Deed Mortgage Releases			
1203. Transfer taxes	(from GFE #8)		
1204. City/County tax/stamps Deed Mortgage			
1205. State tax/stamps Deed Mortgage			
1206.			
1207.			
1208.			
1300. Additional Settlement Charges			
1301. Required services that you can shop for	(from GFE #6)		
1302.			
1303.			
1304.			
1305.			
1306.			
1307.			
1400. Total Settlement Charges (enter on lines 103, Section J and 502, Section K)		0.00	0.00

HUD-1 Settlement Statement page 3 of 3

Comparison of Good Faith Estimate (GFE) and HUD-1 Charges		Good Faith Estimate	HUD-1
Charges That Cannot Increase	HUD-1 Line Number		
Our origination charge	# 801		
Your credit or charge (points) for the specific interest rate chosen	# 802		
Your adjusted origination charges	# 803		
Transfer taxes	# 1203		
Charges That in Total Cannot Increase More Than 10%		Good Faith Estimate	HUD-1
Government recording charges	# 1201		
	#		
	#		
	#		
	#		
	#		
	#		
	#		
	#		
	#		
	#		
	Total	0.00	0.00
	Increase between GFE and HUD-1 Charges	$ 0.00 or	N/A
Charges That Can Change		Good Faith Estimate	HUD-1
Initial deposit for your escrow	# 1001		
Daily interest charges	# 901 /day		
Homeowner's insurance	# 903		
	#		
	#		
	#		
	#		
	#		
	#		
	#		

Loan Terms

Your initial loan amount is	$
Your loan term is	Years
Your initial interest rate is	%
Your initial monthly amount owed for principal, interest, and any mortgage insurance is	$ includes ☐ Principal ☐ Interest ☐ Mortgage Insurance
Can your interest rate rise?	☐ No ☐ Yes, it can rise to a maximum of %. The first change will be on and can change again every after . Every change date, your interest rate can increase or decrease by %. Over the life of the loan, your interest rate is guaranteed to never be **lower** than % or **higher** than %.
Even if you make payments on time, can your loan balance rise?	☐ No ☐ Yes, it can rise to a maximum of $.
Even if you make payments on time, can your monthly amount owed for principal, interest, and mortgage insurance rise?	☐ No ☐ Yes, the first increase can be on and the monthly amount owed can rise to $. The maximum amount it can ever rise to is $.
Does your loan have a prepayment penalty?	☐ No ☐ Yes, your maximum prepayment penalty is $.
Does your loan have a balloon payment?	☐ No ☐ Yes, you have a balloon payment of $ due in years on .
Total monthly amount owed including escrow account payments.	☐ You do not have a monthly escrow payment for items, such as property taxes and homeowner's insurance. You must pay these items directly yourself. ☐ You have an additional monthly escrow payment of $ that results in a total initial monthly amount owed of $. This includes principal, interest, any mortgage insurance and any items checked below: ☐ Property taxes ☐ Homeowner's insurance ☐ Flood insurance ☐ ☐

Note: If you have any questions about the Settlement Charges and Loan Terms listed on this form, please contact your lender.

Using the Internet to Find Data

In today's world of technology, most readers of this book will have all the skills they need to access the information available on the Internet. However, not everyone has the full range of available skills to access information on the internet. Some may find tips in this section.

A high speed connection. The best use of the Internet requires having a reliable high speed connection. The most efficient way is to have the computer at your home hard wired into the Internet. Public libraries also offer both computers and access for little to no charge. There are also computer Internet cafés that will rent you a computer with Internet access.

Libraries are often a Wi-Fi hotspot so you can access the Internet from your laptop. WI-FI is an abbreviation of "Wireless Fidelity." Wi-Fi allows a device to transmit information through the air without a wire connection. A Wi-Fi enabled laptop has a transmission device that sends and receives signals to a Wi-Fi enabled device.

The receiving device is usually a router. The router is designed to receive the signals sent from the laptop and forward them to the transmission cable connected to the Internet. When your Wi-Fi enabled laptop is in a Wi-Fi enabled area, you are connected to the Internet just as if you were at home with a computer hard wired to your cable system.

If you have a laptop computer with a Wi-Fi connection you may use many Wi-Fi hotspot access centers. Access centers include fast food restaurants (Burger King, McDonalds, Panera Bread, and Wendy's), coffee shops (Dunkin Donuts, Starbucks, and many small local companies), bookstores (Barnes & Noble), and shipping companies (FedEx), etc. Some centers are free while others charge for usage. The list grows daily. Use the Internet to find other Wi-Fi spots near you. Search on your [city state Wi-Fi] such as [Waltham MA Wi-Fi]

Search for Information on the Internet Using Google. Next I show how to use Google to search for content. Yahoo works in a similar fashion. There may be other search engines you prefer such as Ask.com, AOL.com, or altavista.com

Brackets [ ] are used as a convention in this book to show the data that you type into the search field. The computer looks for the bracketed data. You do not enter the brackets, just the information within the brackets. For example, if you were searching for information on dogs it is shown in the book as [dogs]. It means you only enter dogs.

To find the assessing information for your town, city or county enter [town name state assessor]. Town name is the name of the town you are looking for such as Waltham, state is the state you are looking for such as MA. It can be spelled out as Massachusetts, but it's not necessary. Assessor is the keyword for the information that you are looking for in Waltham, MA.

For example, to find the assessor's information for Waltham MA enter [Waltham MA assessor]. This gets you to a list of potential sites for your local assessor's office. Look at the list and find the one that looks like the official city, town, parish, or county web site.

By carefully looking at the web pages you may find a link to the assessor's on-line property database. Click on this link and it shows the search page for the assessor's database.

You can typically search by address, owners' name, or map-block and lot. If you cannot find a link, call the assessor's office. The phone number is usually listed on the municipality's web sites. They can tell you if the assessor's data is online and if so how to find it. If it is not on line, you will have to visit the assessor's office to get the field card data.

Searching Tips. You can refine your search using quotes and/or other search logic. For example [House Sale] gets a broad range of sites while ["House Sale" Arlington MA] narrows it down significantly.

The quote marks tell Google to search for sites with the exact wording compared to sites that contain any of the words in any part of the site. True Boolean logic uses the operators AND, OR, NOT. Google simplifies this to plus [+], minus [-] and [OR]. The plus or minus sign is typed just in front of the word to include or exclude with no space following it. There must be a space in front of it. ["Arlington MA" +"House Sale"] gets sites with both word groups, while ["Arlington MA" -"House Sale"] excludes sites that have "House Sale" as a key word.

This specific search should focus on information about the town but not properties for sale. To search for either group use ["Arlington MA" OR "House Sale"] this gets sites with either word grouping.

The tilde symbol [~] indicates that Google should search for synonyms for the word [Zoning ~law] not only finds laws, but regulations, ordinances, rules, statutes, and bylaws.

Finding Properties for Sale. Ideally you would have access to the actual Multiple Listing Service (MLS) that serves your area. An MLS system is a proprietary system that requires a subscription and is limited to members and associate members of the real estate boards they serve.

However, real estate brokers may let you have a glimpse of it. When you search for homes for sale in your home town and state, you usually will get a large list of real estate brokerage firms offering a list of properties for sale. They vary in flexibility and generally want your e-mail address and/or contact information to register to use the site. It does not take long before you may be overwhelmed with information from various real estate firms.

The brokers want to sign you as a client to let them use their expertise with the real MLS system to focus in on your exact needs.

Realtor.com. This is a site sponsored by the National Association of Realtors® (NAR). It shows both active listings and properties that sold. It can be helpful to get an understanding of values in your area of interest. It has a powerful mapping tool that will show listings and/or sales in a given neighborhood.

Local real estate companies may place their listings on this site. It is fairly comprehensive and allows you to select the city or town in which you are interested. You may select by price range, number of bedrooms, and baths.

The advanced search on this site is powerful in allowing refinements for Nearby Areas (essentially neighborhoods), Property Features (size, age, garage, number of stories, heating and cooling, indoor and outdoor amenities), and other features such as pets allowed.

Lot and Community allows refinements on lot size, waterfront, golf course, etc., while Community allows searches for properties near a pool, park, horses, senior, boating, clubhouse, tennis, and golf.

You will not see every property available for sale. The property owner has the option of excluding their listing from the web sites. Also remember that real estate is a volatile market. Things change by the hour. New properties come on the market, list prices change, properties are withdrawn, expire, or go under agreement.

Use these sites to gain an understanding of the market, and to find the most active brokers. Eventually you may decide to select a broker to represent you either as a listing or buyer's broker.

Trulia.com and Zillow.com are general web sites showing both current listings and sales information. Both allow you to look at sales on a map and get details on a property and nearby sales and listings.

This is a sampling of FSBO web sites:

Forsalebyowner.com, Isoldmyhouse.com, and FSBO.com. There are many others. Most are new and at this time have only a few listings.

Finding Other Information That May Be Helpful. Besides finding data on properties for sale, there is a wide range of data that may be useful to you at various times. This is a brief list of topics:

Consumer Confidence Index
Tax rate/taxes
Unemployment rates
Schools
Community services
Parks, recreation areas
Zoning
Field Card
Assessor maps
Registry of deeds
Flood Zone
Environmental/contaminated sites
Aerial views

Web Sites

Category	Web Site	Purpose
Appraiser	appraisalinstitute.org	Appraisal institute, dick on find an appraiser
Assessor Data	Assessors office	Search for municipality state assessor [Springfield MA assessor]
Auto	zipcar.com	Short tern auto rental
Auto	consumerreports.org	Consumer reports - automobile quality reviews
Cost Vs. Value	remodeling.hw.net	Click on facts & Figures Click on Cost vs. Value report
Credit	annualcreditreport.com	Free credit report
Credit	myfico.com	Click on EDUCATION Tab for additional info on FICO scores
Deeds	Deeds by county	Search for state, county [FL Lee County deeds]
FSBO	Forsalebyowner.com	Website for a For Sale by Owner (FSBO)
FSBO	Isoldmyhouse.com	Website for a For Sale by Owner (FSBO)
FSBO	FSBO.com	Website for a For Sale by Owner (FSBO)
House data	ListMLSbyowner.com	Website for a For Sale by Owner (FSBO)
Hazardous Material	Lead paint	search for state Lead Paint ~Law, i.e. [MA lead paint ~law]
Hazardous Material	Asbestos	search for state Asbestos ~Law, i.e. [CA asbestos ~law]
Hazardous Material	UFFI	search for state UFFI ~Law, i.e. [TX UFFI ~law]
Hazardous Material	RADON gas	search for state RADON Gas ~Law, i.e. [PA Radon Gas ~law]
Hazardous Material	EPA.gov	Click on Mold
Home Inspector	ASHI.com	American Society of Home Inspectors - Find a home inspector
House data	Realtor.com	Listings and sales
House data	Trulia.com	Listings and sales
House data	Zillow.com	Listings and sales
Insulation R Factor	energystar.gov	Click on home improvement dick on Seal and Insulate Under Adding Insulation.... Click on Recommended Levels of Insulation This displays a map of the US with R levels
Insurance Agent	by state	in Google search for [MA "independent Insurance agents"] ---use your state name
Loan Application	Freddie Mac Loan Application	Search for [Freddie Mac Form 65]
Loans, FHA	HUD.gov	hud.gov/buying/loans.cfm
Loans, VA	va.gov	Click on Veteran Services, select home loans from drop down box
Maps, aerial	bing.com	Aerial Map search, enter address, dick on birds eye view use compass arrows to rotate view
Maps, aerial	maps.google.com	Aerial Map search, enter address, dick on satellite or map view use compass move view Use person icon to get a street view, many options
Rehab Loans	HUD.gov	Search for [203K rehab] Information on rehab loans
Reverse Mortgage	HUD.gov	Click on Learn about Reverse mortgages for Seniors
Title Insurance	by state	in Google search for [MA "Title Insurance"] ---use your state name

Index

U

UFFI · 28, 40, 154, 181
unit deed · 145
Urea Formaldehyde Foam Insulation
· See UFFI
Using a Financial Calculator · 234
utility lines · 119, 138, 226

V

VA · 3, 9
Vacation Home Alternative · 96
Veterans Affairs · See VA

W

Walk throiugh · See property
inspection
Walls & Ceilings · See Interior
Finishes
water and sewer · 28, 121, 169, 193,
213
Web Sites · 272
worksheet program · 191, 197, 237

Z

Zoning · 122, 270, 271

About The Author

DON GRIFFIN

Is a real estate appraiser with twenty plus years' experience in many states. He was a computer programmer, systems analyst, and manager. Don has written many technical software manuals and has taught international project leaders the principals of software project management.

Don has a Bachelor of Science in Business Administration, and an Associate Degree in Computer Science. Don holds the MAI designation from the Appraisal Institute indicating expertise in commercial Real Estate Appraising and the SRA designation indicating expertise in residential Real Estate Appraising.

He has testified in court as an expert witness. Don's ability to synthesize complex topics and to explain them to a lay audience is valued not only on the witness stand but in his written appraisal reports.

Don brings all of his experience in technical writing and real estate appraising coupled with a lifetime of personal home ownership to this wonderfully broad treatment of real estate. His experience in multiple states makes this a truly national book..